Jesus Reigns in Me!

Living Daily in the Power of His Resurrection

Sarah Hornsby

Chosen Books

A Division of Baker Book House Co
Grand Rapids, Michigan 49516

Published by Chosen Books
a division of Baker Book House Company
P.O. Box 6287, Grand Rapids, MI 49516-6287

Printed in the United States of America

Library of Congress Cataloging-in-Publication Data

Hornsby, Sarah.
    Jesus reigns in me! : living daily in the power of his
  resurrection / Sarah Hornsby.
       p. cm.
    ISBN 0-8007-9241-6 (cloth)
    1. Jesus Christ—Resurrection—Meditations. 2. Christian
  life. 3. Devotional literature. I. Title
    BT481.H65 1996
    232'.5—dc20   96-10233

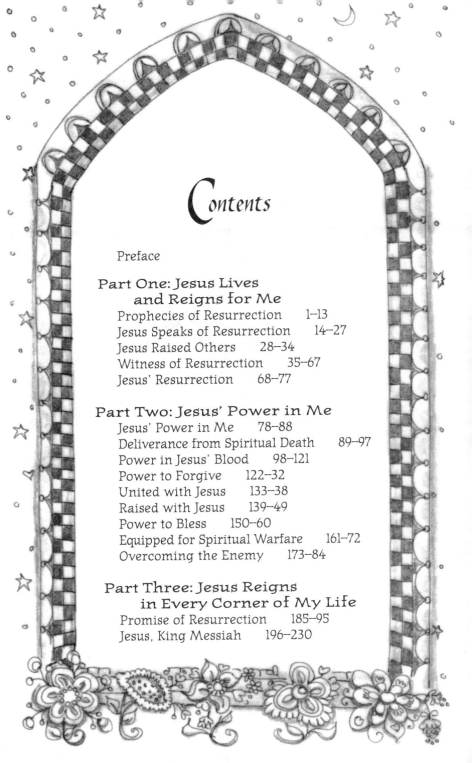

Contents

$\mathcal{S}$pecial $\mathcal{T}$hanks to

Ms. Nancy, who was in the room with Mama and never failed to say, "I'm praying for you and your loved ones; you pray for me and my loved ones."

Eleanor Cheney, prayer partner and friend.

Andy Hornsby, encourager, healing person, who guided me in understanding more about the meaning of resurrection through resources from his church, Evangel Cathedral, Spartanburg, South Carolina.

Jane Campbell, for her steady encouragement and editing.

Preface

This book is the third of a trilogy: *Jesus, Be in Me*, a book of Lenten messages; *Jesus, Be in My Christmas*, a book of Advent messages; and now *Jesus Reigns in Me*, a book about Jesus' resurrection and the Easter joy that leads to Pentecost and beyond.

Jesus Reigns in Me is special, since I began the research for it after being called from Nicaragua (where my husband, Jim, and I are missionaries) to be with my dying mother. I stayed at the Presbyterian Home in Lexington, South Carolina, in my mother's empty apartment. Complications after her surgery brought her close to death. Her chances of pulling through at age 87 were not good.

Every day for a month I visited her at the home's health care center, as did my sister, Ebba, and her husband, John. Daily Mama made improvements, moving from a firm desire to be rid of her body of pain to a renewed desire to live.

I did not consciously pray for her to live, because Mama, the source of wisdom for our family, has always known best. My own need drew me to her. Being with her each day, reading poems she liked, singing her favorite hymns, making her hot coffee and bringing it to her in a Thermos—these were ways I showed my love. Rubbing her feet every evening before leaving for the night became a ritual. Before my eyes she was transformed, renewed, encouraged and strengthened. She had me take down the sign *No Visitors Allowed* that she had scrawled on a piece of paper, and had me wheel her out to see the last roses of summer and her many favorite garden spots and friends at the home.

This was my personal introduction to resurrection, and how sweet it was! The day before I returned to Nicaragua, not knowing if I would ever see her again, Mama read my fifteen-page outline for this book, tears flowing, head nodding in assent at the Scriptures. She was my wise Mama again, approving and enabling me. When I had first come, she could not read anything, and instead of the bright, positive remarks she usually wrote in her journal and on her calendar, she had the desire only to mark a large, black X through each day. We had come a long way.

That was a year ago. Now Mama is faithful in an exercise group at the home. She lives in a small apartment inside the home instead of in her cottage on the hill. She visits the others in the health care center. She has moved with admirable courage into her "last phase" (as she calls it). As energy allows, she is gathering my daddy's memorabilia to make a biography of his life for our family.

When I was writing *Jesus, Be in Me*, Daddy was dying of cancer and I did not know it. The Lord ministered to my grief in the words He gave me as I meditated on Jesus' death. Now, in this resurrection book, Jesus has given me another wonderful reason to praise Him: the gracious gift of another year with my mother.

When I began this trilogy, I went through *Strong's Concordance* and listed hundreds of Scriptures about Jesus being in me. It stretched my imagination to consider that Jesus reigns over all activities or situations, good and bad. As I have written this book, I referred to my list to choose one quality for each day. Studying these qualities, I pray, will bring a whole new blessing to you, with the risen Jesus coming alive in you. Read each Scripture. Ask Jesus in what ways He can be in you in this area. And listen to Him. You will become aware of new ways He can enter and touch your life, and the lives of others through you.

For the border drawings I chose windows and doorways (but not because I learned to use a new computer with Windows as I wrote this book!). The Bible speaks of the world Jesus made as He intended it to be, and of us, His beloved children, walking and talking with Him in the garden. So enter through the door of resurrection and let Him reign over every area of your life.

Sarah Hornsby
Matagalpa, Nicaragua, Central America

Part One

Jesus Lives and Reigns for Me

1

Prophecies of Resurrection
A Righteous Branch Raised

"I shall raise up for David a righteous Branch; and He will reign as king and act wisely and do justice and righteousness in the land."

Jeremiah 23:5, NASB

*T*ree or *branch* implies a life in right relation to God, rooted and growing luxuriantly in His presence. I am grafted into Jesus as the Vine in such a permanent, integral connection that His life flows through me. Jesus' reign can be recognized where wisdom, justice and righteousness are done. Lord Jesus, raise me above the pettiness of my everyday circumstances; enable me to be aware of Your life surging through me today. Grow ever green in me. Jesus, be in my growing.

"Their leaves will not wither, nor will their fruit fail. Every month they will bear, because the water from the sanctuary flows to them. Their fruit will serve for food and their leaves for healing."

Ezekiel 47:12

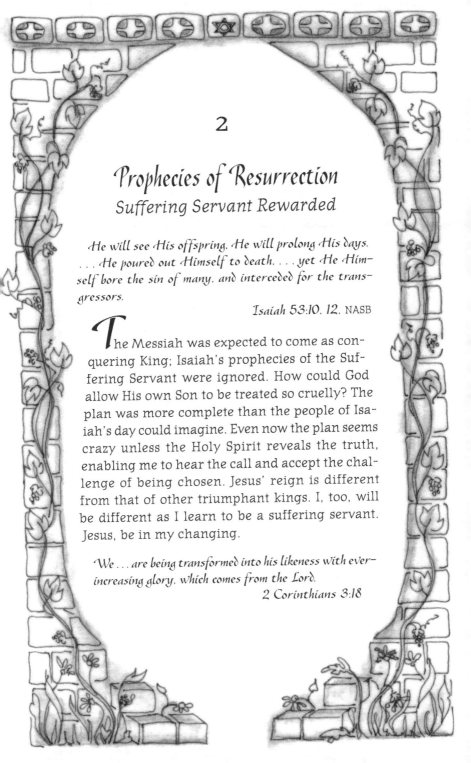

2

Prophecies of Resurrection
Suffering Servant Rewarded

*He will see His offspring. He will prolong His days.
. . . He poured out Himself to death. . . . yet He Himself bore the sin of many, and interceded for the transgressors.*

Isaiah 53:10, 12, NASB

The Messiah was expected to come as conquering King; Isaiah's prophecies of the Suffering Servant were ignored. How could God
allow His own Son to be treated so cruelly? The
plan was more complete than the people of Isaiah's day could imagine. Even now the plan seems
crazy unless the Holy Spirit reveals the truth,
enabling me to hear the call and accept the chal-
lenge of being chosen. Jesus' reign is different
from that of other triumphant kings. I, too, will
be different as I learn to be a suffering servant.
Jesus, be in my changing.

*We . . . are being transformed into his likeness with ever-
increasing glory, which comes from the Lord.*

2 Corinthians 3:18

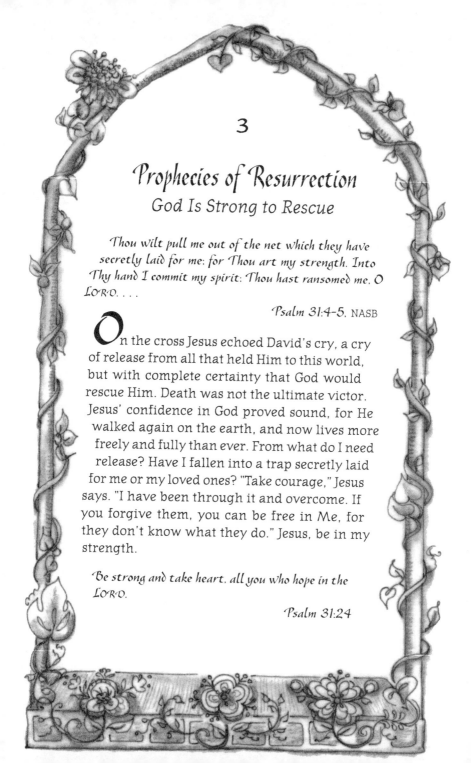

3

Prophecies of Resurrection
God Is Strong to Rescue

Thou wilt pull me out of the net which they have secretly laid for me; for Thou art my strength. Into Thy hand I commit my spirit: Thou hast ransomed me, O LORD. . . .

Psalm 31:4-5, NASB

On the cross Jesus echoed David's cry, a cry of release from all that held Him to this world, but with complete certainty that God would rescue Him. Death was not the ultimate victor. Jesus' confidence in God proved sound, for He walked again on the earth, and now lives more freely and fully than ever. From what do I need release? Have I fallen into a trap secretly laid for me or my loved ones? "Take courage," Jesus says. "I have been through it and overcome. If you forgive them, you can be free in Me, for they don't know what they do." Jesus, be in my strength.

Be strong and take heart, all you who hope in the LORD.

Psalm 31:24

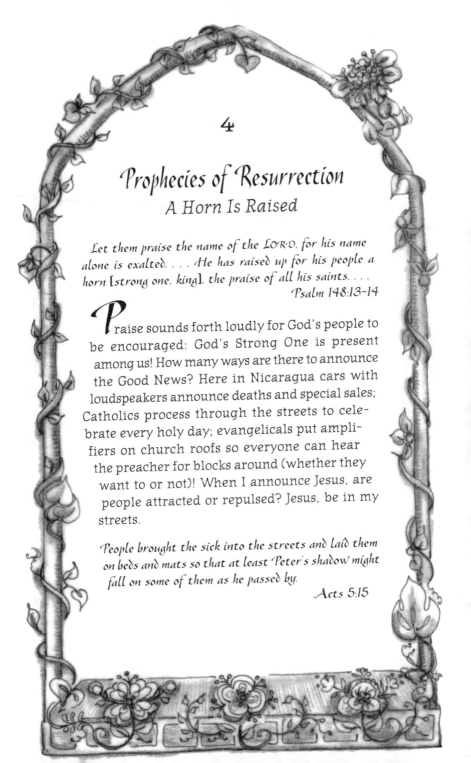

4

Prophecies of Resurrection
A Horn Is Raised

Let them praise the name of the LORD, for his name alone is exalted. . . . He has raised up for his people a horn [strong one, king], the praise of all his saints. . . .
Psalm 148:13-14

*P*raise sounds forth loudly for God's people to be encouraged: God's Strong One is present among us! How many ways are there to announce the Good News? Here in Nicaragua cars with loudspeakers announce deaths and special sales; Catholics process through the streets to celebrate every holy day; evangelicals put amplifiers on church roofs so everyone can hear the preacher for blocks around (whether they want to or not)! When I announce Jesus, are people attracted or repulsed? Jesus, be in my streets.

People brought the sick into the streets and laid them on beds and mats so that at least Peter's shadow might fall on some of them as he passed by.
Acts 5:15

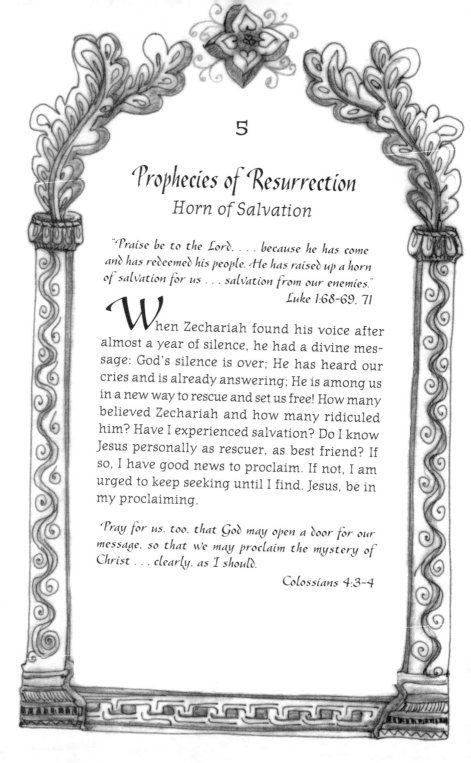

5

Prophecies of Resurrection
Horn of Salvation

"Praise be to the Lord. . . . because he has come and has redeemed his people. He has raised up a horn of salvation for us . . . salvation from our enemies."

Luke 1:68-69. 71

When Zechariah found his voice after almost a year of silence, he had a divine message: God's silence is over; He has heard our cries and is already answering; He is among us in a new way to rescue and set us free! How many believed Zechariah and how many ridiculed him? Have I experienced salvation? Do I know Jesus personally as rescuer, as best friend? If so, I have good news to proclaim. If not, I am urged to keep seeking until I find. Jesus, be in my proclaiming.

Pray for us. too, that God may open a door for our message. so that we may proclaim the mystery of Christ . . . clearly. as I should.

Colossians 4:3-4

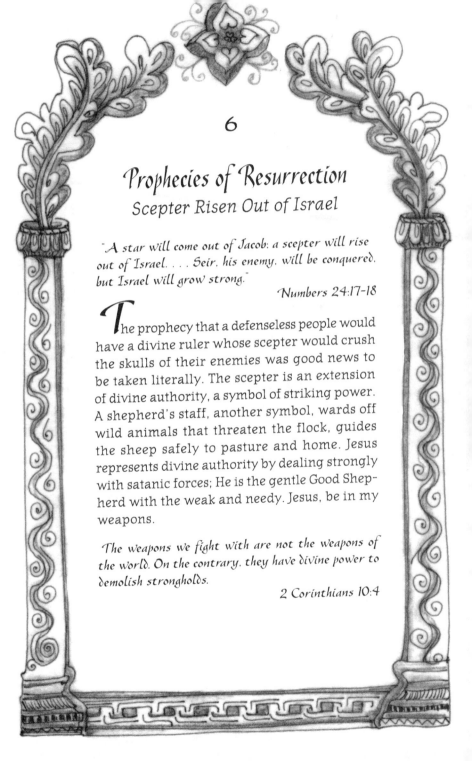

6

Prophecies of Resurrection
Scepter Risen Out of Israel

"A star will come out of Jacob; a scepter will rise out of Israel. . . . Seir, his enemy, will be conquered, but Israel will grow strong."

Numbers 24:17-18

The prophecy that a defenseless people would have a divine ruler whose scepter would crush the skulls of their enemies was good news to be taken literally. The scepter is an extension of divine authority, a symbol of striking power. A shepherd's staff, another symbol, wards off wild animals that threaten the flock, guides the sheep safely to pasture and home. Jesus represents divine authority by dealing strongly with satanic forces; He is the gentle Good Shepherd with the weak and needy. Jesus, be in my weapons.

The weapons we fight with are not the weapons of the world. On the contrary, they have divine power to demolish strongholds.

2 Corinthians 10:4

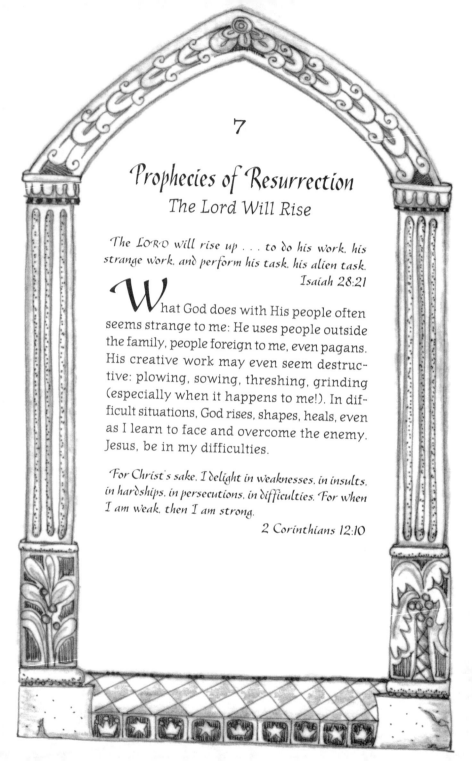

Prophecies of Resurrection
The Lord Will Rise

The LORD will rise up . . . to do his work, his strange work, and perform his task, his alien task.
Isaiah 28:21

What God does with His people often seems strange to me: He uses people outside the family, people foreign to me, even pagans. His creative work may even seem destructive: plowing, sowing, threshing, grinding (especially when it happens to me!). In difficult situations, God rises, shapes, heals, even as I learn to face and overcome the enemy. Jesus, be in my difficulties.

For Christ's sake, I delight in weaknesses, in insults, in hardships, in persecutions, in difficulties. For when I am weak, then I am strong.

2 Corinthians 12:10

8

Prophecies of Resurrection
A Light Rises in Darkness

"If you spend yourselves in behalf of the hungry and satisfy the needs of the oppressed. then your light will rise in the darkness, and your night will become like the noonday."

Isaiah 58:10

*T*he prophet Isaiah said that a new day will dawn when God's people (in Archbishop Oscar Romero's words) "stop the oppression." Stop accusing others, stop malicious gossip, but don't stop there! The light will rise in the darkness when God's people use their energy, influence, money to help those who are in need, hungry, oppressed. How? That is why I have Jesus, the Light of the world, to show the way. Jesus, be in my energy.

We proclaim him. admonishing and teaching everyone with all wisdom. so that we may present everyone perfect in Christ. To this end I labor. struggling with all his energy. which so powerfully works in me.

Colossians 1:28-29

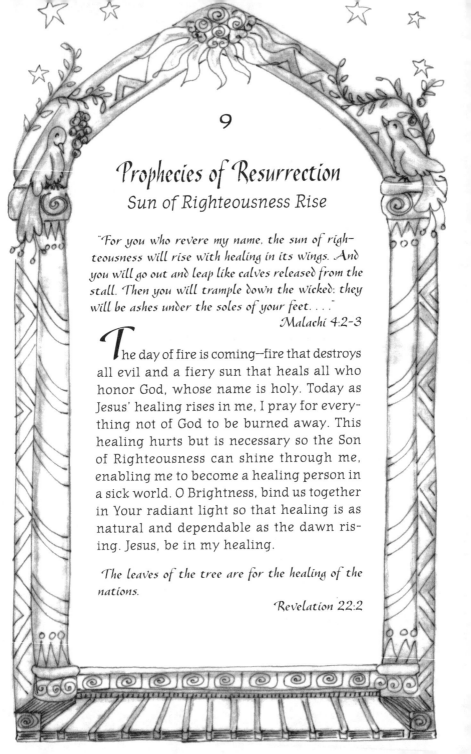

9

Prophecies of Resurrection
Sun of Righteousness Rise

"For you who revere my name, the sun of righteousness will rise with healing in its wings. And you will go out and leap like calves released from the stall. Then you will trample down the wicked; they will be ashes under the soles of your feet. . . ."

Malachi 4:2-3

The day of fire is coming—fire that destroys all evil and a fiery sun that heals all who honor God, whose name is holy. Today as Jesus' healing rises in me, I pray for everything not of God to be burned away. This healing hurts but is necessary so the Son of Righteousness can shine through me, enabling me to become a healing person in a sick world. O Brightness, bind us together in Your radiant light so that healing is as natural and dependable as the dawn rising. Jesus, be in my healing.

The leaves of the tree are for the healing of the nations.

Revelation 22:2

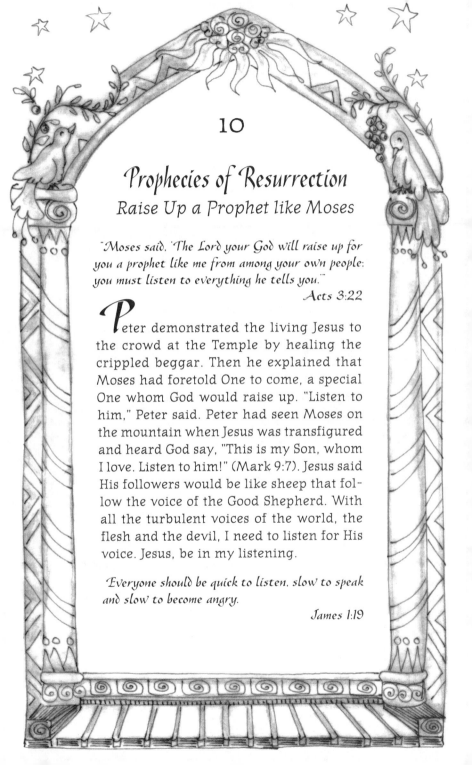

10

Prophecies of Resurrection
Raise Up a Prophet like Moses

"Moses said, 'The Lord your God will raise up for you a prophet like me from among your own people; you must listen to everything he tells you.'"

Acts 3:22

Peter demonstrated the living Jesus to the crowd at the Temple by healing the crippled beggar. Then he explained that Moses had foretold One to come, a special One whom God would raise up. "Listen to him," Peter said. Peter had seen Moses on the mountain when Jesus was transfigured and heard God say, "This is my Son, whom I love. Listen to him!" (Mark 9:7). Jesus said His followers would be like sheep that follow the voice of the Good Shepherd. With all the turbulent voices of the world, the flesh and the devil, I need to listen for His voice. Jesus, be in my listening.

Everyone should be quick to listen, slow to speak and slow to become angry.

James 1:19

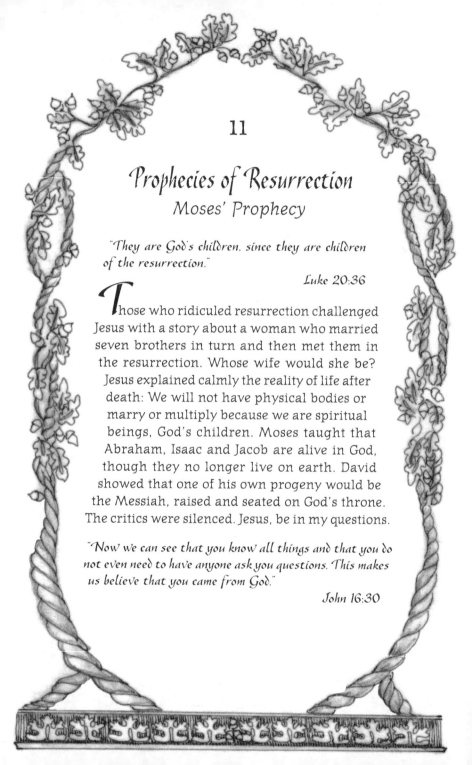

Prophecies of Resurrection
Moses' Prophecy

"They are God's children, since they are children of the resurrection."

Luke 20:36

*T*hose who ridiculed resurrection challenged Jesus with a story about a woman who married seven brothers in turn and then met them in the resurrection. Whose wife would she be? Jesus explained calmly the reality of life after death: We will not have physical bodies or marry or multiply because we are spiritual beings, God's children. Moses taught that Abraham, Isaac and Jacob are alive in God, though they no longer live on earth. David showed that one of his own progeny would be the Messiah, raised and seated on God's throne. The critics were silenced. Jesus, be in my questions.

"Now we can see that you know all things and that you do not even need to have anyone ask you questions. This makes us believe that you came from God."

John 16:30

12

Prophecies of Resurrection
David's Prophecy

"I saw the Lord always before me. Because he is at my right hand, I will not be shaken."

Acts 2:25

Seeing what was ahead, David said the Messiah would not be abandoned in the grave. David was a man of words and deeds, of passion and compassion. The psalms he wrote are a poignant record of his vital relationship with the living God. God's healing came in the midst of David's most desperate circumstances. His words, though expressing harsh realities and the gamut of emotions, are permeated with and culminate in faith and praise. Am I as honest as David with myself and God? Are my words expressive of faith, forgiveness and praise? Jesus, be in my words.

Let the word of Christ dwell in you richly as you teach and admonish one another . . . [and] sing psalms, hymns and spiritual songs with gratitude in your hearts to God.

Colossians 3:16

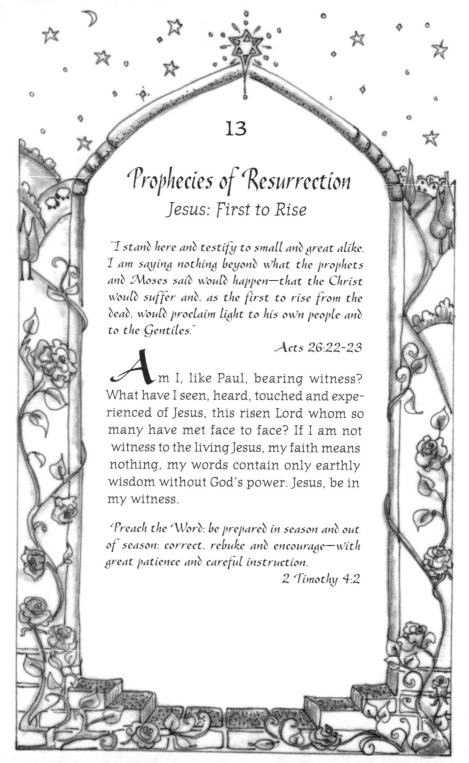

Prophecies of Resurrection
Jesus: First to Rise

"I stand here and testify to small and great alike. I am saying nothing beyond what the prophets and Moses said would happen—that the Christ would suffer and, as the first to rise from the dead, would proclaim light to his own people and to the Gentiles."

Acts 26:22-23

Am I, like Paul, bearing witness? What have I seen, heard, touched and experienced of Jesus, this risen Lord whom so many have met face to face? If I am not witness to the living Jesus, my faith means nothing, my words contain only earthly wisdom without God's power. Jesus, be in my witness.

Preach the Word; be prepared in season and out of season; correct, rebuke and encourage—with great patience and careful instruction.

2 Timothy 4:2

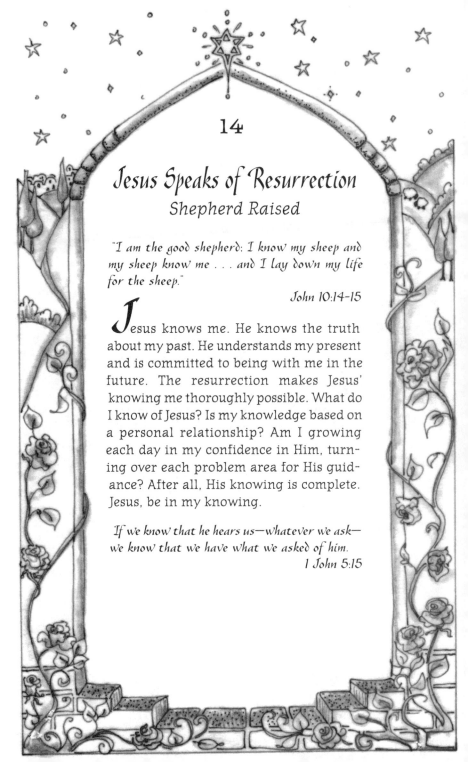

14

Jesus Speaks of Resurrection
Shepherd Raised

"I am the good shepherd: I know my sheep and my sheep know me . . . and I lay down my life for the sheep."

John 10:14-15

Jesus knows me. He knows the truth about my past. He understands my present and is committed to being with me in the future. The resurrection makes Jesus' knowing me thoroughly possible. What do I know of Jesus? Is my knowledge based on a personal relationship? Am I growing each day in my confidence in Him, turning over each problem area for His guidance? After all, His knowing is complete. Jesus, be in my knowing.

If we know that he hears us—whatever we ask— we know that we have what we asked of him.

1 John 5:15

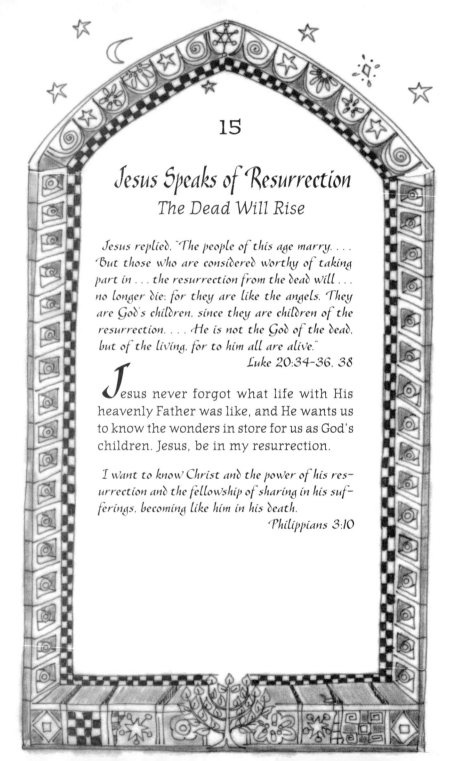

15

Jesus Speaks of Resurrection
The Dead Will Rise

Jesus replied, "The people of this age marry. . . .
But those who are considered worthy of taking
part in . . . the resurrection from the dead will . . .
no longer die; for they are like the angels. They
are God's children, since they are children of the
resurrection. . . . He is not the God of the dead,
but of the living, for to him all are alive."
                                              Luke 20:34-36, 38

Jesus never forgot what life with His
heavenly Father was like, and He wants us
to know the wonders in store for us as God's
children. Jesus, be in my resurrection.

I want to know Christ and the power of his res-
urrection and the fellowship of sharing in his suf-
ferings, becoming like him in his death.
                                              Philippians 3:10

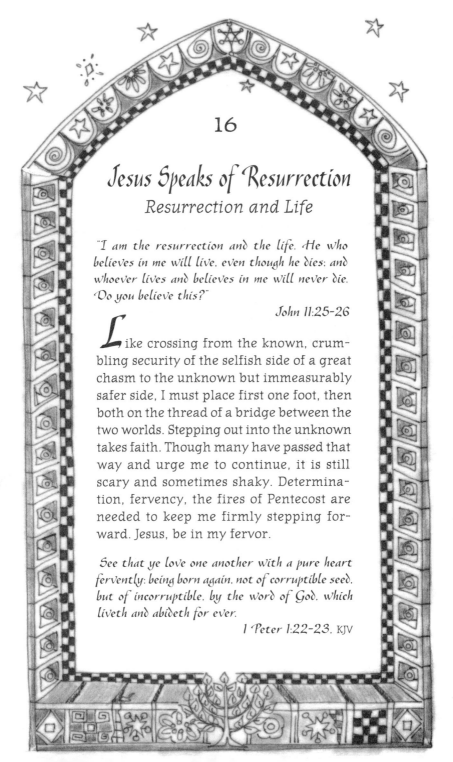

16

Jesus Speaks of Resurrection
Resurrection and Life

"I am the resurrection and the life. He who believes in me will live, even though he dies; and whoever lives and believes in me will never die. Do you believe this?"

John 11:25-26

*L*ike crossing from the known, crumbling security of the selfish side of a great chasm to the unknown but immeasurably safer side, I must place first one foot, then both on the thread of a bridge between the two worlds. Stepping out into the unknown takes faith. Though many have passed that way and urge me to continue, it is still scary and sometimes shaky. Determination, fervency, the fires of Pentecost are needed to keep me firmly stepping forward. Jesus, be in my fervor.

See that ye love one another with a pure heart fervently: being born again, not of corruptible seed, but of incorruptible, by the word of God, which liveth and abideth for ever.

1 Peter 1:22-23, KJV

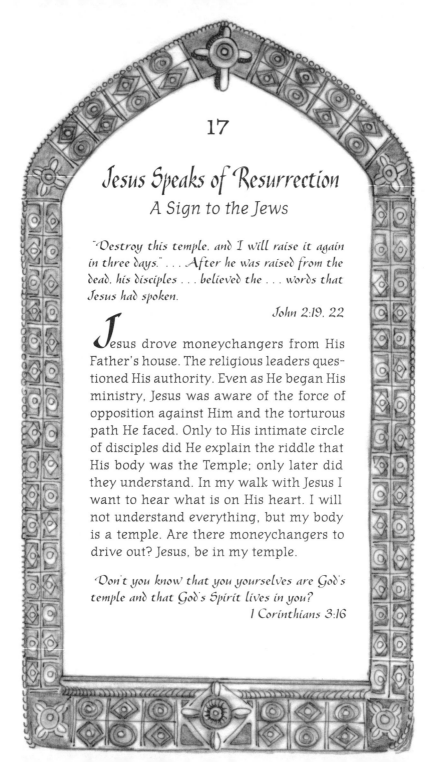

17

Jesus Speaks of Resurrection
A Sign to the Jews

"Destroy this temple, and I will raise it again in three days." . . . After he was raised from the dead, his disciples . . . believed the . . . words that Jesus had spoken.

John 2:19, 22

Jesus drove moneychangers from His Father's house. The religious leaders questioned His authority. Even as He began His ministry, Jesus was aware of the force of opposition against Him and the torturous path He faced. Only to His intimate circle of disciples did He explain the riddle that His body was the Temple; only later did they understand. In my walk with Jesus I want to hear what is on His heart. I will not understand everything, but my body is a temple. Are there moneychangers to drive out? Jesus, be in my temple.

Don't you know that you yourselves are God's temple and that God's Spirit lives in you?

1 Corinthians 3:16

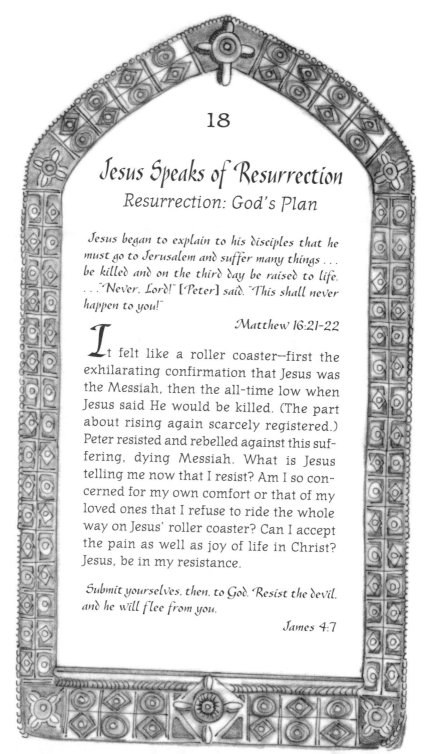

18

Jesus Speaks of Resurrection
Resurrection: God's Plan

Jesus began to explain to his disciples that he must go to Jerusalem and suffer many things . . . be killed and on the third day be raised to life. . . ."Never, Lord!" [Peter] said. "This shall never happen to you!"

Matthew 16:21-22

It felt like a roller coaster—first the exhilarating confirmation that Jesus was the Messiah, then the all-time low when Jesus said He would be killed. (The part about rising again scarcely registered.) Peter resisted and rebelled against this suffering, dying Messiah. What is Jesus telling me now that I resist? Am I so concerned for my own comfort or that of my loved ones that I refuse to ride the whole way on Jesus' roller coaster? Can I accept the pain as well as joy of life in Christ? Jesus, be in my resistance.

Submit yourselves, then, to God. Resist the devil, and he will flee from you.

James 4:7

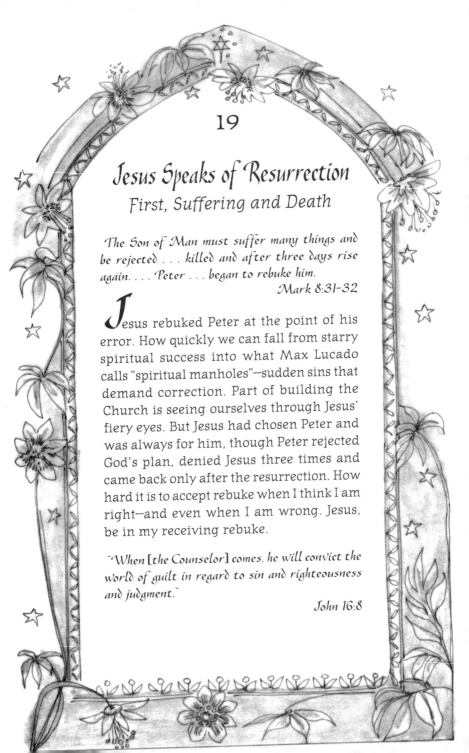

19

Jesus Speaks of Resurrection
First, Suffering and Death

The Son of Man must suffer many things and be rejected . . . killed and after three days rise again. . . . Peter . . . began to rebuke him.

Mark 8:31-32

Jesus rebuked Peter at the point of his error. How quickly we can fall from starry spiritual success into what Max Lucado calls "spiritual manholes"—sudden sins that demand correction. Part of building the Church is seeing ourselves through Jesus' fiery eyes. But Jesus had chosen Peter and was always for him, though Peter rejected God's plan, denied Jesus three times and came back only after the resurrection. How hard it is to accept rebuke when I think I am right—and even when I am wrong. Jesus, be in my receiving rebuke.

"When [the Counselor] comes, he will convict the world of guilt in regard to sin and righteousness and judgment."

John 16:8

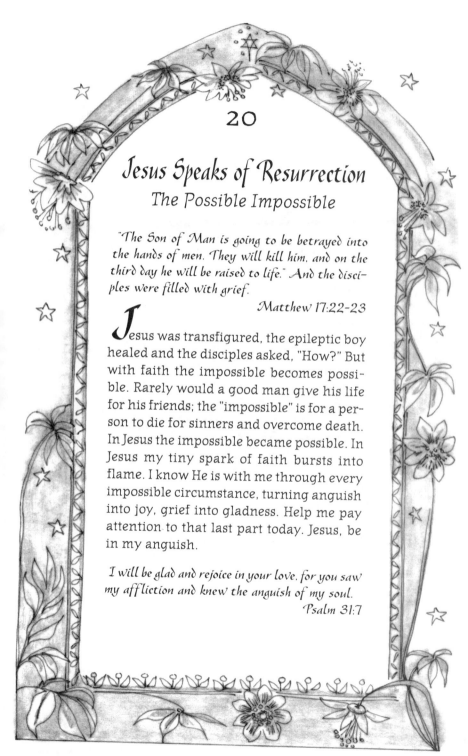

20

Jesus Speaks of Resurrection
The Possible Impossible

"The Son of Man is going to be betrayed into the hands of men. They will kill him, and on the third day he will be raised to life." And the disciples were filled with grief.

Matthew 17:22-23

Jesus was transfigured, the epileptic boy healed and the disciples asked, "How?" But with faith the impossible becomes possible. Rarely would a good man give his life for his friends; the "impossible" is for a person to die for sinners and overcome death. In Jesus the impossible became possible. In Jesus my tiny spark of faith bursts into flame. I know He is with me through every impossible circumstance, turning anguish into joy, grief into gladness. Help me pay attention to that last part today. Jesus, be in my anguish.

I will be glad and rejoice in your love. for you saw my affliction and knew the anguish of my soul.

Psalm 31:7

21

Jesus Speaks of Resurrection
Fearful Unknown

*"The Son of Man is going to be betrayed. . . .
They will kill him, and after three days he will
rise." But they did not understand what he
meant and were afraid to ask him about it.*
                                        Mark 9:31–32

So much was happening that they did not understand. Jesus was great and their faith little. When He spoke of death and resurrection, uncertainty churned within and they were afraid to ask Jesus, who called them friends. They did not know Him who would send the Holy Spirit to explain everything. I question and do not understand many things. At times unnecessary fear and worry rob me of faith and full, active life. Jesus, be in my fears.

*God is love. Whoever lives in love lives in God, and
God in him. . . . Perfect love drives out fear. . . .*
                                        1 John 4:16, 18

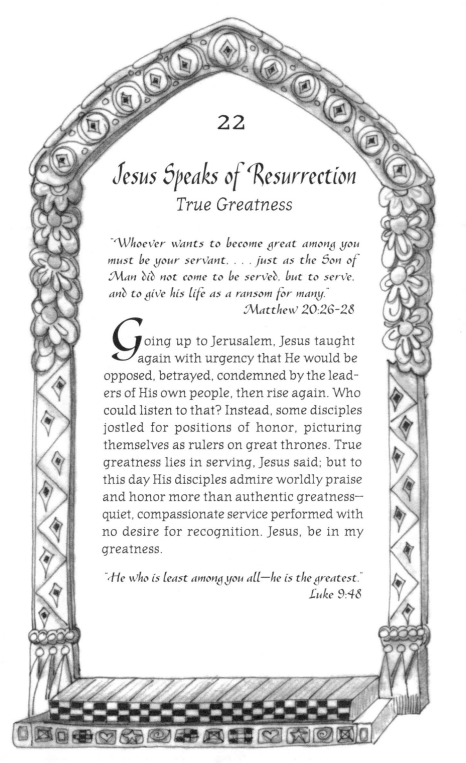

22

Jesus Speaks of Resurrection
True Greatness

"Whoever wants to become great among you must be your servant. . . . just as the Son of Man did not come to be served, but to serve, and to give his life as a ransom for many."
                                        Matthew 20:26-28

Going up to Jerusalem, Jesus taught again with urgency that He would be opposed, betrayed, condemned by the leaders of His own people, then rise again. Who could listen to that? Instead, some disciples jostled for positions of honor, picturing themselves as rulers on great thrones. True greatness lies in serving, Jesus said; but to this day His disciples admire worldly praise and honor more than authentic greatness—quiet, compassionate service performed with no desire for recognition. Jesus, be in my greatness.

"He who is least among you all—he is the greatest."
                                        Luke 9:48

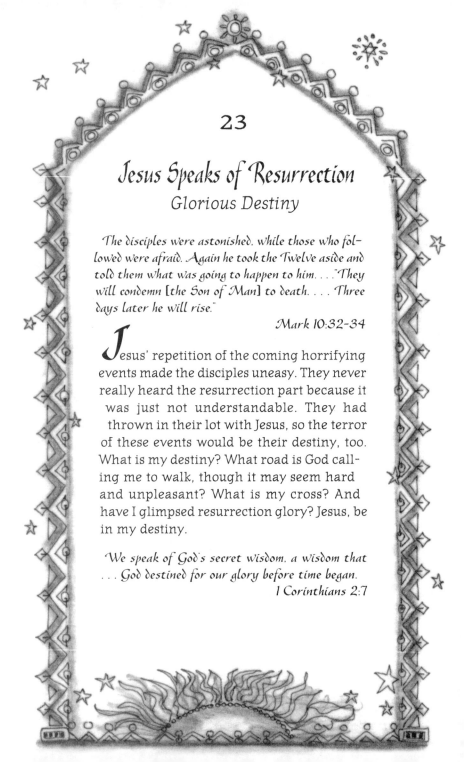

23

Jesus Speaks of Resurrection
Glorious Destiny

*The disciples were astonished, while those who fol-
lowed were afraid. Again he took the Twelve aside and
told them what was going to happen to him. . . ."They
will condemn [the Son of Man] to death. . . . Three
days later he will rise."*

Mark 10:32-34

Jesus' repetition of the coming horrifying
events made the disciples uneasy. They never
really heard the resurrection part because it
was just not understandable. They had
thrown in their lot with Jesus, so the terror
of these events would be their destiny, too.
What is my destiny? What road is God calling me to walk, though it may seem hard
and unpleasant? What is my cross? And
have I glimpsed resurrection glory? Jesus, be
in my destiny.

*We speak of God's secret wisdom, a wisdom that
. . . God destined for our glory before time began.*

1 Corinthians 2:7

Jesus Speaks of Resurrection
He Opened Their Minds

*Then he opened their minds so they could under-
stand the Scriptures. . . . "The Christ will suffer and
rise from the dead . . . and repentance and forgiveness
of sins will be preached . . . to all nations. . . . You are
witnesses."*

Luke 24:45-48

The disciples viewed God and the world—and
had interpreted Scripture over the years—through
the traditions and customs of their people. Jesus
opened their minds to a new way of thinking, a
new perception of who God is, personified in Himself, Jesus, their Friend and Lord. How is my mind
closed or filled with junk that needs to be thrown
out? Are there precious, hidden truths to be found,
dusted and shared? Jesus, be in my mind.

*. . . Then make my joy complete by being like-minded,
having the same love, being one in spirit and purpose. . . . Your attitude . . . [like] Jesus. . . . He
humbled himself. . . .*

Philippians 2:2, 5, 8

Jesus Speaks of Resurrection
Meeting in Galilee

*"This very night you will all fall away on account
of me. . . . But after I have risen, I will go ahead
of you into Galilee."*

Matthew 26:31-32

Jesus knew beforehand not only of His sufferings, but of the reaction of the disciples.
Even so, He promised to meet them on their
own ground, Galilee. His forgiveness of their
falling away was generous and complete.
How do I relate to people I know will fail me
or not fulfill their part? Do I reject them in
disgust, or am I willing to forgive the hurt
they cause and begin anew, meeting them
in Galilee? How do I treat my own failures
and shortcomings? Can I forgive myself?
Jesus, be in my failing.

*To him who is able to keep you from falling and to
present you before his glorious presence without
fault and with great joy. . . .*

Jude 24

Jesus Speaks of Resurrection
Don't Tell Until . . .

As they were coming down the mountain, Jesus instructed them, "Don't tell anyone what you have seen, until the Son of Man has been raised from the dead."

Matthew 17:9

There is a time to keep quiet and a time to tell what I have seen and experienced. The three at the Transfiguration had to keep a marvelous secret for a time, but after the resurrection they could fit it into the whole picture of the risen Jesus. I will keep quiet not because I am afraid what people will think, but awaiting inner certainty of what God wants told and when. As a writer I have learned the value of an editor and word processor; my words can be cut, pasted, sharpened and honed to penetrate the heart. Jesus, be in my telling.

It gave me great joy to have some brothers come and tell about your faithfulness to the truth and how you continue to walk in the truth.

3 John 3

Jesus Speaks of Resurrection
Then They Understood

After he was raised from the dead, his disciples recalled what he had said. Then they believed the Scripture and the words that Jesus had spoken.

John 2:22

Jesus' ministry was colored by His thorough understanding of God's plan for His life, death and resurrection. He walked, ate, slept and performed all the ordinary necessities of life in the daily consciousness of that fact. Yet no one understood Him until afterward. If I feel others do not understand me, I remember Jesus was in that place. As I relate to others, Lord, help me to be understanding. Jesus, be in my understanding.

My purpose is that they may be encouraged in heart and united in love, so that they may have the full riches of complete understanding, in order that they may know . . . Christ.

Colossians 2:2

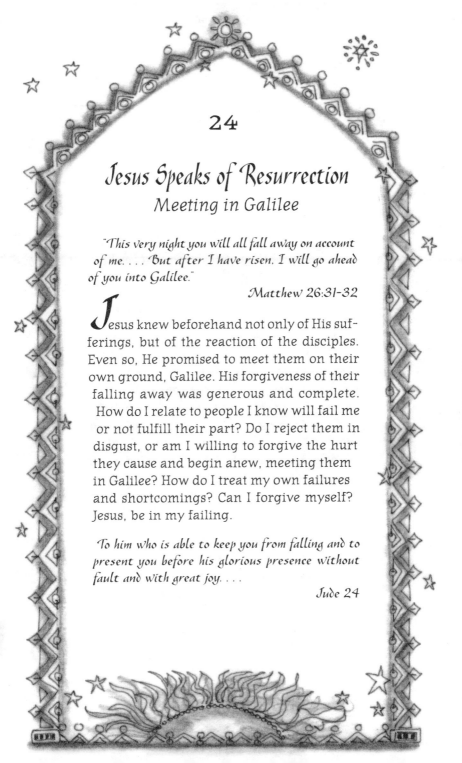

24

Jesus Speaks of Resurrection
Meeting in Galilee

"This very night you will all fall away on account of me. . . . But after I have risen, I will go ahead of you into Galilee."

Matthew 26:31-32

Jesus knew beforehand not only of His sufferings, but of the reaction of the disciples. Even so, He promised to meet them on their own ground, Galilee. His forgiveness of their falling away was generous and complete. How do I relate to people I know will fail me or not fulfill their part? Do I reject them in disgust, or am I willing to forgive the hurt they cause and begin anew, meeting them in Galilee? How do I treat my own failures and shortcomings? Can I forgive myself? Jesus, be in my failing.

To him who is able to keep you from falling and to present you before his glorious presence without fault and with great joy. . . .

Jude 24

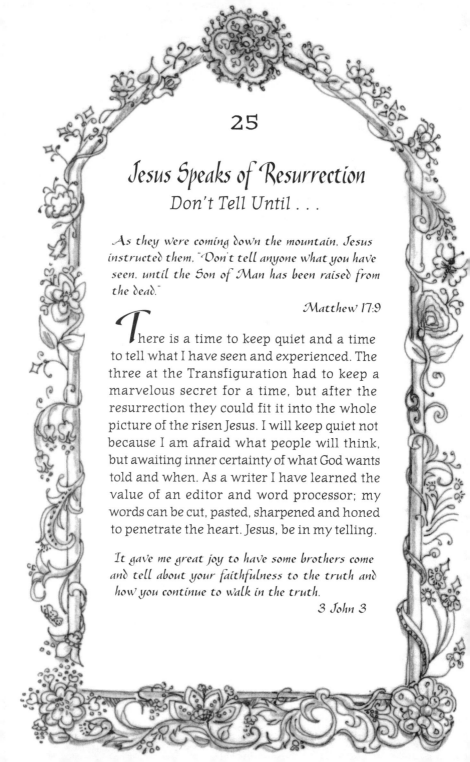

25

Jesus Speaks of Resurrection
Don't Tell Until . . .

As they were coming down the mountain, Jesus instructed them, "Don't tell anyone what you have seen, until the Son of Man has been raised from the dead."

Matthew 17:9

There is a time to keep quiet and a time to tell what I have seen and experienced. The three at the Transfiguration had to keep a marvelous secret for a time, but after the resurrection they could fit it into the whole picture of the risen Jesus. I will keep quiet not because I am afraid what people will think, but awaiting inner certainty of what God wants told and when. As a writer I have learned the value of an editor and word processor; my words can be cut, pasted, sharpened and honed to penetrate the heart. Jesus, be in my telling.

It gave me great joy to have some brothers come and tell about your faithfulness to the truth and how you continue to walk in the truth.

3 John 3

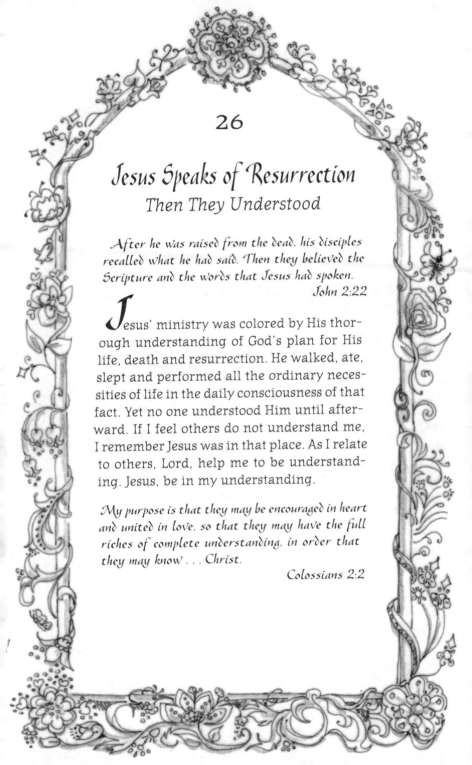

26

Jesus Speaks of Resurrection
Then They Understood

After he was raised from the dead, his disciples recalled what he had said. Then they believed the Scripture and the words that Jesus had spoken.
John 2:22

Jesus' ministry was colored by His thorough understanding of God's plan for His life, death and resurrection. He walked, ate, slept and performed all the ordinary necessities of life in the daily consciousness of that fact. Yet no one understood Him until afterward. If I feel others do not understand me, I remember Jesus was in that place. As I relate to others, Lord, help me to be understanding. Jesus, be in my understanding.

My purpose is that they may be encouraged in heart and united in love, so that they may have the full riches of complete understanding, in order that they may know . . . Christ.
Colossians 2:2

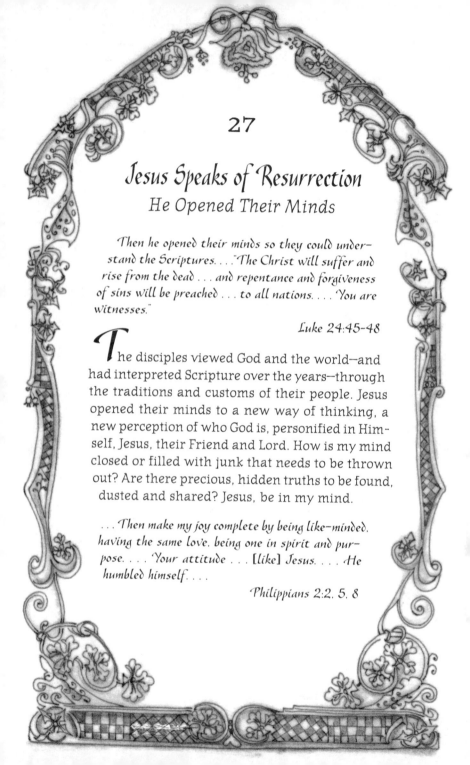

27

Jesus Speaks of Resurrection
He Opened Their Minds

*Then he opened their minds so they could under-
stand the Scriptures. . . . "The Christ will suffer and
rise from the dead . . . and repentance and forgiveness
of sins will be preached . . . to all nations. . . . 'You are
witnesses."*

Luke 24:45-48

The disciples viewed God and the world—and
had interpreted Scripture over the years—through
the traditions and customs of their people. Jesus
opened their minds to a new way of thinking, a
new perception of who God is, personified in Himself, Jesus, their Friend and Lord. How is my mind
closed or filled with junk that needs to be thrown
out? Are there precious, hidden truths to be found,
dusted and shared? Jesus, be in my mind.

*. . . Then make my joy complete by being like-minded,
having the same love, being one in spirit and purpose. . . . Your attitude . . . [like] Jesus. . . . He
humbled himself. . . .*

Philippians 2:2, 5, 8

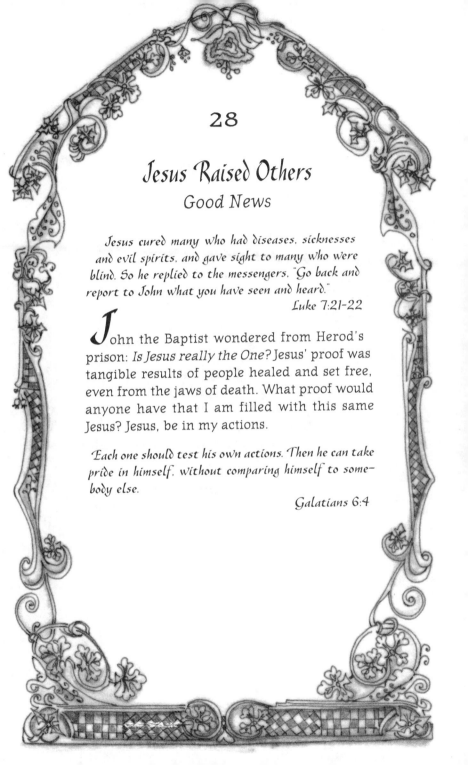

28

Jesus Raised Others
Good News

Jesus cured many who had diseases, sicknesses and evil spirits, and gave sight to many who were blind. So he replied to the messengers, "Go back and report to John what you have seen and heard."

Luke 7:21-22

John the Baptist wondered from Herod's prison: *Is Jesus really the One?* Jesus' proof was tangible results of people healed and set free, even from the jaws of death. What proof would anyone have that I am filled with this same Jesus? Jesus, be in my actions.

Each one should test his own actions. Then he can take pride in himself, without comparing himself to somebody else.

Galatians 6:4

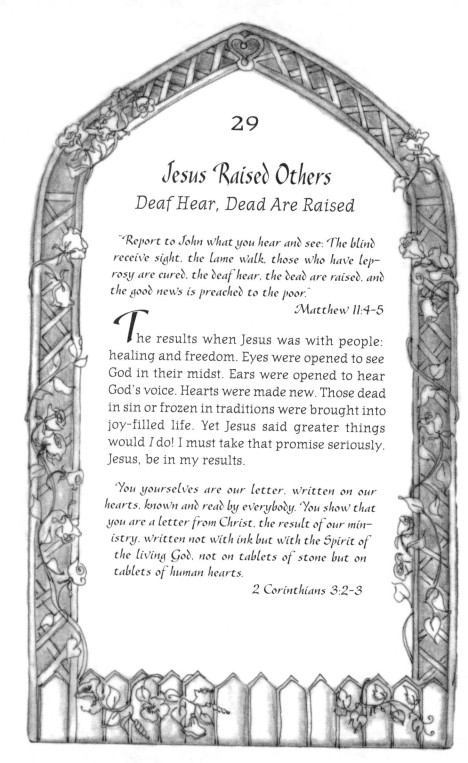

Jesus Raised Others
Deaf Hear, Dead Are Raised

"Report to John what you hear and see: The blind receive sight, the lame walk, those who have leprosy are cured, the deaf hear, the dead are raised, and the good news is preached to the poor."

Matthew 11:4-5

The results when Jesus was with people: healing and freedom. Eyes were opened to see God in their midst. Ears were opened to hear God's voice. Hearts were made new. Those dead in sin or frozen in traditions were brought into joy-filled life. Yet Jesus said greater things would *I* do! I must take that promise seriously. Jesus, be in my results.

You yourselves are our letter, written on our hearts, known and read by everybody. You show that you are a letter from Christ, the result of our ministry, written not with ink but with the Spirit of the living God, not on tablets of stone but on tablets of human hearts.

2 Corinthians 3:2-3

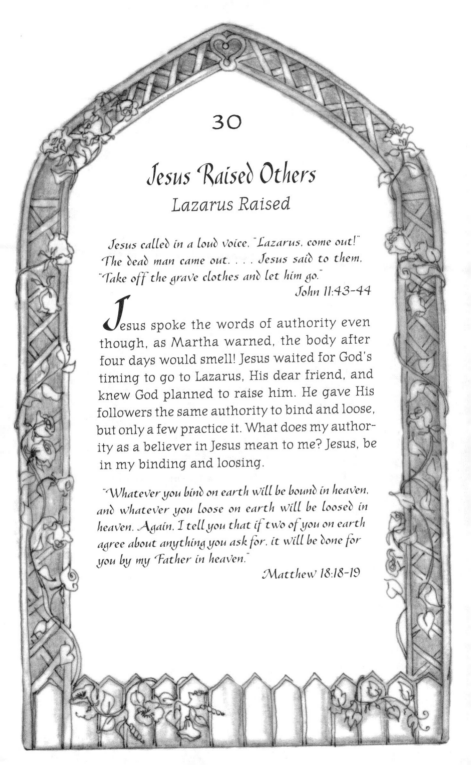

30

Jesus Raised Others
Lazarus Raised

*Jesus called in a loud voice, "Lazarus, come out!"
The dead man came out. . . . Jesus said to them,
"Take off the grave clothes and let him go."*
John 11:43-44

Jesus spoke the words of authority even though, as Martha warned, the body after four days would smell! Jesus waited for God's timing to go to Lazarus, His dear friend, and knew God planned to raise him. He gave His followers the same authority to bind and loose, but only a few practice it. What does my authority as a believer in Jesus mean to me? Jesus, be in my binding and loosing.

*"Whatever you bind on earth will be bound in heaven,
and whatever you loose on earth will be loosed in
heaven. Again, I tell you that if two of you on earth
agree about anything you ask for, it will be done for
you by my Father in heaven."*
Matthew 18:18-19

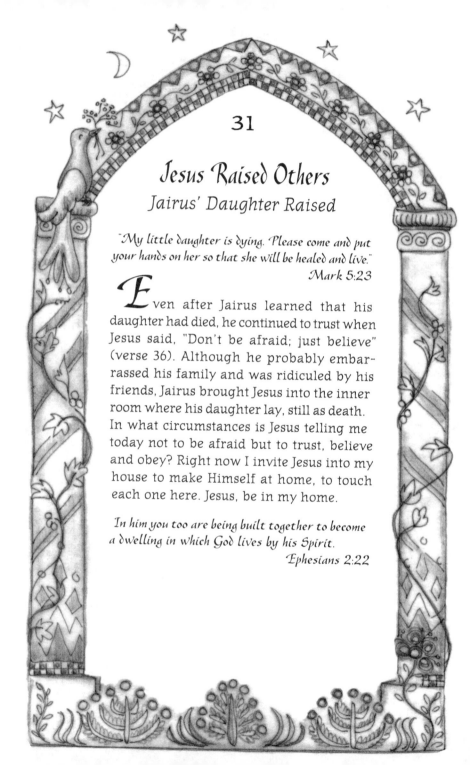

Jesus Raised Others
Jairus' Daughter Raised

*"My little daughter is dying. Please come and put
your hands on her so that she will be healed and live."*
Mark 5:23

*E*ven after Jairus learned that his
daughter had died, he continued to trust when
Jesus said, "Don't be afraid; just believe"
(verse 36). Although he probably embarrassed his family and was ridiculed by his
friends, Jairus brought Jesus into the inner
room where his daughter lay, still as death.
In what circumstances is Jesus telling me
today not to be afraid but to trust, believe
and obey? Right now I invite Jesus into my
house to make Himself at home, to touch
each one here. Jesus, be in my home.

*In him you too are being built together to become
a dwelling in which God lives by his Spirit.*
Ephesians 2:22

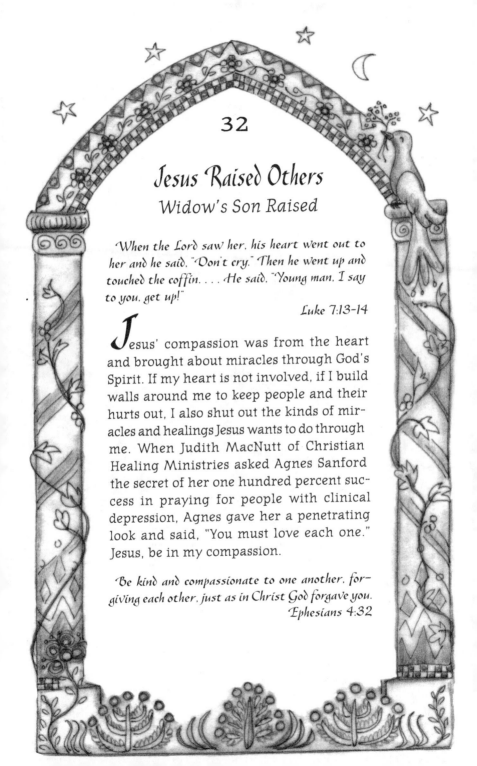

32

Jesus Raised Others
Widow's Son Raised

When the Lord saw her, his heart went out to her and he said, "Don't cry." Then he went up and touched the coffin. . . . He said, "Young man, I say to you, get up!"

Luke 7:13-14

Jesus' compassion was from the heart and brought about miracles through God's Spirit. If my heart is not involved, if I build walls around me to keep people and their hurts out, I also shut out the kinds of miracles and healings Jesus wants to do through me. When Judith MacNutt of Christian Healing Ministries asked Agnes Sanford the secret of her one hundred percent success in praying for people with clinical depression, Agnes gave her a penetrating look and said, "You must love each one." Jesus, be in my compassion.

Be kind and compassionate to one another, forgiving each other, just as in Christ God forgave you.

Ephesians 4:32

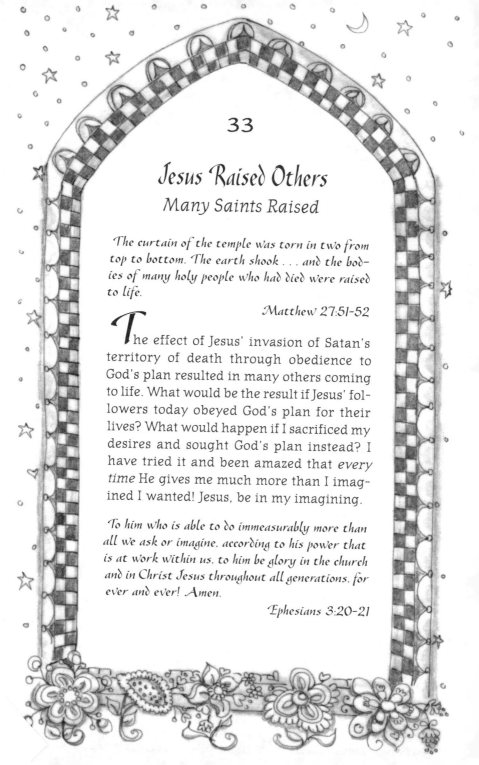

33

Jesus Raised Others
Many Saints Raised

The curtain of the temple was torn in two from top to bottom. The earth shook . . . and the bodies of many holy people who had died were raised to life.

Matthew 27:51-52

The effect of Jesus' invasion of Satan's territory of death through obedience to God's plan resulted in many others coming to life. What would be the result if Jesus' followers today obeyed God's plan for their lives? What would happen if I sacrificed my desires and sought God's plan instead? I have tried it and been amazed that *every time* He gives me much more than I imagined I wanted! Jesus, be in my imagining.

To him who is able to do immeasurably more than all we ask or imagine, according to his power that is at work within us, to him be glory in the church and in Christ Jesus throughout all generations, for ever and ever! Amen.

Ephesians 3:20-21

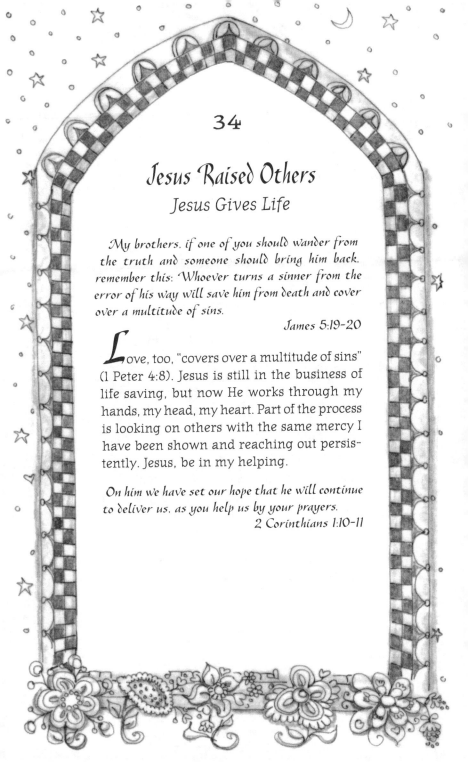

Jesus Raised Others
Jesus Gives Life

My brothers, if one of you should wander from the truth and someone should bring him back, remember this: Whoever turns a sinner from the error of his way will save him from death and cover over a multitude of sins.

James 5:19-20

*L*ove, too, "covers over a multitude of sins" (1 Peter 4:8). Jesus is still in the business of life saving, but now He works through my hands, my head, my heart. Part of the process is looking on others with the same mercy I have been shown and reaching out persistently. Jesus, be in my helping.

On him we have set our hope that he will continue to deliver us, as you help us by your prayers.

2 Corinthians 1:10-11

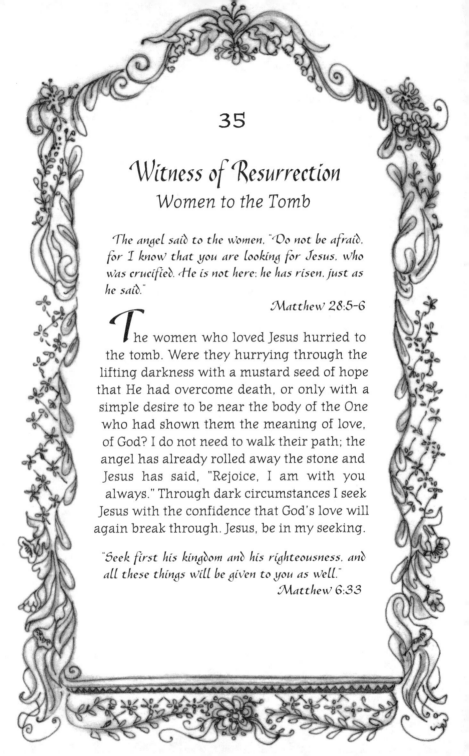

Witness of Resurrection
Women to the Tomb

*The angel said to the women. "Do not be afraid.
for I know that you are looking for Jesus. who
was crucified. He is not here: he has risen, just as
he said."*

Matthew 28:5-6

The women who loved Jesus hurried to
the tomb. Were they hurrying through the
lifting darkness with a mustard seed of hope
that He had overcome death, or only with a
simple desire to be near the body of the One
who had shown them the meaning of love,
of God? I do not need to walk their path; the
angel has already rolled away the stone and
Jesus has said, "Rejoice, I am with you
always." Through dark circumstances I seek
Jesus with the confidence that God's love will
again break through. Jesus, be in my seeking.

*"Seek first his kingdom and his righteousness. and
all these things will be given to you as well."*

Matthew 6:33

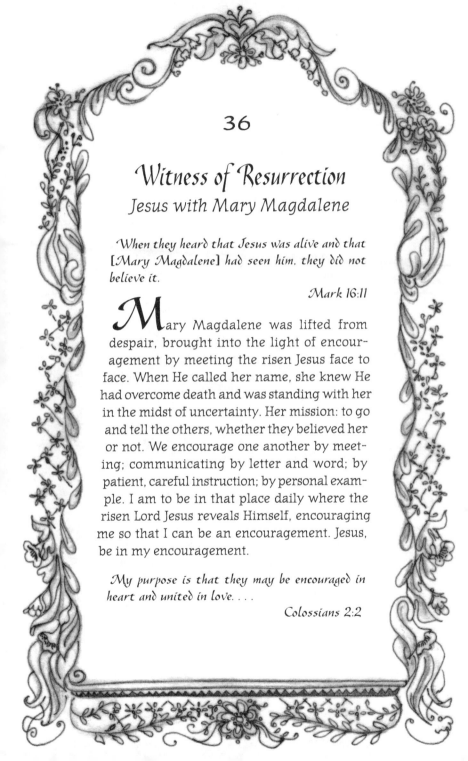

36

Witness of Resurrection
Jesus with Mary Magdalene

When they heard that Jesus was alive and that [Mary Magdalene] had seen him, they did not believe it.

Mark 16:11

Mary Magdalene was lifted from despair, brought into the light of encouragement by meeting the risen Jesus face to face. When He called her name, she knew He had overcome death and was standing with her in the midst of uncertainty. Her mission: to go and tell the others, whether they believed her or not. We encourage one another by meeting; communicating by letter and word; by patient, careful instruction; by personal example. I am to be in that place daily where the risen Lord Jesus reveals Himself, encouraging me so that I can be an encouragement. Jesus, be in my encouragement.

My purpose is that they may be encouraged in heart and united in love. . . .

Colossians 2:2

Witness of Resurrection
Jesus with the Other Women

The women hurried away from the tomb, afraid yet filled with joy. . . . Suddenly Jesus met them. "Greetings," he said. They came to him, clasped his feet and worshiped him.

Matthew 28:8-9

*I*n encountering the resurrected Jesus, the grieving women received hope, joy and purpose. My mother, confronted with the death of her husband of 56 years, noticed that the grief of others was reopened. By comforting, listening to, loving one another, they received strength in a circle of consolation. In God's great plan, which includes life and death for every creature, Jesus is ever-present, close as our breathing. Jesus, be in my consolation.

May . . . [God], who loved us and by his grace gave us eternal encouragement and good hope, encourage your hearts and strengthen you in every good deed and word.

2 Thessalonians 2:16-17

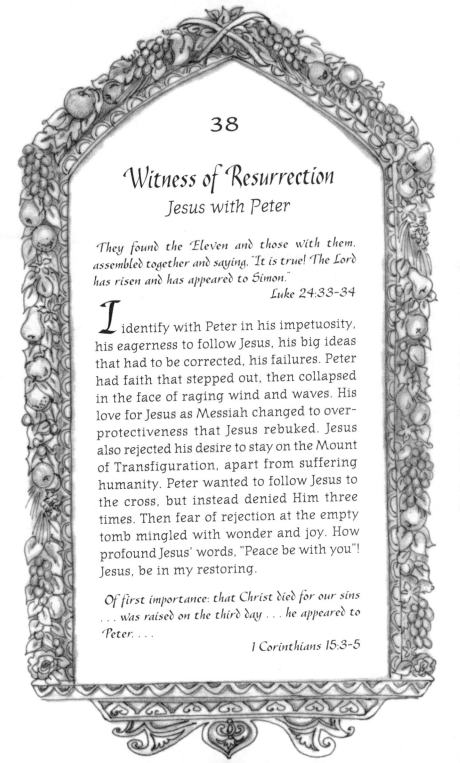

38

Witness of Resurrection
Jesus with Peter

They found the Eleven and those with them,
assembled together and saying, "It is true! The Lord
has risen and has appeared to Simon."

Luke 24:33-34

I identify with Peter in his impetuosity,
his eagerness to follow Jesus, his big ideas
that had to be corrected, his failures. Peter
had faith that stepped out, then collapsed
in the face of raging wind and waves. His
love for Jesus as Messiah changed to over-
protectiveness that Jesus rebuked. Jesus
also rejected his desire to stay on the Mount
of Transfiguration, apart from suffering
humanity. Peter wanted to follow Jesus to
the cross, but instead denied Him three
times. Then fear of rejection at the empty
tomb mingled with wonder and joy. How
profound Jesus' words, "Peace be with you"!
Jesus, be in my restoring.

Of first importance: that Christ died for our sins
. . . was raised on the third day . . . he appeared to
Peter. . . .

1 Corinthians 15:3-5

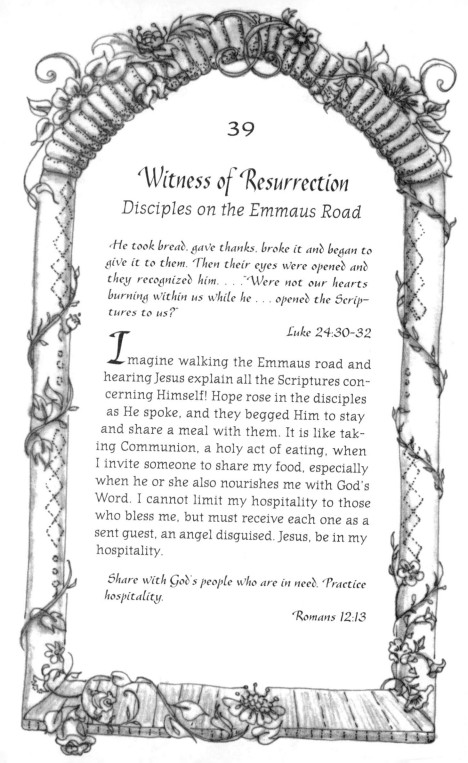

Witness of Resurrection
Disciples on the Emmaus Road

He took bread, gave thanks, broke it and began to give it to them. Then their eyes were opened and they recognized him. . . ."Were not our hearts burning within us while he . . . opened the Scriptures to us?"

Luke 24:30-32

*I*magine walking the Emmaus road and hearing Jesus explain all the Scriptures concerning Himself! Hope rose in the disciples as He spoke, and they begged Him to stay and share a meal with them. It is like taking Communion, a holy act of eating, when I invite someone to share my food, especially when he or she also nourishes me with God's Word. I cannot limit my hospitality to those who bless me, but must receive each one as a sent guest, an angel disguised. Jesus, be in my hospitality.

Share with God's people who are in need. Practice hospitality.

Romans 12:13

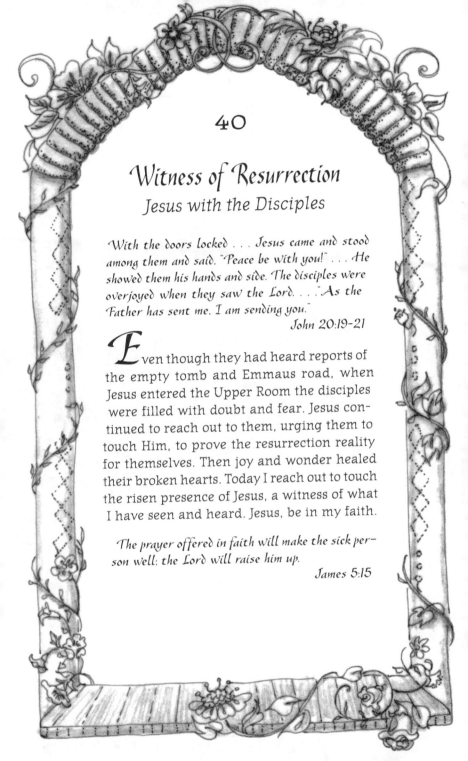

40

Witness of Resurrection
Jesus with the Disciples

With the doors locked . . . Jesus came and stood among them and said, "Peace be with you!" . . . He showed them his hands and side. The disciples were overjoyed when they saw the Lord. . . . "As the Father has sent me, I am sending you."

John 20:19-21

*E*ven though they had heard reports of the empty tomb and Emmaus road, when Jesus entered the Upper Room the disciples were filled with doubt and fear. Jesus continued to reach out to them, urging them to touch Him, to prove the resurrection reality for themselves. Then joy and wonder healed their broken hearts. Today I reach out to touch the risen presence of Jesus, a witness of what I have seen and heard. Jesus, be in my faith.

The prayer offered in faith will make the sick person well: the Lord will raise him up.

James 5:15

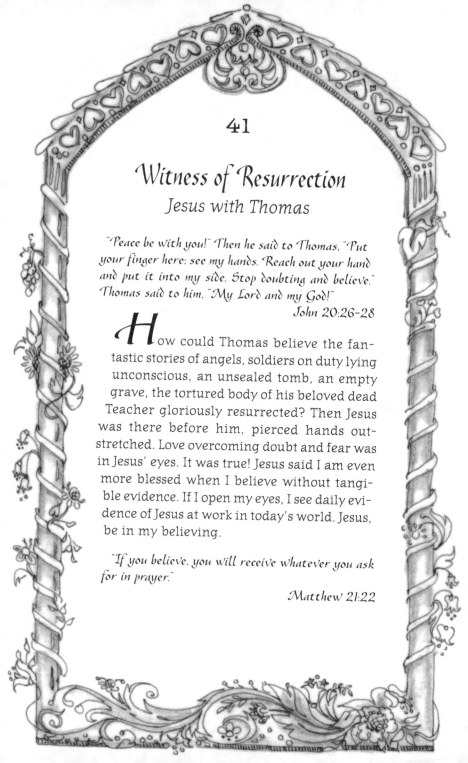

41

Witness of Resurrection
Jesus with Thomas

"Peace be with you!" Then he said to Thomas, "Put your finger here: see my hands. Reach out your hand and put it into my side. Stop doubting and believe." Thomas said to him, "My Lord and my God!"

John 20:26-28

How could Thomas believe the fantastic stories of angels, soldiers on duty lying unconscious, an unsealed tomb, an empty grave, the tortured body of his beloved dead Teacher gloriously resurrected? Then Jesus was there before him, pierced hands outstretched. Love overcoming doubt and fear was in Jesus' eyes. It was true! Jesus said I am even more blessed when I believe without tangible evidence. If I open my eyes, I see daily evidence of Jesus at work in today's world. Jesus, be in my believing.

"If you believe, you will receive whatever you ask for in prayer."

Matthew 21:22

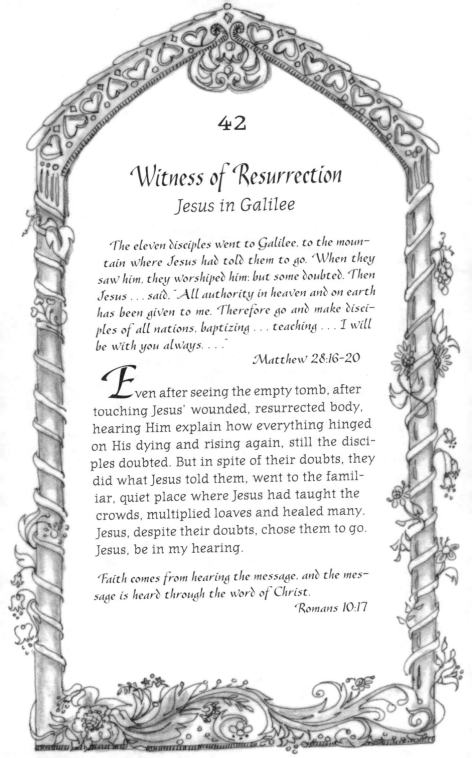

42

Witness of Resurrection
Jesus in Galilee

The eleven disciples went to Galilee, to the mountain where Jesus had told them to go. When they saw him, they worshiped him; but some doubted. Then Jesus . . . said, "All authority in heaven and on earth has been given to me. Therefore go and make disciples of all nations, baptizing . . . teaching . . . I will be with you always. . . ."

Matthew 28:16-20

*E*ven after seeing the empty tomb, after touching Jesus' wounded, resurrected body, hearing Him explain how everything hinged on His dying and rising again, still the disciples doubted. But in spite of their doubts, they did what Jesus told them, went to the familiar, quiet place where Jesus had taught the crowds, multiplied loaves and healed many. Jesus, despite their doubts, chose them to go. Jesus, be in my hearing.

Faith comes from hearing the message, and the message is heard through the word of Christ.

Romans 10:17

43

Witness of Resurrection
Jesus with Peter

*It was Jesus. He called out to them. "Friends. . . .
throw your net on the right side of the boat and you
will find some." When they did. they were unable to
haul the net in because of the large number of fish.*

John 21:4-6

Jesus had told them to wait for Him in
Galilee, but Peter could not hang around
doing nothing. Yet all his fishing that night
amounted to nothing until Jesus called instructions from the shore. I am so like Peter, wanting to get the job done in my way, in my timing. Yesterday the computer stopped me four
times from writing. I prayed over it, yet real-
ized Jesus wanted me to visit several sick
people. I left the house and was able to minister with peace. Today the computer works!
Jesus, be in my doing.

*Let us not become weary in doing good. for at the
proper time we will reap a harvest if we do not
give up.*

Galatians 6:9

44

Witness of Resurrection
Jesus' Question to Peter

Jesus said to Simon Peter, "Simon son of John, do you truly love me more than these? . . . Feed my lambs. . . . Take care of my sheep. . . . Feed my sheep. . . ."

John 21:15-17

By the fire, with the smell of fried fish in the early morning light, Jesus asked Peter one question three times about his motives and mission: "Do you have sacrificial love?" I feel Jesus is taking me aside to ask in the kindest way possible: "Is your love the kind that gives even when it is not returned? Do you care enough for those in your circle despite rejection, misunderstanding or apathy?" I need God's great love to overcome my smallness, His warmth to melt my coldness and indifference. Jesus, be in my caring.

Be shepherds of God's flock that is under your care, serving as overseers . . . because you are willing . . . eager to serve.

1 Peter 5:2

45

Witness of Resurrection
Jesus with the Five Hundred

He appeared to more than five hundred of the brothers at the same time, most of whom are still living. . . .
                                    1 Corinthians 15:6

Jesus wanted those who had followed Him, who were confused and disheartened by His death, to see the reality of the resurrection, so He appeared to them in person. In the midst of their gathering, Jesus came to strengthen them. Jesus still appears to those who seek Him earnestly—to save, set free, empower. His healing touch is present in our midst. Jesus, be in my strengthening.

When you come together, everyone has a hymn, or a word of instruction, a revelation, a tongue or an interpretation. All of these must be done for the strengthening of the church.
                                    1 Corinthians 14:26

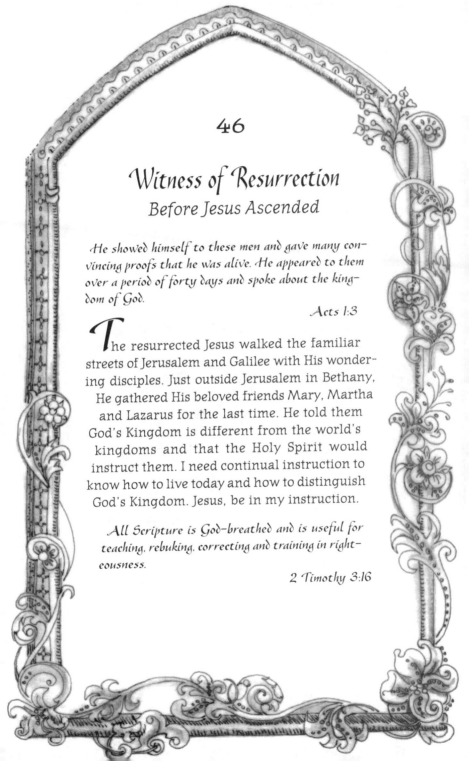

46

Witness of Resurrection
Before Jesus Ascended

He showed himself to these men and gave many convincing proofs that he was alive. He appeared to them over a period of forty days and spoke about the kingdom of God.

Acts 1:3

The resurrected Jesus walked the familiar streets of Jerusalem and Galilee with His wondering disciples. Just outside Jerusalem in Bethany, He gathered His beloved friends Mary, Martha and Lazarus for the last time. He told them God's Kingdom is different from the world's kingdoms and that the Holy Spirit would instruct them. I need continual instruction to know how to live today and how to distinguish God's Kingdom. Jesus, be in my instruction.

All Scripture is God-breathed and is useful for teaching, rebuking, correcting and training in righteousness.

2 Timothy 3:16

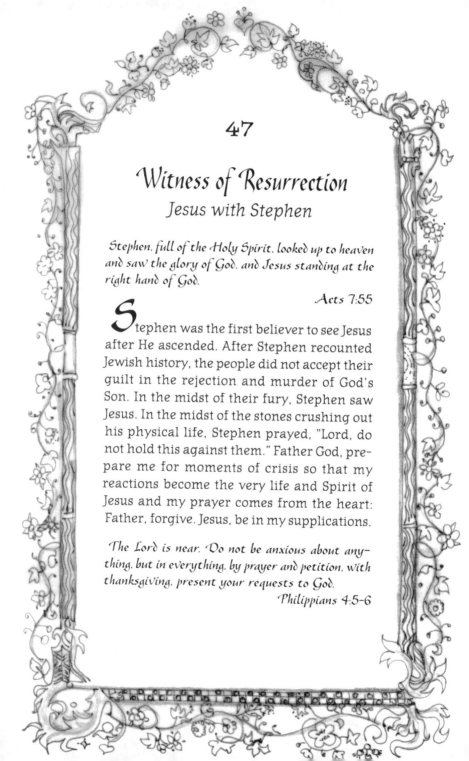

47

Witness of Resurrection
Jesus with Stephen

Stephen, full of the Holy Spirit, looked up to heaven and saw the glory of God, and Jesus standing at the right hand of God.

Acts 7:55

Stephen was the first believer to see Jesus after He ascended. After Stephen recounted Jewish history, the people did not accept their guilt in the rejection and murder of God's Son. In the midst of their fury, Stephen saw Jesus. In the midst of the stones crushing out his physical life, Stephen prayed, "Lord, do not hold this against them." Father God, prepare me for moments of crisis so that my reactions become the very life and Spirit of Jesus and my prayer comes from the heart: Father, forgive. Jesus, be in my supplications.

The Lord is near. Do not be anxious about anything, but in everything, by prayer and petition, with thanksgiving, present your requests to God.

Philippians 4:5-6

48

Witness of Resurrection
Jesus with Paul

*"About noon . . . as I was on the road, I saw a light
from heaven, brighter than the sun, blazing around
me and my companions. We all fell to the ground,
and I heard a voice saying to me in Aramaic, 'Saul,
Saul, why do you persecute me?' . . . 'Who are you,
Lord?' 'I am Jesus, whom you are persecuting.'"*
Acts 26:13-15

Saul was fervent in the pharisaical beliefs
that drove him to persecute, even kill Christians, until he met Jesus on the Damascus
road. Jesus converted that furious energy into
enduring, compassionate stamina. When
swords are beaten into plowshares, plenty of
work remains to be done, but the result is
harvest, not destruction. Jesus, be in my fight.

*Man of God . . . pursue righteousness, godliness,
faith, love, endurance and gentleness. Fight the good
fight of the faith. Take hold of . . . eternal life. . . .*
1 Timothy 6:11-12

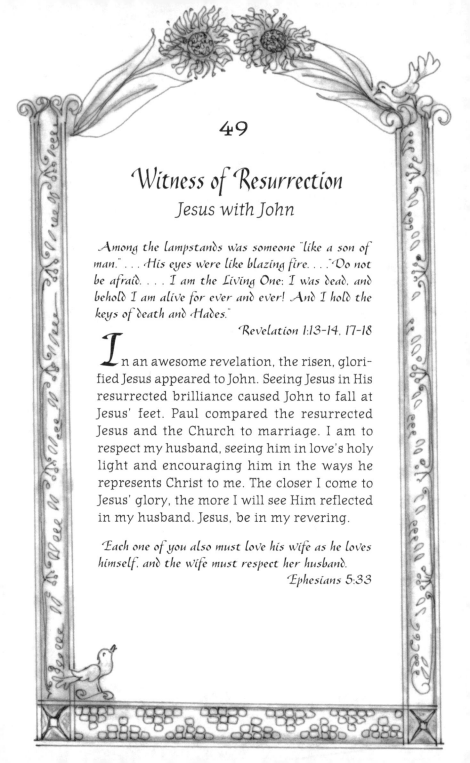

49

Witness of Resurrection
Jesus with John

Among the lampstands was someone "like a son of man." . . . His eyes were like blazing fire. . . . "Do not be afraid. . . . I am the Living One; I was dead, and behold I am alive for ever and ever! And I hold the keys of death and Hades."

Revelation 1:13-14, 17-18

In an awesome revelation, the risen, glorified Jesus appeared to John. Seeing Jesus in His resurrected brilliance caused John to fall at Jesus' feet. Paul compared the resurrected Jesus and the Church to marriage. I am to respect my husband, seeing him in love's holy light and encouraging him in the ways he represents Christ to me. The closer I come to Jesus' glory, the more I will see Him reflected in my husband. Jesus, be in my revering.

Each one of you also must love his wife as he loves himself, and the wife must respect her husband.

Ephesians 5:33

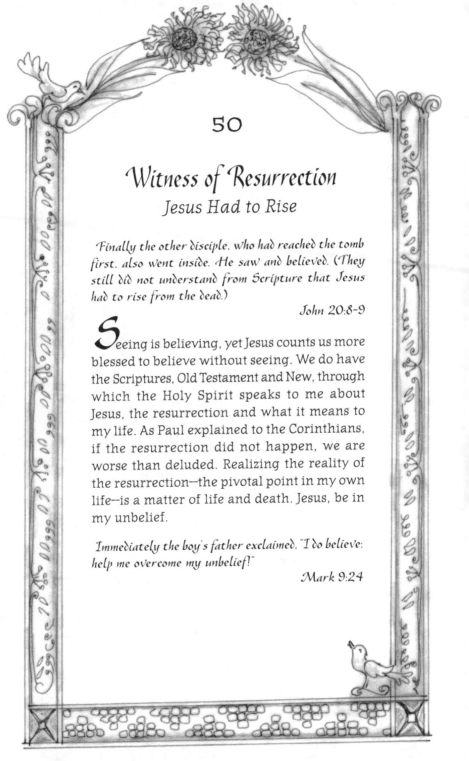

Witness of Resurrection
Jesus Had to Rise

Finally the other disciple, who had reached the tomb first, also went inside. He saw and believed. (They still did not understand from Scripture that Jesus had to rise from the dead.)

John 20:8-9

*S*eeing is believing, yet Jesus counts us more blessed to believe without seeing. We do have the Scriptures, Old Testament and New, through which the Holy Spirit speaks to me about Jesus, the resurrection and what it means to my life. As Paul explained to the Corinthians, if the resurrection did not happen, we are worse than deluded. Realizing the reality of the resurrection—the pivotal point in my own life—is a matter of life and death. Jesus, be in my unbelief.

Immediately the boy's father exclaimed, "I do believe: help me overcome my unbelief!"

Mark 9:24

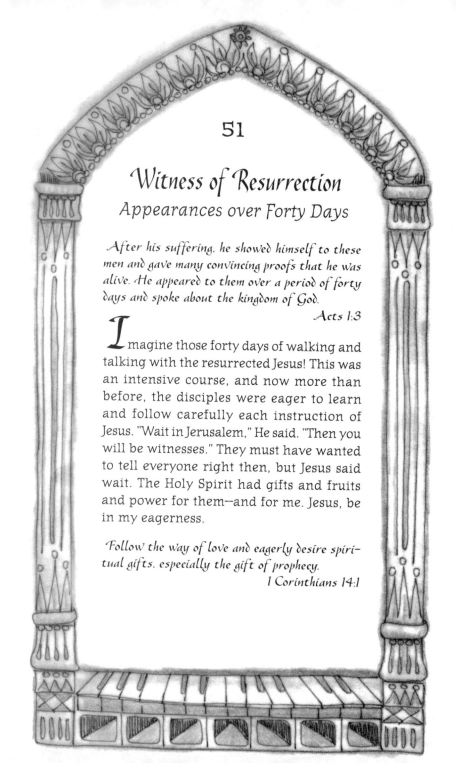

51

Witness of Resurrection
Appearances over Forty Days

After his suffering, he showed himself to these men and gave many convincing proofs that he was alive. He appeared to them over a period of forty days and spoke about the kingdom of God.

Acts 1:3

*I*magine those forty days of walking and talking with the resurrected Jesus! This was an intensive course, and now more than before, the disciples were eager to learn and follow carefully each instruction of Jesus. "Wait in Jerusalem," He said. "Then you will be witnesses." They must have wanted to tell everyone right then, but Jesus said wait. The Holy Spirit had gifts and fruits and power for them—and for me. Jesus, be in my eagerness.

Follow the way of love and eagerly desire spiritual gifts, especially the gift of prophecy.

1 Corinthians 14:1

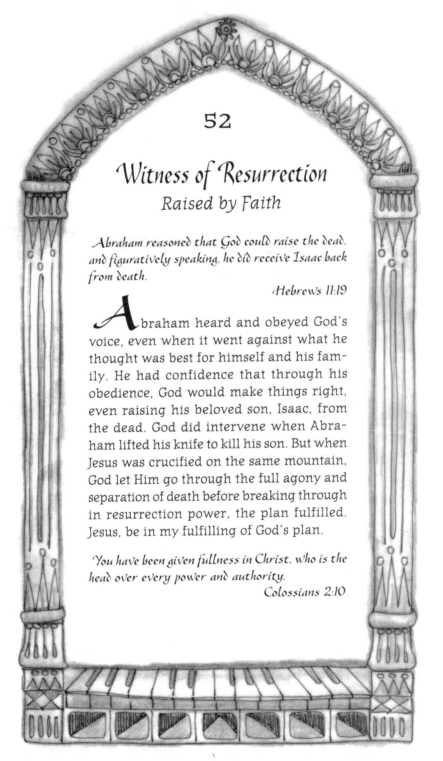

52

Witness of Resurrection
Raised by Faith

Abraham reasoned that God could raise the dead, and figuratively speaking, he did receive Isaac back from death.

Hebrews 11:19

Abraham heard and obeyed God's voice, even when it went against what he thought was best for himself and his family. He had confidence that through his obedience, God would make things right, even raising his beloved son, Isaac, from the dead. God did intervene when Abraham lifted his knife to kill his son. But when Jesus was crucified on the same mountain, God let Him go through the full agony and separation of death before breaking through in resurrection power, the plan fulfilled. Jesus, be in my fulfilling of God's plan.

You have been given fullness in Christ, who is the head over every power and authority.

Colossians 2:10

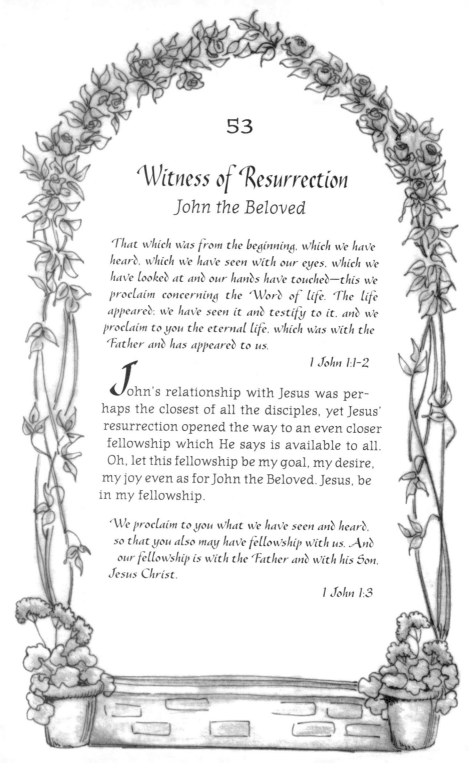

53

Witness of Resurrection
John the Beloved

That which was from the beginning, which we have heard, which we have seen with our eyes, which we have looked at and our hands have touched—this we proclaim concerning the Word of life. The life appeared; we have seen it and testify to it, and we proclaim to you the eternal life, which was with the Father and has appeared to us.

1 John 1:1-2

Iohn's relationship with Jesus was perhaps the closest of all the disciples, yet Jesus' resurrection opened the way to an even closer fellowship which He says is available to all. Oh, let this fellowship be my goal, my desire, my joy even as for John the Beloved. Jesus, be in my fellowship.

We proclaim to you what we have seen and heard, so that you also may have fellowship with us. And our fellowship is with the Father and with his Son, Jesus Christ.

1 John 1:3

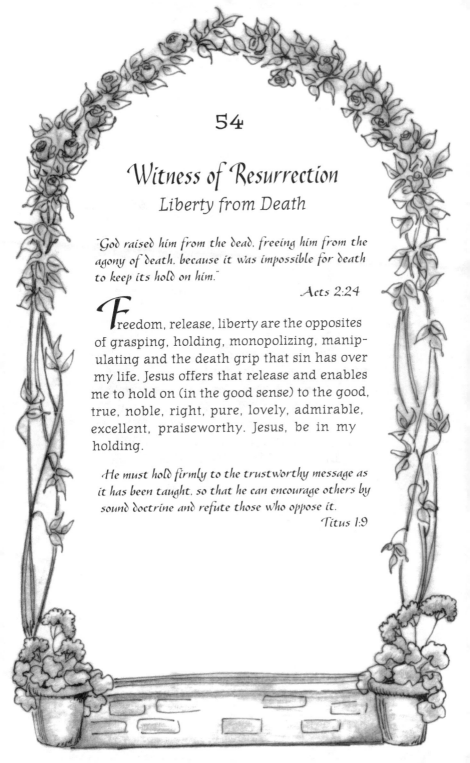

54

Witness of Resurrection
Liberty from Death

"God raised him from the dead, freeing him from the agony of death, because it was impossible for death to keep its hold on him."

Acts 2:24

Freedom, release, liberty are the opposites of grasping, holding, monopolizing, manipulating and the death grip that sin has over my life. Jesus offers that release and enables me to hold on (in the good sense) to the good, true, noble, right, pure, lovely, admirable, excellent, praiseworthy. Jesus, be in my holding.

He must hold firmly to the trustworthy message as it has been taught, so that he can encourage others by sound doctrine and refute those who oppose it.

Titus 1:9

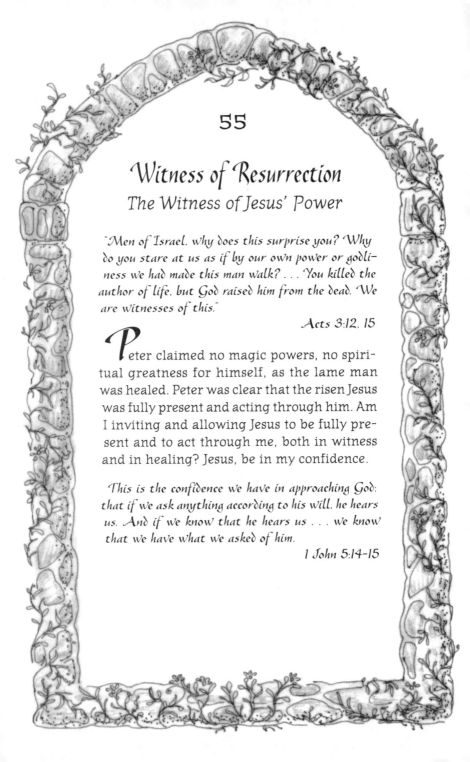

Witness of Resurrection
The Witness of Jesus' Power

"Men of Israel, why does this surprise you? Why
do you stare at us as if by our own power or godliness we had made this man walk? . . . You killed the
author of life, but God raised him from the dead. We
are witnesses of this."

Acts 3:12, 15

Peter claimed no magic powers, no spiritual greatness for himself, as the lame man
was healed. Peter was clear that the risen Jesus
was fully present and acting through him. Am
I inviting and allowing Jesus to be fully present and to act through me, both in witness
and in healing? Jesus, be in my confidence.

This is the confidence we have in approaching God:
that if we ask anything according to his will, he hears
us. And if we know that he hears us . . . we know
that we have what we asked of him.

1 John 5:14-15

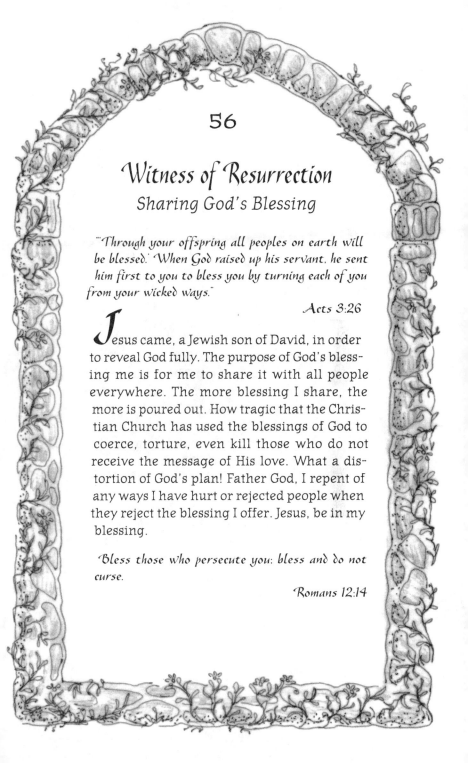

Witness of Resurrection
Sharing God's Blessing

"Through your offspring all peoples on earth will be blessed." When God raised up his servant, he sent him first to you to bless you by turning each of you from your wicked ways."

Acts 3:26

Jesus came, a Jewish son of David, in order to reveal God fully. The purpose of God's blessing me is for me to share it with all people everywhere. The more blessing I share, the more is poured out. How tragic that the Christian Church has used the blessings of God to coerce, torture, even kill those who do not receive the message of His love. What a distortion of God's plan! Father God, I repent of any ways I have hurt or rejected people when they reject the blessing I offer. Jesus, be in my blessing.

Bless those who persecute you: bless and do not curse.

Romans 12:14

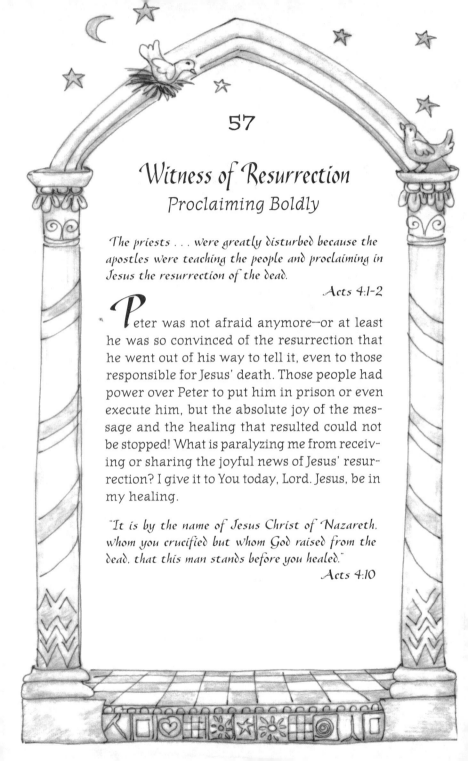

Witness of Resurrection
Proclaiming Boldly

The priests . . . were greatly disturbed because the apostles were teaching the people and proclaiming in Jesus the resurrection of the dead.

Acts 4:1-2

*P*eter was not afraid anymore—or at least he was so convinced of the resurrection that he went out of his way to tell it, even to those responsible for Jesus' death. Those people had power over Peter to put him in prison or even execute him, but the absolute joy of the message and the healing that resulted could not be stopped! What is paralyzing me from receiving or sharing the joyful news of Jesus' resurrection? I give it to You today, Lord. Jesus, be in my healing.

"It is by the name of Jesus Christ of Nazareth, whom you crucified but whom God raised from the dead, that this man stands before you healed."

Acts 4:10

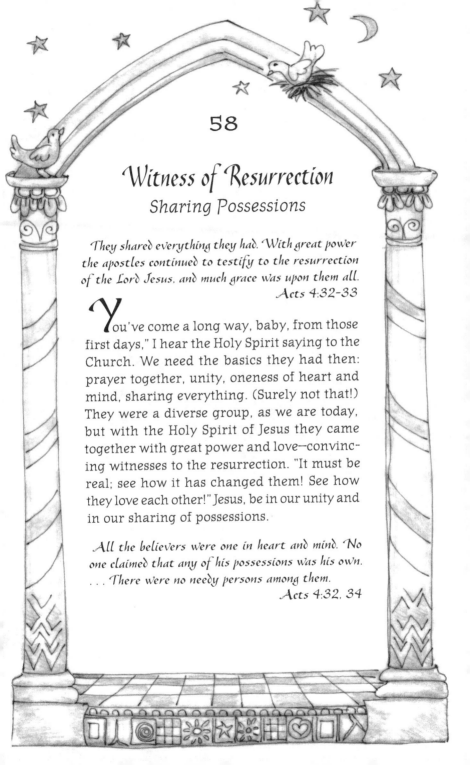

58

Witness of Resurrection
Sharing Possessions

They shared everything they had. With great power the apostles continued to testify to the resurrection of the Lord Jesus, and much grace was upon them all.
Acts 4:32-33

Y ou've come a long way, baby, from those first days," I hear the Holy Spirit saying to the Church. We need the basics they had then: prayer together, unity, oneness of heart and mind, sharing everything. (Surely not that!) They were a diverse group, as we are today, but with the Holy Spirit of Jesus they came together with great power and love—convincing witnesses to the resurrection. "It must be real; see how it has changed them! See how they love each other!" Jesus, be in our unity and in our sharing of possessions.

All the believers were one in heart and mind. No one claimed that any of his possessions was his own. . . . There were no needy persons among them.
Acts 4:32, 34

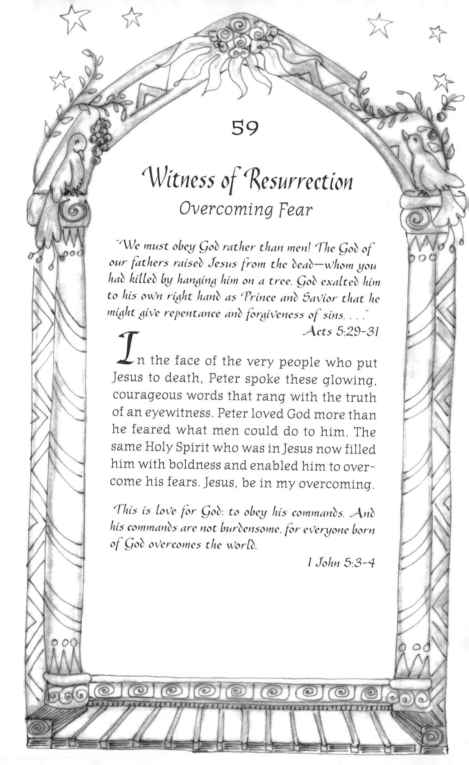

59

Witness of Resurrection
Overcoming Fear

"We must obey God rather than men! The God of our fathers raised Jesus from the dead—whom you had killed by hanging him on a tree. God exalted him to his own right hand as Prince and Savior that he might give repentance and forgiveness of sins. . . ."

Acts 5:29-31

In the face of the very people who put Jesus to death, Peter spoke these glowing, courageous words that rang with the truth of an eyewitness. Peter loved God more than he feared what men could do to him. The same Holy Spirit who was in Jesus now filled him with boldness and enabled him to overcome his fears. Jesus, be in my overcoming.

This is love for God: to obey his commands. And his commands are not burdensome, for everyone born of God overcomes the world.

1 John 5:3-4

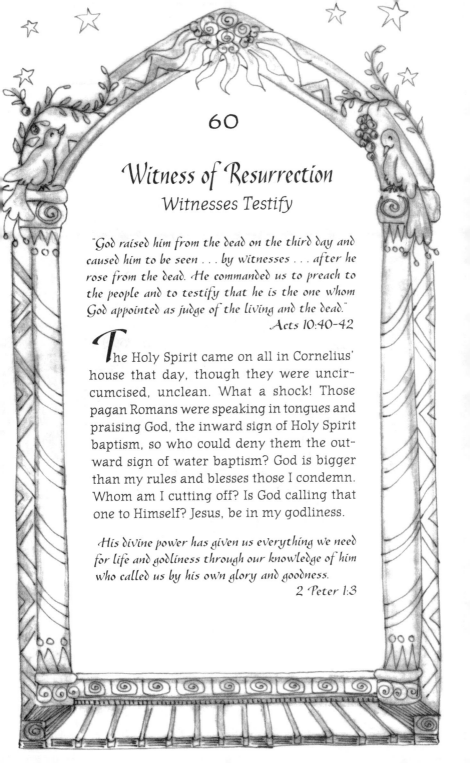

60

Witness of Resurrection
Witnesses Testify

"God raised him from the dead on the third day and caused him to be seen . . . by witnesses . . . after he rose from the dead. He commanded us to preach to the people and to testify that he is the one whom God appointed as judge of the living and the dead."
Acts 10:40-42

The Holy Spirit came on all in Cornelius' house that day, though they were uncircumcised, unclean. What a shock! Those pagan Romans were speaking in tongues and praising God, the inward sign of Holy Spirit baptism, so who could deny them the outward sign of water baptism? God is bigger than my rules and blesses those I condemn. Whom am I cutting off? Is God calling that one to Himself? Jesus, be in my godliness.

His divine power has given us everything we need for life and godliness through our knowledge of him who called us by his own glory and goodness.
2 Peter 1:3

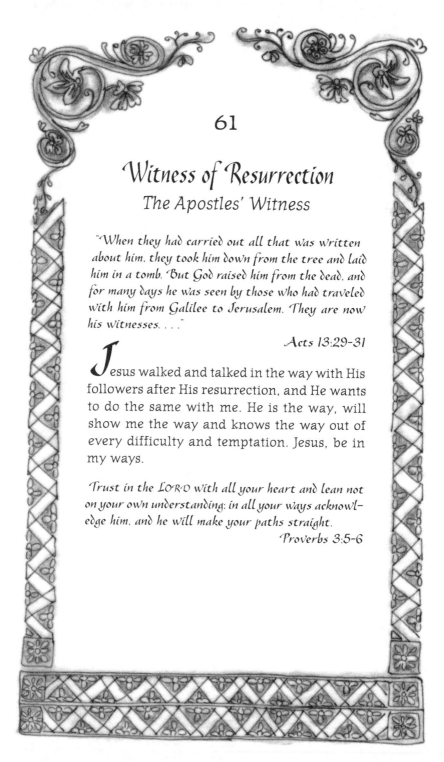

61

Witness of Resurrection
The Apostles' Witness

"When they had carried out all that was written about him, they took him down from the tree and laid him in a tomb. But God raised him from the dead, and for many days he was seen by those who had traveled with him from Galilee to Jerusalem. They are now his witnesses. . . ."

Acts 13:29-31

Jesus walked and talked in the way with His followers after His resurrection, and He wants to do the same with me. He is the way, will show me the way and knows the way out of every difficulty and temptation. Jesus, be in my ways.

Trust in the LORD with all your heart and lean not on your own understanding; in all your ways acknowledge him, and he will make your paths straight.

Proverbs 3:5-6

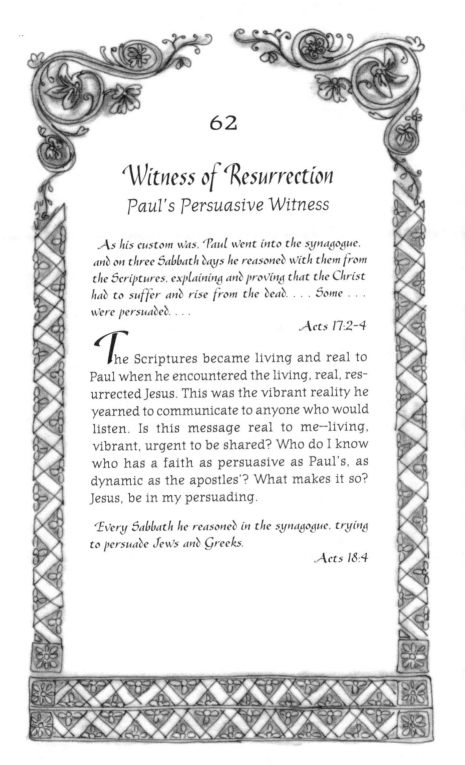

62

Witness of Resurrection
Paul's Persuasive Witness

As his custom was, Paul went into the synagogue, and on three Sabbath days he reasoned with them from the Scriptures, explaining and proving that the Christ had to suffer and rise from the dead. . . . Some . . . were persuaded. . . .

Acts 17:2-4

The Scriptures became living and real to Paul when he encountered the living, real, resurrected Jesus. This was the vibrant reality he yearned to communicate to anyone who would listen. Is this message real to me—living, vibrant, urgent to be shared? Who do I know who has a faith as persuasive as Paul's, as dynamic as the apostles'? What makes it so? Jesus, be in my persuading.

Every Sabbath he reasoned in the synagogue, trying to persuade Jews and Greeks.

Acts 18:4

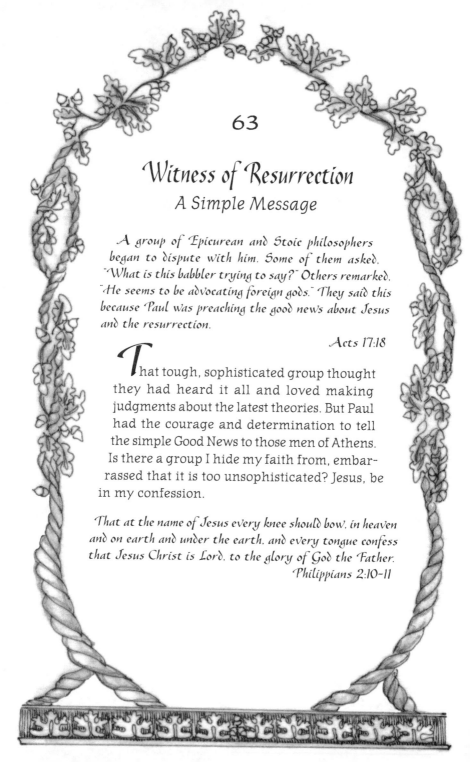

63

Witness of Resurrection
A Simple Message

*A group of Epicurean and Stoic philosophers
began to dispute with him. Some of them asked,
"What is this babbler trying to say?" Others remarked,
"He seems to be advocating foreign gods." They said this
because Paul was preaching the good news about Jesus
and the resurrection.*

Acts 17:18

That tough, sophisticated group thought
they had heard it all and loved making
judgments about the latest theories. But Paul
had the courage and determination to tell
the simple Good News to those men of Athens.
Is there a group I hide my faith from, embarrassed that it is too unsophisticated? Jesus, be
in my confession.

*That at the name of Jesus every knee should bow, in heaven
and on earth and under the earth, and every tongue confess
that Jesus Christ is Lord, to the glory of God the Father.*

Philippians 2:10-11

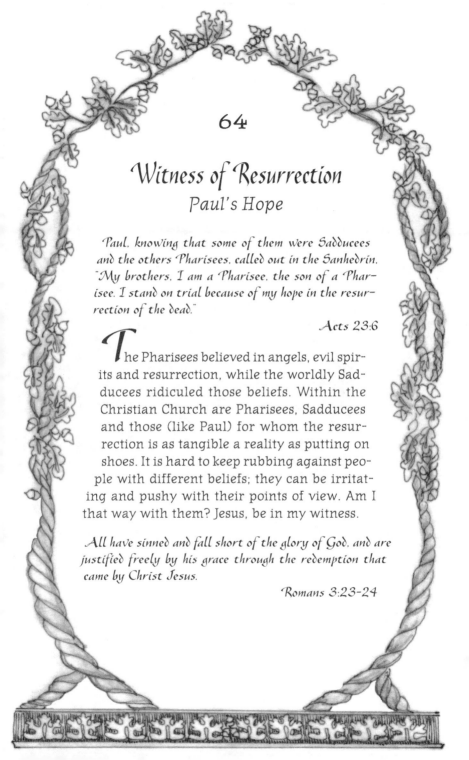

64

Witness of Resurrection
Paul's Hope

Paul, knowing that some of them were Sadducees and the others Pharisees, called out in the Sanhedrin, "My brothers, I am a Pharisee, the son of a Pharisee. I stand on trial because of my hope in the resurrection of the dead."

Acts 23:6

The Pharisees believed in angels, evil spirits and resurrection, while the worldly Sadducees ridiculed those beliefs. Within the Christian Church are Pharisees, Sadducees and those (like Paul) for whom the resurrection is as tangible a reality as putting on shoes. It is hard to keep rubbing against people with different beliefs; they can be irritating and pushy with their points of view. Am I that way with them? Jesus, be in my witness.

All have sinned and fall short of the glory of God, and are justified freely by his grace through the redemption that came by Christ Jesus.

Romans 3:23-24

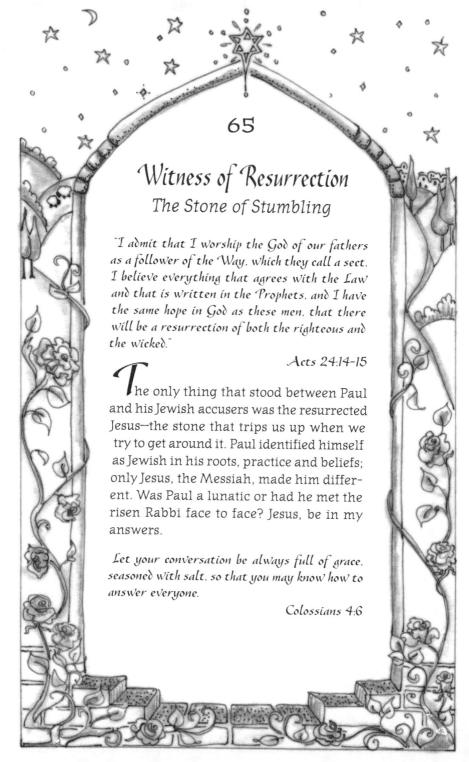

Witness of Resurrection
The Stone of Stumbling

"I admit that I worship the God of our fathers as a follower of the Way, which they call a sect. I believe everything that agrees with the Law and that is written in the Prophets, and I have the same hope in God as these men, that there will be a resurrection of both the righteous and the wicked."

Acts 24:14-15

The only thing that stood between Paul and his Jewish accusers was the resurrected Jesus—the stone that trips us up when we try to get around it. Paul identified himself as Jewish in his roots, practice and beliefs; only Jesus, the Messiah, made him different. Was Paul a lunatic or had he met the risen Rabbi face to face? Jesus, be in my answers.

Let your conversation be always full of grace, seasoned with salt, so that you may know how to answer everyone.

Colossians 4:6

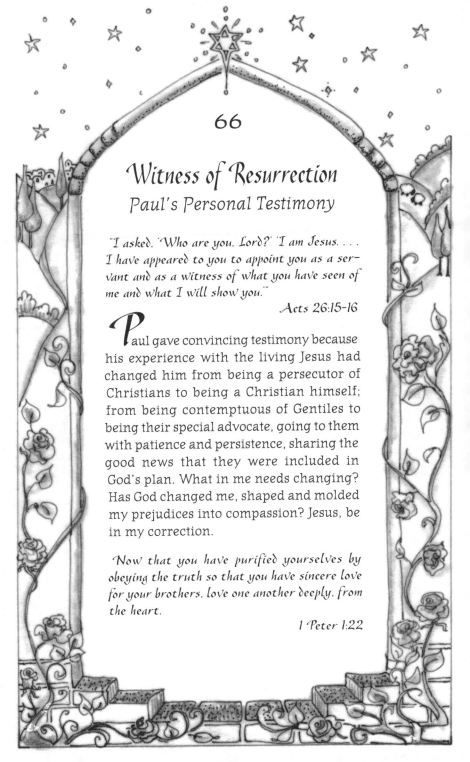

Witness of Resurrection
Paul's Personal Testimony

"I asked, 'Who are you, Lord?' 'I am Jesus. . . .
I have appeared to you to appoint you as a ser-
vant and as a witness of what you have seen of
me and what I will show you."

Acts 26:15-16

*P*aul gave convincing testimony because his experience with the living Jesus had changed him from being a persecutor of Christians to being a Christian himself; from being contemptuous of Gentiles to being their special advocate, going to them with patience and persistence, sharing the good news that they were included in God's plan. What in me needs changing? Has God changed me, shaped and molded my prejudices into compassion? Jesus, be in my correction.

Now that you have purified yourselves by
obeying the truth so that you have sincere love
for your brothers, love one another deeply, from
the heart.

1 Peter 1:22

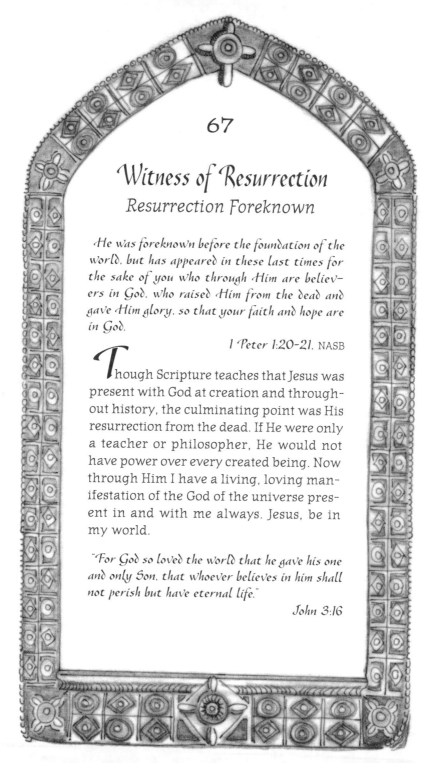

Witness of Resurrection
Resurrection Foreknown

He was foreknown before the foundation of the world, but has appeared in these last times for the sake of you who through Him are believers in God, who raised Him from the dead and gave Him glory, so that your faith and hope are in God.

1 Peter 1:20-21, NASB

Though Scripture teaches that Jesus was present with God at creation and throughout history, the culminating point was His resurrection from the dead. If He were only a teacher or philosopher, He would not have power over every created being. Now through Him I have a living, loving manifestation of the God of the universe present in and with me always. Jesus, be in my world.

"For God so loved the world that he gave his one and only Son, that whoever believes in him shall not perish but have eternal life."

John 3:16

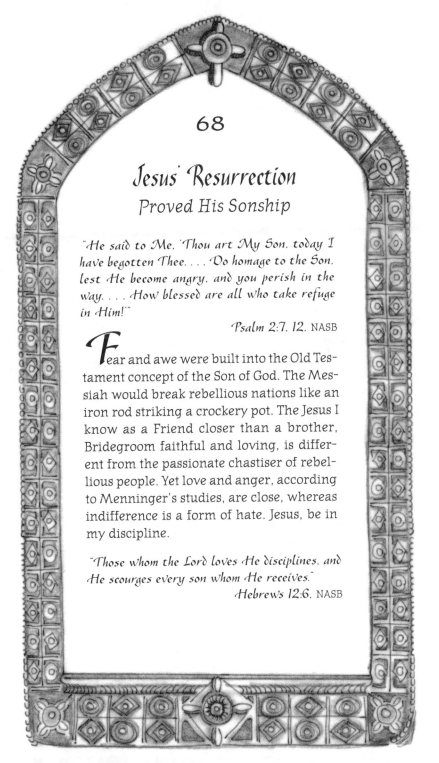

68

Jesus' Resurrection
Proved His Sonship

"He said to Me. 'Thou art My Son. today I have begotten Thee. . . . Do homage to the Son. lest He become angry. and you perish in the way. . . . How blessed are all who take refuge in Him!'"

Psalm 2:7. 12. NASB

Fear and awe were built into the Old Testament concept of the Son of God. The Messiah would break rebellious nations like an iron rod striking a crockery pot. The Jesus I know as a Friend closer than a brother, Bridegroom faithful and loving, is different from the passionate chastiser of rebellious people. Yet love and anger, according to Menninger's studies, are close, whereas indifference is a form of hate. Jesus, be in my discipline.

"Those whom the Lord loves He disciplines. and He scourges every son whom He receives."

Hebrews 12:6. NASB

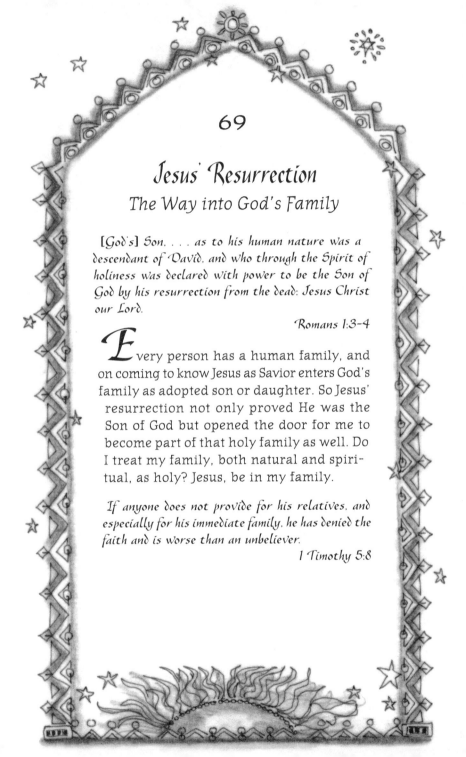

69

Jesus' Resurrection
The Way into God's Family

[God's] Son. . . . as to his human nature was a descendant of David, and who through the Spirit of holiness was declared with power to be the Son of God by his resurrection from the dead: Jesus Christ our Lord.

Romans 1:3-4

*E*very person has a human family, and on coming to know Jesus as Savior enters God's family as adopted son or daughter. So Jesus' resurrection not only proved He was the Son of God but opened the door for me to become part of that holy family as well. Do I treat my family, both natural and spiritual, as holy? Jesus, be in my family.

If anyone does not provide for his relatives, and especially for his immediate family, he has denied the faith and is worse than an unbeliever.

1 Timothy 5:8

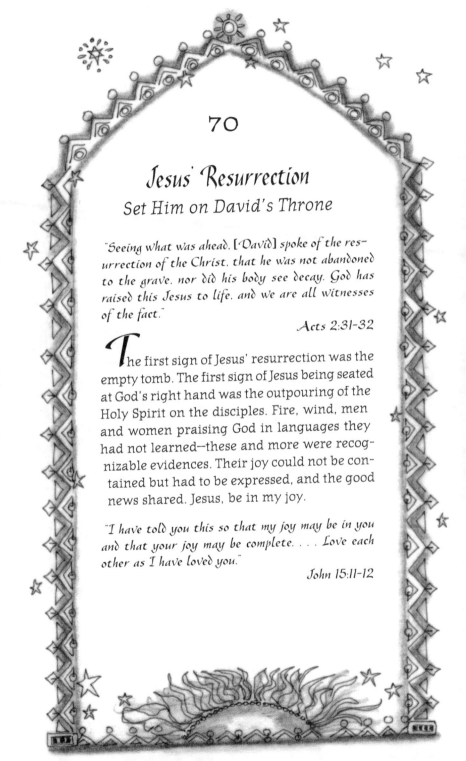

70

Jesus' Resurrection
Set Him on David's Throne

"Seeing what was ahead, [David] spoke of the resurrection of the Christ, that he was not abandoned to the grave, nor did his body see decay. God has raised this Jesus to life, and we are all witnesses of the fact."

Acts 2:31-32

The first sign of Jesus' resurrection was the empty tomb. The first sign of Jesus being seated at God's right hand was the outpouring of the Holy Spirit on the disciples. Fire, wind, men and women praising God in languages they had not learned—these and more were recognizable evidences. Their joy could not be contained but had to be expressed, and the good news shared. Jesus, be in my joy.

"I have told you this so that my joy may be in you and that your joy may be complete. . . . Love each other as I have loved you."

John 15:11-12

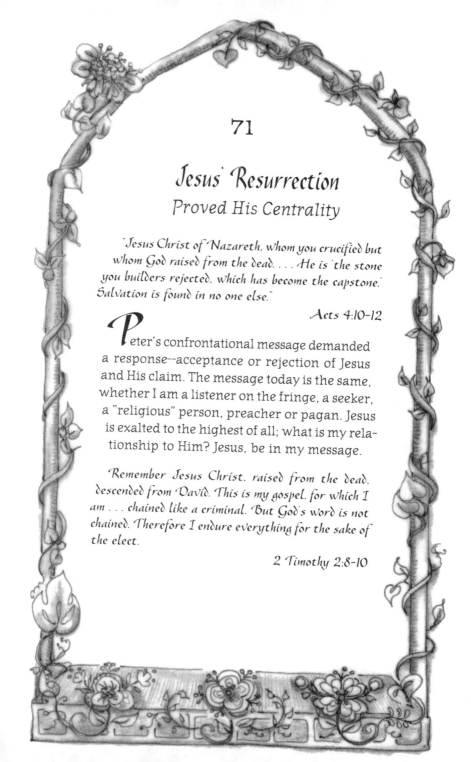

71

Jesus' Resurrection
Proved His Centrality

"Jesus Christ of Nazareth, whom you crucified but whom God raised from the dead. . . . He is 'the stone you builders rejected, which has become the capstone.' Salvation is found in no one else."

Acts 4:10-12

Peter's confrontational message demanded a response—acceptance or rejection of Jesus and His claim. The message today is the same, whether I am a listener on the fringe, a seeker, a "religious" person, preacher or pagan. Jesus is exalted to the highest of all; what is my relationship to Him? Jesus, be in my message.

Remember Jesus Christ, raised from the dead, descended from David. This is my gospel, for which I am . . . chained like a criminal. But God's word is not chained. Therefore I endure everything for the sake of the elect.

2 Timothy 2:8-10

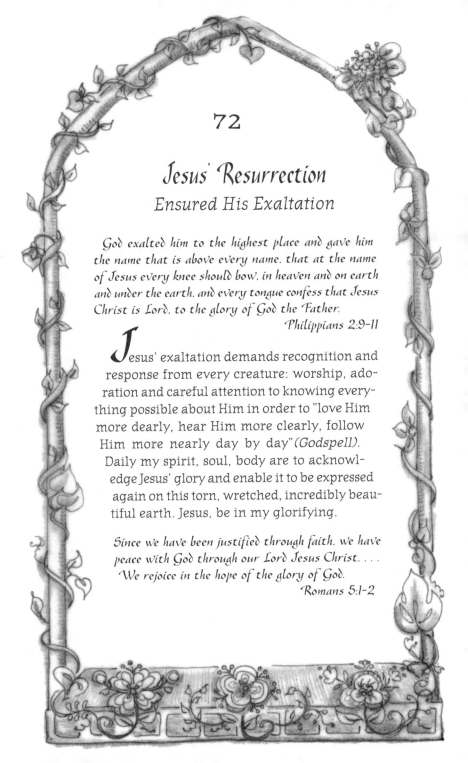

Jesus' Resurrection
Ensured His Exaltation

God exalted him to the highest place and gave him the name that is above every name, that at the name of Jesus every knee should bow, in heaven and on earth and under the earth, and every tongue confess that Jesus Christ is Lord, to the glory of God the Father.
Philippians 2:9-11

*J*esus' exaltation demands recognition and response from every creature: worship, adoration and careful attention to knowing everything possible about Him in order to "love Him more dearly, hear Him more clearly, follow Him more nearly day by day" *(Godspell).* Daily my spirit, soul, body are to acknowledge Jesus' glory and enable it to be expressed again on this torn, wretched, incredibly beautiful earth. Jesus, be in my glorifying.

Since we have been justified through faith, we have peace with God through our Lord Jesus Christ. . . . We rejoice in the hope of the glory of God.
Romans 5:1-2

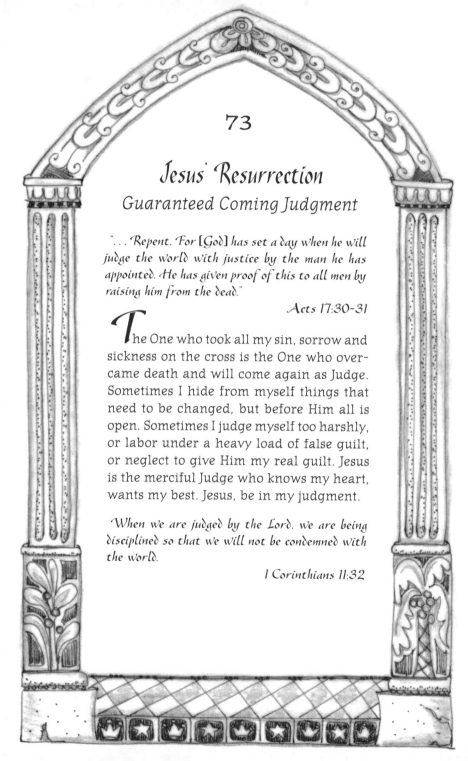

73

Jesus' Resurrection
Guaranteed Coming Judgment

"... Repent. For [God] has set a day when he will
judge the world with justice by the man he has
appointed. He has given proof of this to all men by
raising him from the dead."

Acts 17:30-31

The One who took all my sin, sorrow and
sickness on the cross is the One who overcame death and will come again as Judge.
Sometimes I hide from myself things that
need to be changed, but before Him all is
open. Sometimes I judge myself too harshly,
or labor under a heavy load of false guilt,
or neglect to give Him my real guilt. Jesus
is the merciful Judge who knows my heart,
wants my best. Jesus, be in my judgment.

When we are judged by the Lord. we are being
disciplined so that we will not be condemned with
the world.

1 Corinthians 11:32

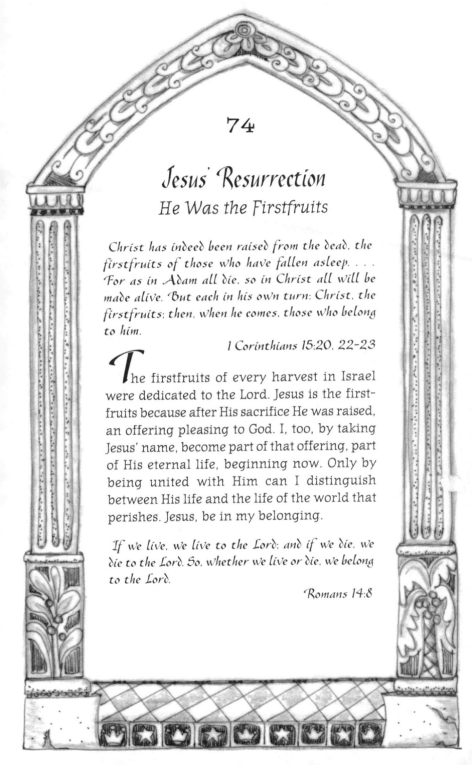

74

Jesus' Resurrection
He Was the Firstfruits

Christ has indeed been raised from the dead, the firstfruits of those who have fallen asleep. . . . For as in Adam all die, so in Christ all will be made alive. But each in his own turn: Christ, the firstfruits; then, when he comes, those who belong to him.

1 Corinthians 15:20, 22-23

The firstfruits of every harvest in Israel were dedicated to the Lord. Jesus is the first-fruits because after His sacrifice He was raised, an offering pleasing to God. I, too, by taking Jesus' name, become part of that offering, part of His eternal life, beginning now. Only by being united with Him can I distinguish between His life and the life of the world that perishes. Jesus, be in my belonging.

If we live, we live to the Lord; and if we die, we die to the Lord. So, whether we live or die, we belong to the Lord.

Romans 14:8

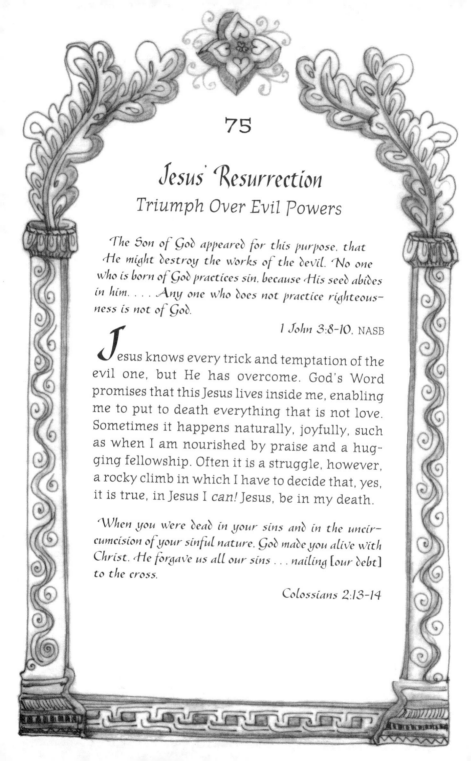

Jesus' Resurrection
Triumph Over Evil Powers

The Son of God appeared for this purpose, that He might destroy the works of the devil. No one who is born of God practices sin, because His seed abides in him. . . . Any one who does not practice righteousness is not of God.

1 John 3:8-10, NASB

Jesus knows every trick and temptation of the evil one, but He has overcome. God's Word promises that this Jesus lives inside me, enabling me to put to death everything that is not love. Sometimes it happens naturally, joyfully, such as when I am nourished by praise and a hugging fellowship. Often it is a struggle, however, a rocky climb in which I have to decide that, yes, it is true, in Jesus I *can!* Jesus, be in my death.

When you were dead in your sins and in the uncircumcision of your sinful nature, God made you alive with Christ. He forgave us all our sins . . . nailing [our debt] to the cross.

Colossians 2:13-14

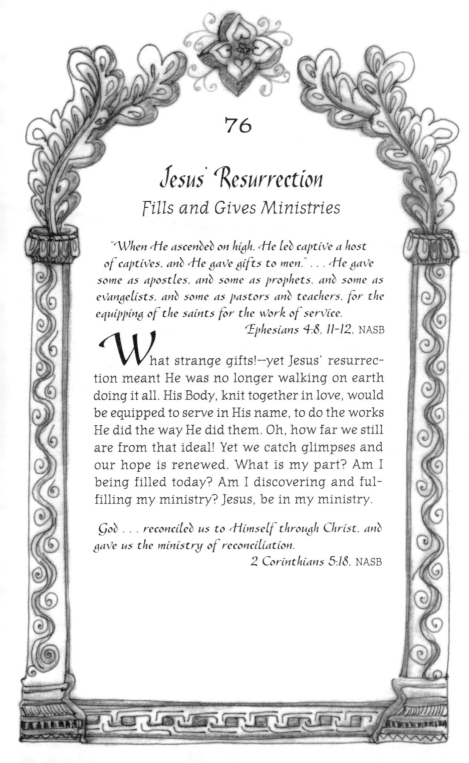

76

Jesus' Resurrection
Fills and Gives Ministries

"When He ascended on high, He led captive a host of captives, and He gave gifts to men." ... He gave some as apostles, and some as prophets, and some as evangelists, and some as pastors and teachers, for the equipping of the saints for the work of service.
Ephesians 4:8, 11-12, NASB

What strange gifts!—yet Jesus' resurrection meant He was no longer walking on earth doing it all. His Body, knit together in love, would be equipped to serve in His name, to do the works He did the way He did them. Oh, how far we still are from that ideal! Yet we catch glimpses and our hope is renewed. What is my part? Am I being filled today? Am I discovering and fulfilling my ministry? Jesus, be in my ministry.

God ... reconciled us to Himself through Christ, and gave us the ministry of reconciliation.
2 Corinthians 5:18, NASB

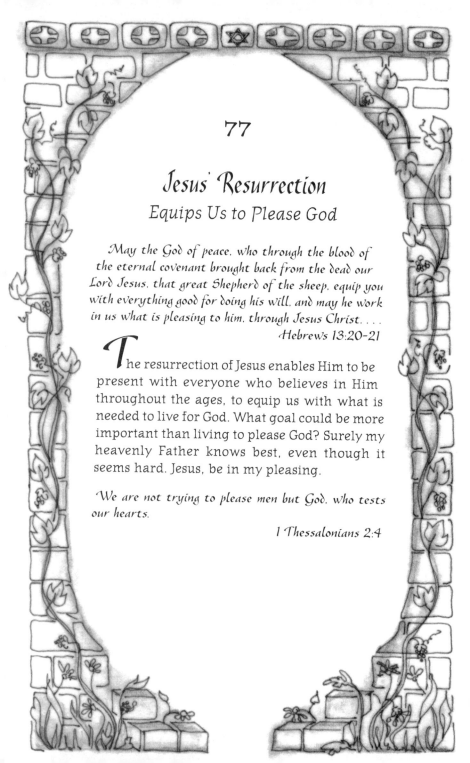

Jesus' Resurrection
Equips Us to Please God

*May the God of peace, who through the blood of
the eternal covenant brought back from the dead our
Lord Jesus, that great Shepherd of the sheep, equip you
with everything good for doing his will, and may he work
in us what is pleasing to him, through Jesus Christ. . . .*
Hebrews 13:20-21

The resurrection of Jesus enables Him to be
present with everyone who believes in Him
throughout the ages, to equip us with what is
needed to live for God. What goal could be more
important than living to please God? Surely my
heavenly Father knows best, even though it
seems hard. Jesus, be in my pleasing.

*We are not trying to please men but God, who tests
our hearts.*

1 Thessalonians 2:4

Part Two

Jesus' Power in Me

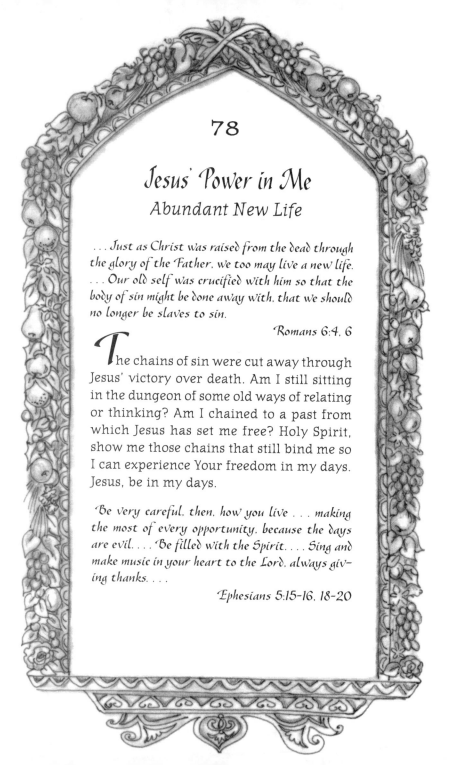

78

Jesus' Power in Me
Abundant New Life

*... Just as Christ was raised from the dead through
the glory of the Father, we too may live a new life.
... Our old self was crucified with him so that the
body of sin might be done away with, that we should
no longer be slaves to sin.*

Romans 6:4, 6

The chains of sin were cut away through
Jesus' victory over death. Am I still sitting
in the dungeon of some old ways of relating
or thinking? Am I chained to a past from
which Jesus has set me free? Holy Spirit,
show me those chains that still bind me so
I can experience Your freedom in my days.
Jesus, be in my days.

*Be very careful, then, how you live ... making
the most of every opportunity, because the days
are evil. ... Be filled with the Spirit. ... Sing and
make music in your heart to the Lord, always giving thanks. ...*

Ephesians 5:15-16, 18-20

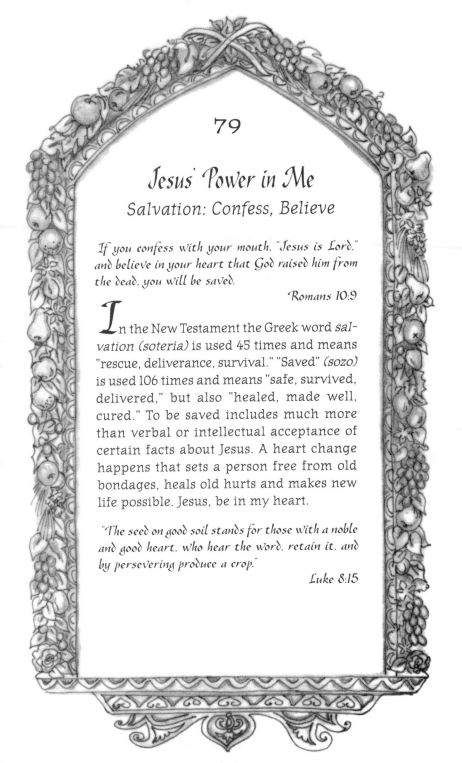

Jesus' Power in Me
Salvation: Confess, Believe

If you confess with your mouth, "Jesus is Lord," and believe in your heart that God raised him from the dead, you will be saved.

Romans 10:9

*I*n the New Testament the Greek word *salvation (soteria)* is used 45 times and means "rescue, deliverance, survival." "Saved" *(sozo)* is used 106 times and means "safe, survived, delivered," but also "healed, made well, cured." To be saved includes much more than verbal or intellectual acceptance of certain facts about Jesus. A heart change happens that sets a person free from old bondages, heals old hurts and makes new life possible. Jesus, be in my heart.

"The seed on good soil stands for those with a noble and good heart, who hear the word, retain it, and by persevering produce a crop."

Luke 8:15

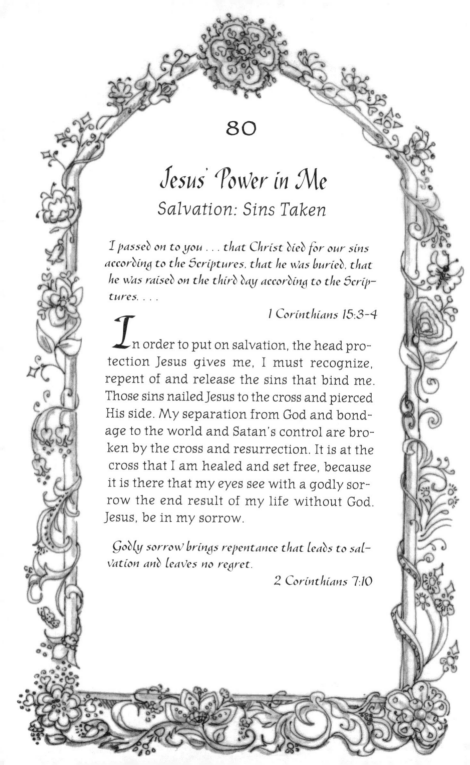

80

Jesus' Power in Me
Salvation: Sins Taken

I passed on to you ... that Christ died for our sins according to the Scriptures, that he was buried, that he was raised on the third day according to the Scriptures....

1 Corinthians 15:3-4

In order to put on salvation, the head protection Jesus gives me, I must recognize, repent of and release the sins that bind me. Those sins nailed Jesus to the cross and pierced His side. My separation from God and bondage to the world and Satan's control are broken by the cross and resurrection. It is at the cross that I am healed and set free, because it is there that my eyes see with a godly sorrow the end result of my life without God. Jesus, be in my sorrow.

Godly sorrow brings repentance that leads to salvation and leaves no regret.

2 Corinthians 7:10

Jesus' Power in Me

Salvation: Works through God

*"Whoever lives by the truth comes into the light,
so that it may be seen plainly that what he has
done has been done through God."*

John 3:21

Eternal life is the promise extended to
all who believe, and that means a quality
life with every crack and corner filled with
God's light. No more are ambition and pride
in my abilities or talents appropriate. Everything I do now is immersed in and formed
by God's loving light. To God be the glory!
Jesus, be in my vocation.

*I urge you to live a life worthy of the calling you
have received. Be completely humble and gentle: be
patient, bearing with one another in love.*

Ephesians 4:1-2

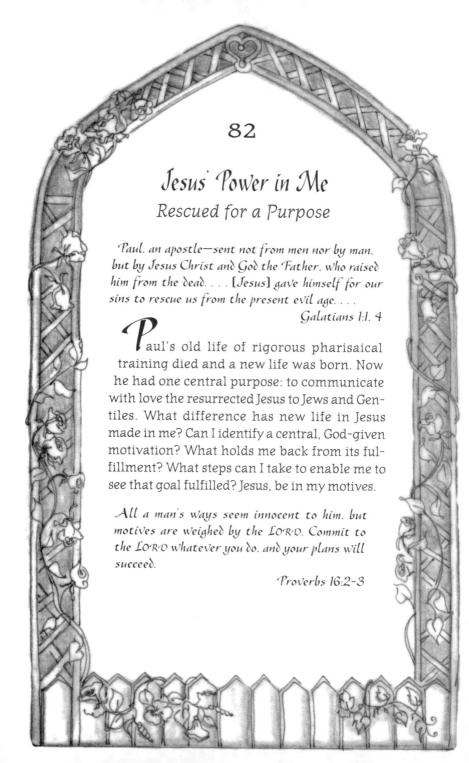

Jesus' Power in Me
Rescued for a Purpose

Paul, an apostle—sent not from men nor by man, but by Jesus Christ and God the Father, who raised him from the dead. . . . [Jesus] gave himself for our sins to rescue us from the present evil age. . . .

Galatians 1:1, 4

Paul's old life of rigorous pharisaical training died and a new life was born. Now he had one central purpose: to communicate with love the resurrected Jesus to Jews and Gentiles. What difference has new life in Jesus made in me? Can I identify a central, God-given motivation? What holds me back from its fulfillment? What steps can I take to enable me to see that goal fulfilled? Jesus, be in my motives.

All a man's ways seem innocent to him, but motives are weighed by the LORD. Commit to the LORD whatever you do, and your plans will succeed.

Proverbs 16:2-3

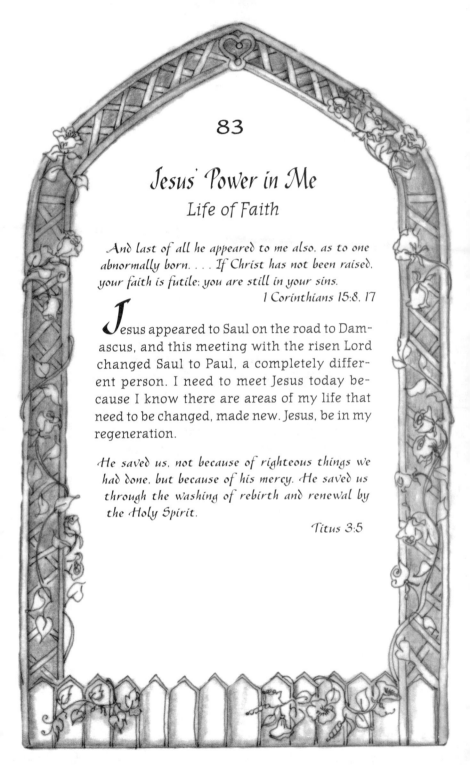

83

Jesus' Power in Me
Life of Faith

And last of all he appeared to me also, as to one abnormally born. . . . If Christ has not been raised, your faith is futile: you are still in your sins.

1 Corinthians 15:8, 17

*J*esus appeared to Saul on the road to Damascus, and this meeting with the risen Lord changed Saul to Paul, a completely different person. I need to meet Jesus today because I know there are areas of my life that need to be changed, made new. Jesus, be in my regeneration.

He saved us, not because of righteous things we had done, but because of his mercy. He saved us through the washing of rebirth and renewal by the Holy Spirit.

Titus 3:5

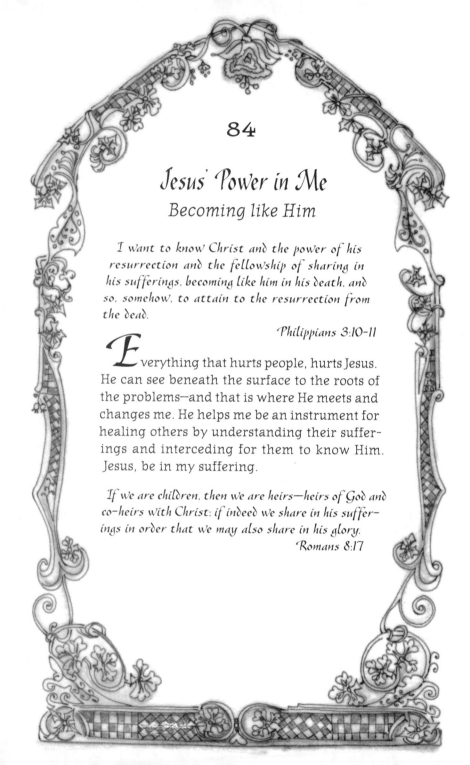

84

Jesus' Power in Me
Becoming like Him

I want to know Christ and the power of his resurrection and the fellowship of sharing in his sufferings, becoming like him in his death, and so, somehow, to attain to the resurrection from the dead.

Philippians 3:10-11

*E*verything that hurts people, hurts Jesus. He can see beneath the surface to the roots of the problems—and that is where He meets and changes me. He helps me be an instrument for healing others by understanding their sufferings and interceding for them to know Him. Jesus, be in my suffering.

If we are children, then we are heirs—heirs of God and co-heirs with Christ; if indeed we share in his sufferings in order that we may also share in his glory.

Romans 8:17

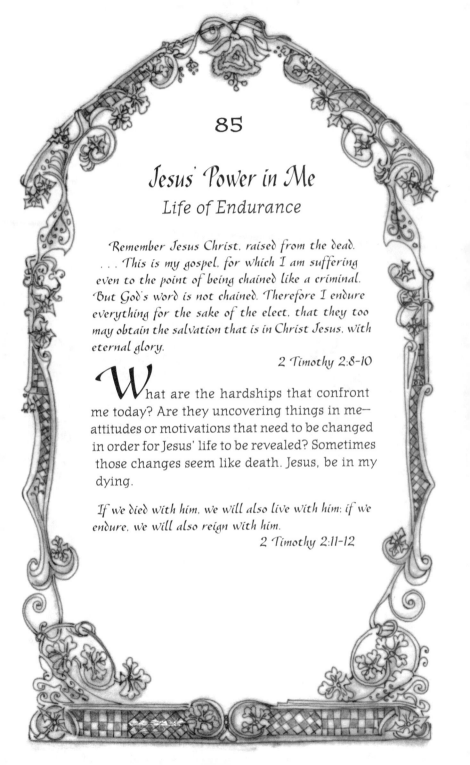

85

Jesus' Power in Me
Life of Endurance

*Remember Jesus Christ, raised from the dead.
. . . This is my gospel, for which I am suffering
even to the point of being chained like a criminal.
But God's word is not chained. Therefore I endure
everything for the sake of the elect, that they too
may obtain the salvation that is in Christ Jesus, with
eternal glory.*

2 Timothy 2:8-10

What are the hardships that confront
me today? Are they uncovering things in me—
attitudes or motivations that need to be changed
in order for Jesus' life to be revealed? Sometimes
those changes seem like death. Jesus, be in my
dying.

*If we died with him, we will also live with him; if we
endure, we will also reign with him.*

2 Timothy 2:11-12

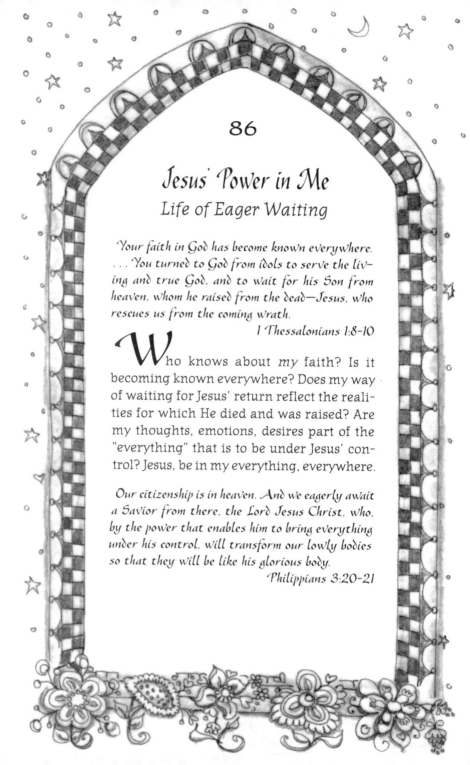

86

Jesus' Power in Me
Life of Eager Waiting

Your faith in God has become known everywhere. . . . You turned to God from idols to serve the living and true God, and to wait for his Son from heaven, whom he raised from the dead—Jesus, who rescues us from the coming wrath.

1 Thessalonians 1:8-10

Who knows about *my* faith? Is it becoming known everywhere? Does my way of waiting for Jesus' return reflect the realities for which He died and was raised? Are my thoughts, emotions, desires part of the "everything" that is to be under Jesus' control? Jesus, be in my everything, everywhere.

Our citizenship is in heaven. And we eagerly await a Savior from there, the Lord Jesus Christ, who, by the power that enables him to bring everything under his control, will transform our lowly bodies so that they will be like his glorious body.

Philippians 3:20-21

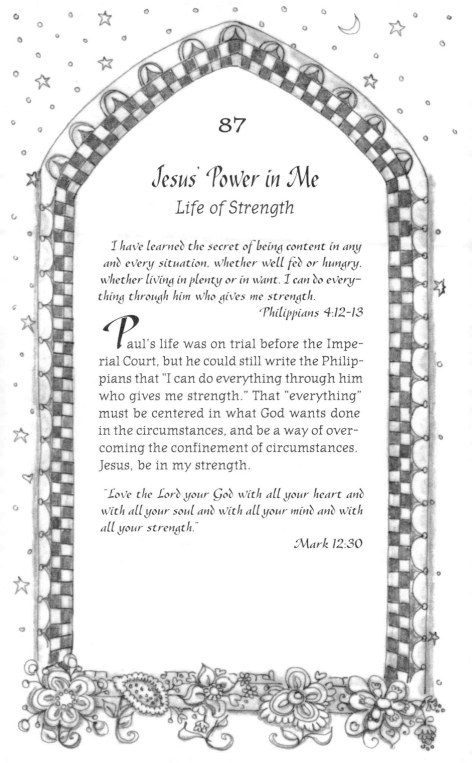

Jesus' Power in Me
Life of Strength

I have learned the secret of being content in any and every situation, whether well fed or hungry, whether living in plenty or in want. I can do everything through him who gives me strength.

Philippians 4:12-13

Paul's life was on trial before the Imperial Court, but he could still write the Philippians that "I can do everything through him who gives me strength." That "everything" must be centered in what God wants done in the circumstances, and be a way of overcoming the confinement of circumstances. Jesus, be in my strength.

"Love the Lord your God with all your heart and with all your soul and with all your mind and with all your strength."

Mark 12:30

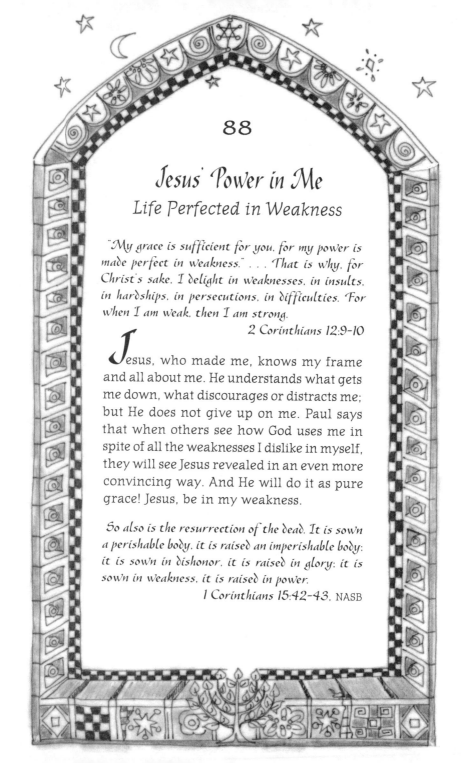

88

Jesus' Power in Me
Life Perfected in Weakness

"My grace is sufficient for you, for my power is made perfect in weakness." . . . That is why, for Christ's sake, I delight in weaknesses, in insults, in hardships, in persecutions, in difficulties. For when I am weak, then I am strong.

2 Corinthians 12:9-10

Jesus, who made me, knows my frame and all about me. He understands what gets me down, what discourages or distracts me; but He does not give up on me. Paul says that when others see how God uses me in spite of all the weaknesses I dislike in myself, they will see Jesus revealed in an even more convincing way. And He will do it as pure grace! Jesus, be in my weakness.

So also is the resurrection of the dead. It is sown a perishable body, it is raised an imperishable body; it is sown in dishonor, it is raised in glory; it is sown in weakness, it is raised in power.

1 Corinthians 15:42-43, NASB

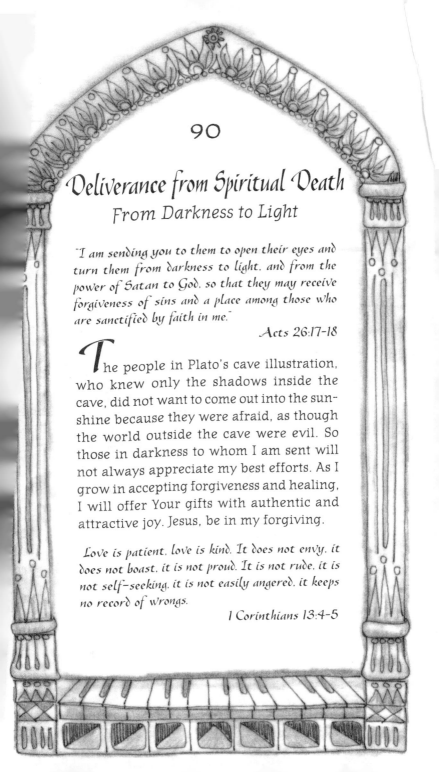

Deliverance from Spiritual Death
From Darkness to Light

"I am sending you to them to open their eyes and turn them from darkness to light, and from the power of Satan to God, so that they may receive forgiveness of sins and a place among those who are sanctified by faith in me."

Acts 26:17-18

The people in Plato's cave illustration, who knew only the shadows inside the cave, did not want to come out into the sunshine because they were afraid, as though the world outside the cave were evil. So those in darkness to whom I am sent will not always appreciate my best efforts. As I grow in accepting forgiveness and healing, I will offer Your gifts with authentic and attractive joy. Jesus, be in my forgiving.

Love is patient, love is kind. It does not envy, it does not boast, it is not proud. It is not rude, it is not self-seeking, it is not easily angered, it keeps no record of wrongs.

1 Corinthians 13:4-5

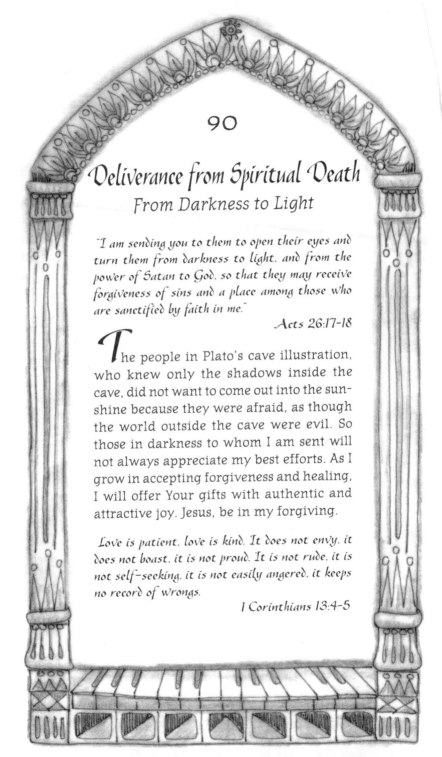

90

Deliverance from Spiritual Death
From Darkness to Light

"I am sending you to them to open their eyes and turn them from darkness to light, and from the power of Satan to God, so that they may receive forgiveness of sins and a place among those who are sanctified by faith in me."

Acts 26:17-18

*T*he people in Plato's cave illustration, who knew only the shadows inside the cave, did not want to come out into the sunshine because they were afraid, as though the world outside the cave were evil. So those in darkness to whom I am sent will not always appreciate my best efforts. As I grow in accepting forgiveness and healing, I will offer Your gifts with authentic and attractive joy. Jesus, be in my forgiving.

Love is patient, love is kind. It does not envy, it does not boast, it is not proud. It is not rude, it is not self-seeking, it is not easily angered, it keeps no record of wrongs.

1 Corinthians 13:4-5

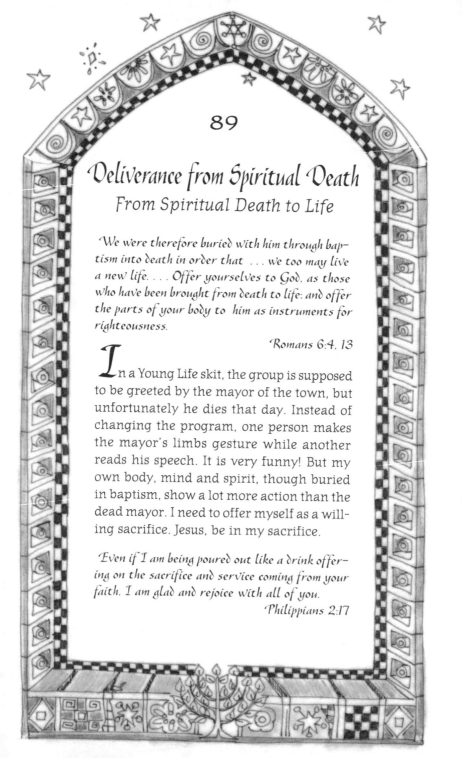

Deliverance from Spiritual Death
From Spiritual Death to Life

We were therefore buried with him through baptism into death in order that ... we too may live a new life. ... Offer yourselves to God, as those who have been brought from death to life: and offer the parts of your body to him as instruments for righteousness.

Romans 6:4, 13

In a Young Life skit, the group is supposed to be greeted by the mayor of the town, but unfortunately he dies that day. Instead of changing the program, one person makes the mayor's limbs gesture while another reads his speech. It is very funny! But my own body, mind and spirit, though buried in baptism, show a lot more action than the dead mayor. I need to offer myself as a willing sacrifice. Jesus, be in my sacrifice.

Even if I am being poured out like a drink offering on the sacrifice and service coming from your faith, I am glad and rejoice with all of you.

Philippians 2:17

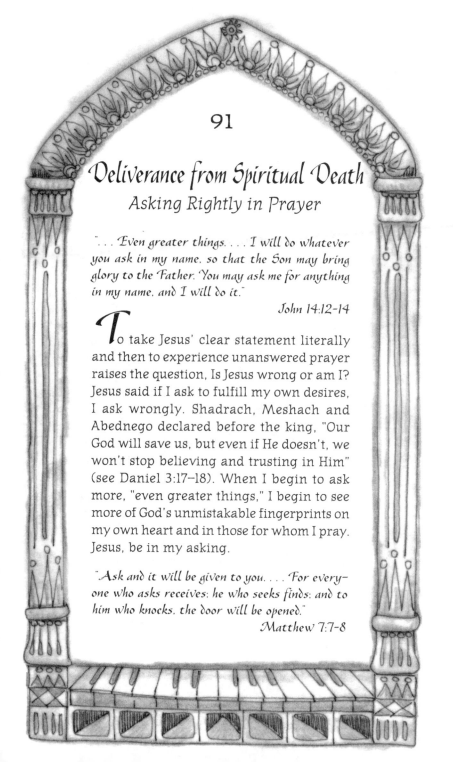

91

Deliverance from Spiritual Death
Asking Rightly in Prayer

". . . Even greater things. . . . I will do whatever you ask in my name, so that the Son may bring glory to the Father. You may ask me for anything in my name, and I will do it."

John 14:12-14

To take Jesus' clear statement literally and then to experience unanswered prayer raises the question, Is Jesus wrong or am I? Jesus said if I ask to fulfill my own desires, I ask wrongly. Shadrach, Meshach and Abednego declared before the king, "Our God will save us, but even if He doesn't, we won't stop believing and trusting in Him" (see Daniel 3:17–18). When I begin to ask more, "even greater things," I begin to see more of God's unmistakable fingerprints on my own heart and in those for whom I pray. Jesus, be in my asking.

"Ask and it will be given to you. . . . For every-one who asks receives; he who seeks finds; and to him who knocks, the door will be opened."

Matthew 7:7-8

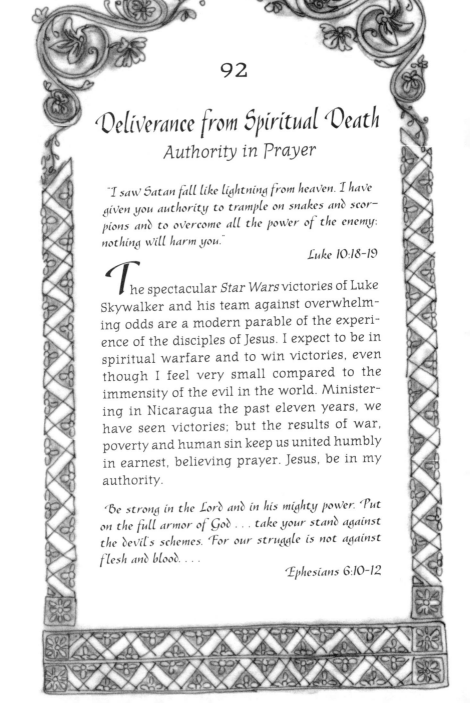

92

Deliverance from Spiritual Death
Authority in Prayer

"I saw Satan fall like lightning from heaven. I have given you authority to trample on snakes and scorpions and to overcome all the power of the enemy: nothing will harm you."

Luke 10:18-19

*T*he spectacular *Star Wars* victories of Luke Skywalker and his team against overwhelming odds are a modern parable of the experience of the disciples of Jesus. I expect to be in spiritual warfare and to win victories, even though I feel very small compared to the immensity of the evil in the world. Ministering in Nicaragua the past eleven years, we have seen victories; but the results of war, poverty and human sin keep us united humbly in earnest, believing prayer. Jesus, be in my authority.

Be strong in the Lord and in his mighty power. Put on the full armor of God . . . take your stand against the devil's schemes. For our struggle is not against flesh and blood. . . .

Ephesians 6:10-12

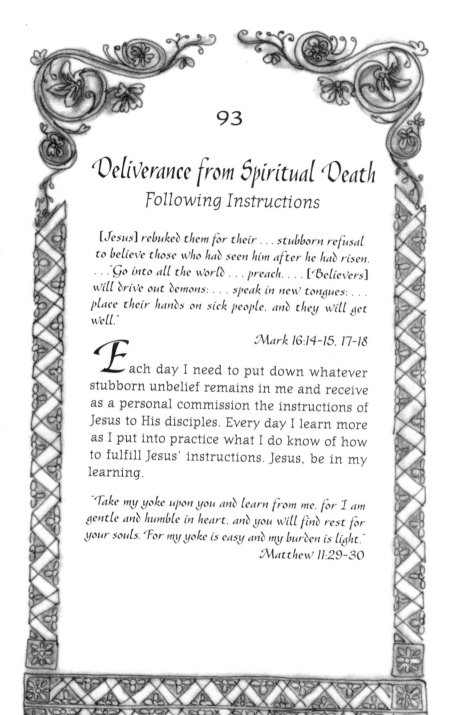

Deliverance from Spiritual Death
Following Instructions

[Jesus] rebuked them for their . . . stubborn refusal to believe those who had seen him after he had risen. . . . "Go into all the world . . . preach. . . . ['Believers] will drive out demons; . . . speak in new tongues; . . . place their hands on sick people, and they will get well."

Mark 16:14-15, 17-18

Each day I need to put down whatever stubborn unbelief remains in me and receive as a personal commission the instructions of Jesus to His disciples. Every day I learn more as I put into practice what I do know of how to fulfill Jesus' instructions. Jesus, be in my learning.

"Take my yoke upon you and learn from me, for I am gentle and humble in heart, and you will find rest for your souls. For my yoke is easy and my burden is light."

Matthew 11:29-30

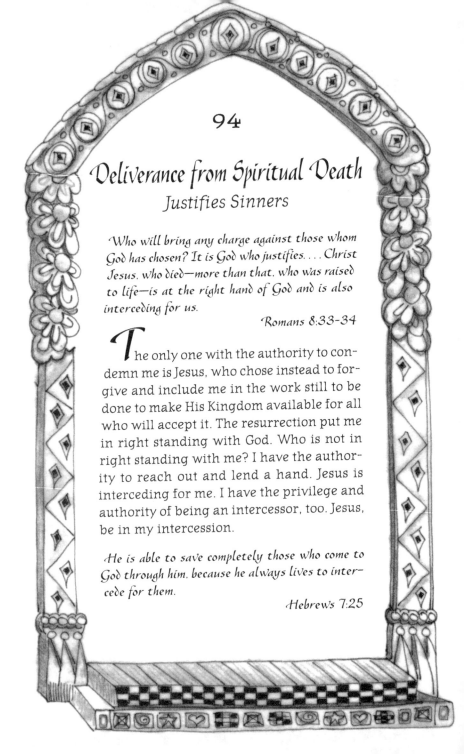

Deliverance from Spiritual Death
Justifies Sinners

Who will bring any charge against those whom God has chosen? It is God who justifies.... Christ Jesus, who died—more than that, who was raised to life—is at the right hand of God and is also interceding for us.

Romans 8:33-34

The only one with the authority to condemn me is Jesus, who chose instead to forgive and include me in the work still to be done to make His Kingdom available for all who will accept it. The resurrection put me in right standing with God. Who is not in right standing with me? I have the authority to reach out and lend a hand. Jesus is interceding for me. I have the privilege and authority of being an intercessor, too. Jesus, be in my intercession.

He is able to save completely those who come to God through him, because he always lives to intercede for them.

Hebrews 7:25

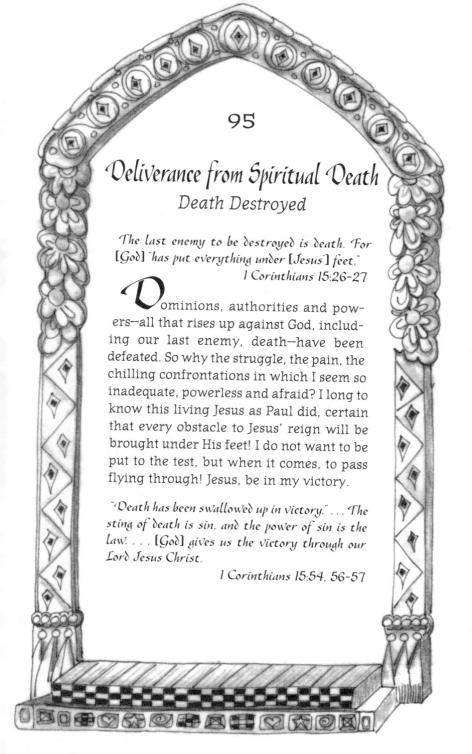

Deliverance from Spiritual Death
Death Destroyed

The last enemy to be destroyed is death. For [God] "has put everything under [Jesus'] feet."
1 Corinthians 15:26-27

Dominions, authorities and powers—all that rises up against God, including our last enemy, death—have been defeated. So why the struggle, the pain, the chilling confrontations in which I seem so inadequate, powerless and afraid? I long to know this living Jesus as Paul did, certain that every obstacle to Jesus' reign will be brought under His feet! I do not want to be put to the test, but when it comes, to pass flying through! Jesus, be in my victory.

"Death has been swallowed up in victory." . . . The sting of death is sin, and the power of sin is the law. . . . [God] gives us the victory through our Lord Jesus Christ.

1 Corinthians 15:54, 56-57

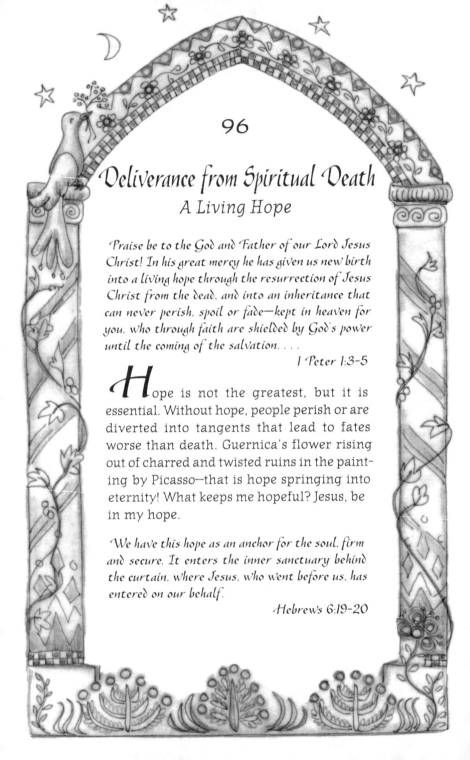

Deliverance from Spiritual Death
A Living Hope

Praise be to the God and Father of our Lord Jesus Christ! In his great mercy he has given us new birth into a living hope through the resurrection of Jesus Christ from the dead, and into an inheritance that can never perish, spoil or fade—kept in heaven for you, who through faith are shielded by God's power until the coming of the salvation. . . .

1 Peter 1:3-5

Hope is not the greatest, but it is essential. Without hope, people perish or are diverted into tangents that lead to fates worse than death. Guernica's flower rising out of charred and twisted ruins in the painting by Picasso—that is hope springing into eternity! What keeps me hopeful? Jesus, be in my hope.

We have this hope as an anchor for the soul, firm and secure. It enters the inner sanctuary behind the curtain, where Jesus, who went before us, has entered on our behalf.

Hebrews 6:19-20

Deliverance from Spiritual Death
Overcomes Temptation

*Because he himself suffered when he was tempted,
he is able to help those who are being tempted.*

Hebrews 2:18

Fire met by greater fire! Jesus, who has been through it all, comes to me, burning away those things that hinder and entangle me. I cannot do it alone, but I am not alone. A simple cry for help, and the Lord Jesus comes as if He had only awaited the recognition that He is the way through. Jesus, be in my refining.

He will be like a refiner's fire or a launderer's soap.

Malachi 3:2

*Worship God acceptably with reverence and awe,
for "our God is a consuming fire."*

Hebrews 12:28-29

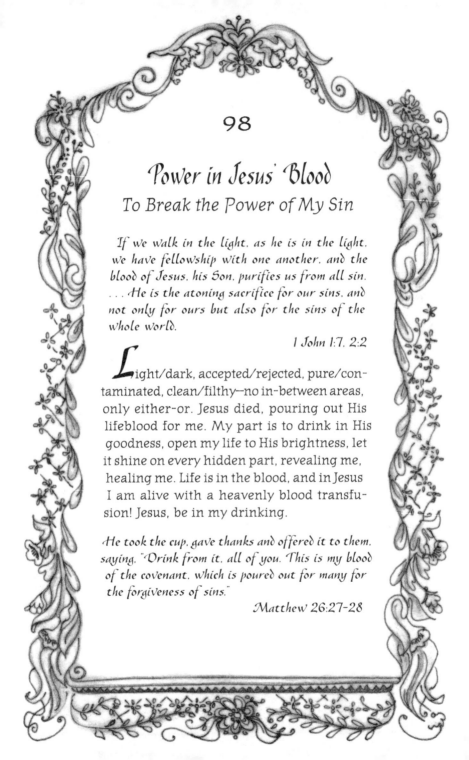

98

Power in Jesus' Blood
To Break the Power of My Sin

If we walk in the light. as he is in the light. we have fellowship with one another. and the blood of Jesus. his Son. purifies us from all sin. . . . He is the atoning sacrifice for our sins. and not only for ours but also for the sins of the whole world.

1 John 1:7, 2:2

Light/dark, accepted/rejected, pure/con-taminated, clean/filthy—no in-between areas, only either-or. Jesus died, pouring out His lifeblood for me. My part is to drink in His goodness, open my life to His brightness, let it shine on every hidden part, revealing me, healing me. Life is in the blood, and in Jesus I am alive with a heavenly blood transfu-sion! Jesus, be in my drinking.

He took the cup. gave thanks and offered it to them. saying. "Drink from it. all of you. This is my blood of the covenant. which is poured out for many for the forgiveness of sins."

Matthew 26:27-28

Power in Jesus' Blood
For Cleansing

The blood of Christ, who through the eternal Spirit offered himself unblemished to God, [will] cleanse our consciences from acts that lead to death, so that we may serve the living God!
Hebrews 9:14

The shining face and vibrant voice of a Brooklyn Tabernacle Choir soloist radiates, "I am clean, washed in the blood of the Lamb." He was a crack cocaine addict living in the doghouse of a vacant lot when his wife covenanted not to give up on him. Such testimonies give hope that this cleansing solution is for me and for those bound in seemingly impossible situations. Jesus, be in my cleansing.

The law requires that nearly everything be cleansed with blood, and without the shedding of blood there is no forgiveness.
Hebrews 9:22

Power in Jesus' Blood
For Forgiveness

He poured out his life unto death, and was numbered with the transgressors. For he bore the sin of many, and made intercession for the transgressors.

Isaiah 53:12

The sight of a lamb being killed, its blood drained as it hung on a wooden post in the pasture, left a memorable impression. Trusting, not understanding, the lamb had come to its death. Jesus understood all too well the cost, yet His love and obedience were so great that He was willing for His lifeblood to be poured out for me and you. Jesus is the source of forgiveness and healing for all my wounds. Being in touch with Him is a matter of life and death. Jesus, be in my wounds.

He himself bore our sins in his body on the tree, so that we might die to sins and live for righteousness; by his wounds you have been healed.

1 Peter 2:24

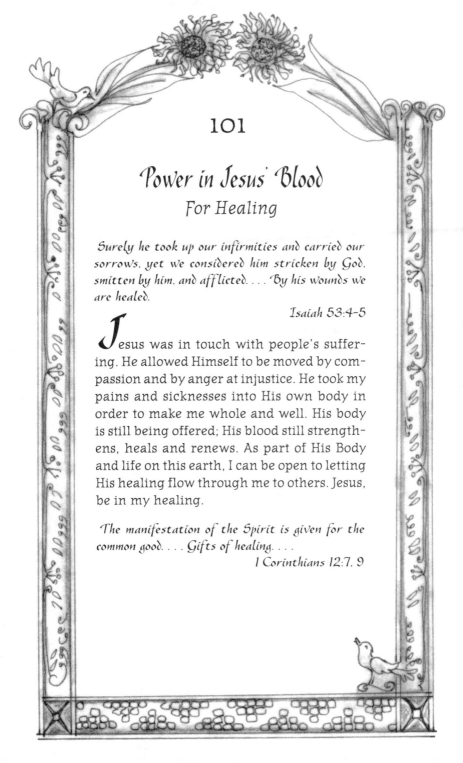

Power in Jesus' Blood
For Healing

Surely he took up our infirmities and carried our sorrows, yet we considered him stricken by God, smitten by him, and afflicted. . . . By his wounds we are healed.

Isaiah 53:4-5

Jesus was in touch with people's suffering. He allowed Himself to be moved by compassion and by anger at injustice. He took my pains and sicknesses into His own body in order to make me whole and well. His body is still being offered; His blood still strengthens, heals and renews. As part of His Body and life on this earth, I can be open to letting His healing flow through me to others. Jesus, be in my healing.

The manifestation of the Spirit is given for the common good. . . . Gifts of healing. . . .

1 Corinthians 12:7, 9

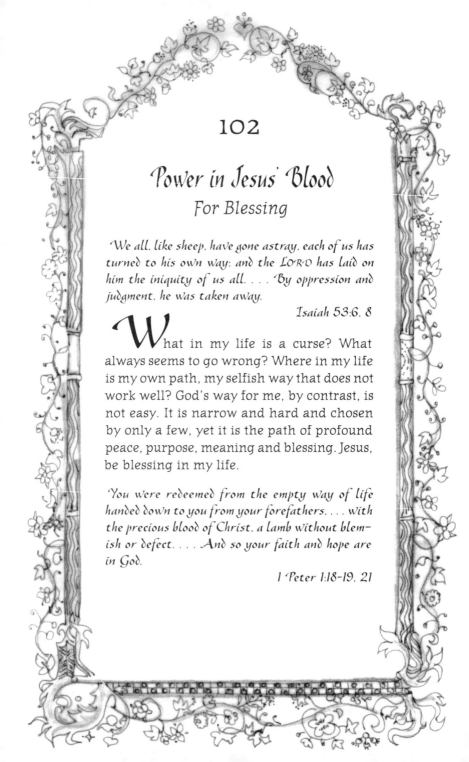

102

Power in Jesus' Blood
For Blessing

We all, like sheep, have gone astray, each of us has turned to his own way; and the LORD has laid on him the iniquity of us all. . . . By oppression and judgment, he was taken away.

Isaiah 53:6, 8

What in my life is a curse? What always seems to go wrong? Where in my life is my own path, my selfish way that does not work well? God's way for me, by contrast, is not easy. It is narrow and hard and chosen by only a few, yet it is the path of profound peace, purpose, meaning and blessing. Jesus, be blessing in my life.

You were redeemed from the empty way of life handed down to you from your forefathers, . . . with the precious blood of Christ, a lamb without blemish or defect. . . . And so your faith and hope are in God.

1 Peter 1:18–19, 21

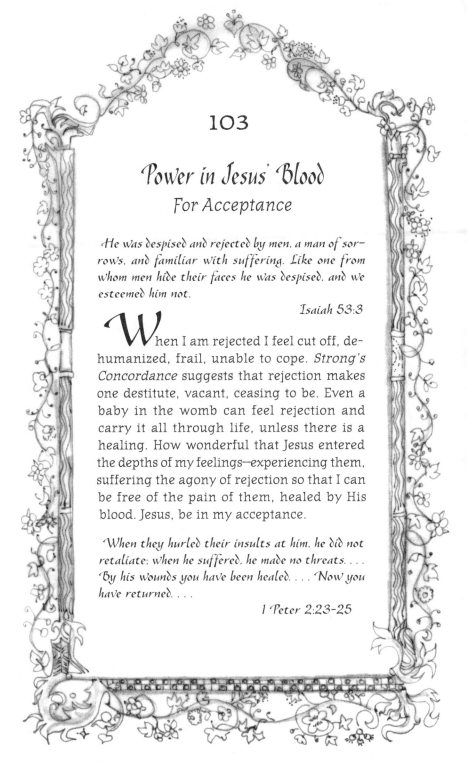

103

Power in Jesus' Blood
For Acceptance

He was despised and rejected by men, a man of sorrows, and familiar with suffering. Like one from whom men hide their faces he was despised, and we esteemed him not.

Isaiah 53:3

When I am rejected I feel cut off, dehumanized, frail, unable to cope. *Strong's Concordance* suggests that rejection makes one destitute, vacant, ceasing to be. Even a baby in the womb can feel rejection and carry it all through life, unless there is a healing. How wonderful that Jesus entered the depths of my feelings—experiencing them, suffering the agony of rejection so that I can be free of the pain of them, healed by His blood. Jesus, be in my acceptance.

When they hurled their insults at him, he did not retaliate; when he suffered, he made no threats. . . . By his wounds you have been healed. . . . Now you have returned. . . .

1 Peter 2:23-25

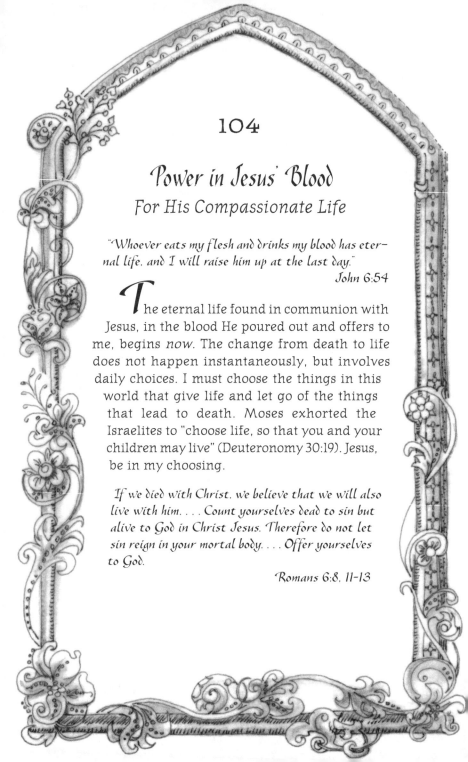

104

Power in Jesus' Blood
For His Compassionate Life

"Whoever eats my flesh and drinks my blood has eternal life, and I will raise him up at the last day."
John 6:54

The eternal life found in communion with Jesus, in the blood He poured out and offers to me, begins *now*. The change from death to life does not happen instantaneously, but involves daily choices. I must choose the things in this world that give life and let go of the things that lead to death. Moses exhorted the Israelites to "choose life, so that you and your children may live" (Deuteronomy 30:19). Jesus, be in my choosing.

If we died with Christ, we believe that we will also live with him. . . . Count yourselves dead to sin but alive to God in Christ Jesus. Therefore do not let sin reign in your mortal body. . . . Offer yourselves to God.

Romans 6:8, 11-13

105

Power in Jesus' Blood
For Being in Him

"Just as the living Father sent me and I live because of the Father, so the one who feeds on me will live because of me."

John 6:57

Sometimes I get the idea that to exchange my ruined, lonely life for Jesus' resurrection life means that I will be fulfilled and happy with a wonderful new family of faith. This is true—but the witness of Paul and saints through the ages reveals that I will not have happy goosebumps when I travel through the valley of the shadow of death. Sometimes God calls me to go where I am not appreciated or respected. There the reality of my being in God is tested. Jesus, be in my being.

We are fools for Christ . . . weak . . . dishonored . . . hungry and thirsty . . . in rags . . . brutally treated . . . homeless . . . the scum of the earth, the refuse of the world.

1 Corinthians 4:10-11, 13

Power in Jesus' Blood
For Grace

*All have sinned and fall short of the glory of God,
and are justified freely by his grace . . . that came
by Christ Jesus. God presented him as a sacrifice of
atonement, through faith in his blood.*
Romans 3:23-25

How many times I fall flat on my face
like a baby learning to walk! The older I get,
it seems, the more those falls hurt. Maybe it
is because I tend to kick myself when I fail,
which prolongs the process of restoration.
Jesus wants me to give Him my failures—even
thank Him for them—for in those times I learn
from the bottom-side up . . . *understanding!*
Jesus, be in my failure.

*Because of the LORD's great love we are not con-
sumed, for his compassions never fail. They are new
every morning; great is your faithfulness.*
Lamentations 3:22-23

Power in Jesus' Blood
For Intimacy

Since we have now been justified by his blood, how much more shall we be saved from God's wrath through him! . . . We were God's enemies. . . . reconciled to him through the death of his Son. . . .
Romans 5:9–10

Making the marvelous exchange of enmity with God for intimacy is not something I can *do*. When I become aware of my true position in front of a holy God, I can, like a child, cry out my need; like a person drowning, I can plead for help. His arms embrace, His will is revealed, His healing enables, His touch is indelible in my life. Jesus, be in my renewing.

Do not conform any longer to the pattern of this world, but be transformed by the renewing of your mind. Then you will be able to test and approve what God's will is—his good, pleasing and perfect will.
Romans 12:2

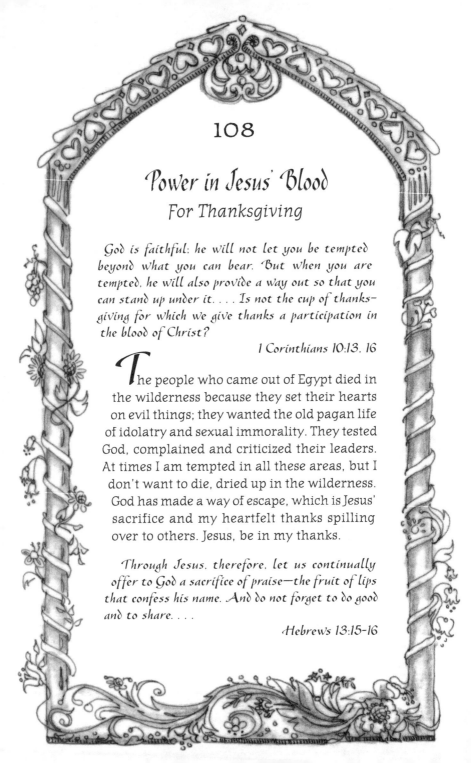

108

Power in Jesus' Blood
For Thanksgiving

God is faithful: he will not let you be tempted beyond what you can bear. But when you are tempted, he will also provide a way out so that you can stand up under it. . . . Is not the cup of thanksgiving for which we give thanks a participation in the blood of Christ?

1 Corinthians 10:13, 16

The people who came out of Egypt died in the wilderness because they set their hearts on evil things; they wanted the old pagan life of idolatry and sexual immorality. They tested God, complained and criticized their leaders. At times I am tempted in all these areas, but I don't want to die, dried up in the wilderness. God has made a way of escape, which is Jesus' sacrifice and my heartfelt thanks spilling over to others. Jesus, be in my thanks.

Through Jesus, therefore, let us continually offer to God a sacrifice of praise—the fruit of lips that confess his name. And do not forget to do good and to share. . . .

Hebrews 13:15-16

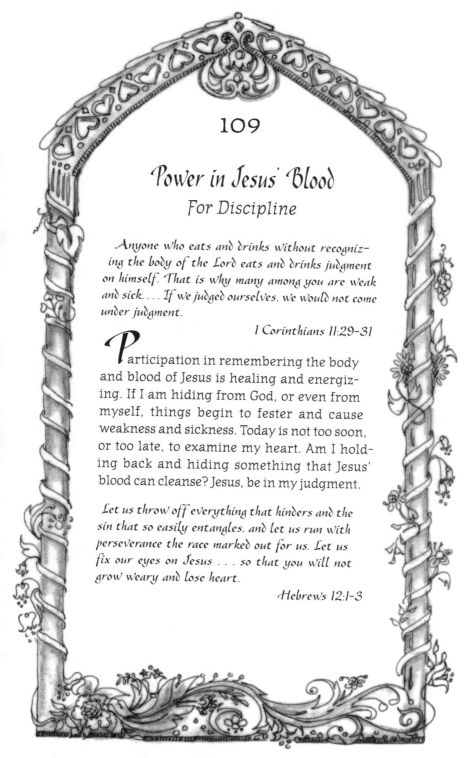

Power in Jesus' Blood
For Discipline

*Anyone who eats and drinks without recogniz-
ing the body of the Lord eats and drinks judgment
on himself. That is why many among you are weak
and sick.... If we judged ourselves, we would not come
under judgment.*

1 Corinthians 11:29-31

Participation in remembering the body
and blood of Jesus is healing and energiz-
ing. If I am hiding from God, or even from
myself, things begin to fester and cause
weakness and sickness. Today is not too soon,
or too late, to examine my heart. Am I holding back and hiding something that Jesus'
blood can cleanse? Jesus, be in my judgment.

*Let us throw off everything that hinders and the
sin that so easily entangles, and let us run with
perseverance the race marked out for us. Let us
fix our eyes on Jesus ... so that you will not
grow weary and lose heart.*

Hebrews 12:1-3

Power in Jesus' Blood
For Imperishable Immortality

Just as we have borne the likeness of the earthly man, so shall we bear the likeness of the man from heaven. . . . We will all be changed. . . .
1 Corinthians 15:49, 51

I n the *Jesus* film, Jesus was almost always walking somewhere and relating with people, not things. It reminds me how much I depend on things, and how I tend to be irritated by people making demands on me. Yet I want to be a healing person like Jesus. Lord, help me find the balance You want for me today in the process of being changed into Your likeness. Jesus, be in my character.

Since we have been justified through faith, we have peace with God through our Lord Jesus Christ, through whom we have gained access by faith. . . . We also rejoice in our sufferings . . . [which produce] perseverance . . . character . . . hope.
Romans 5:1-4

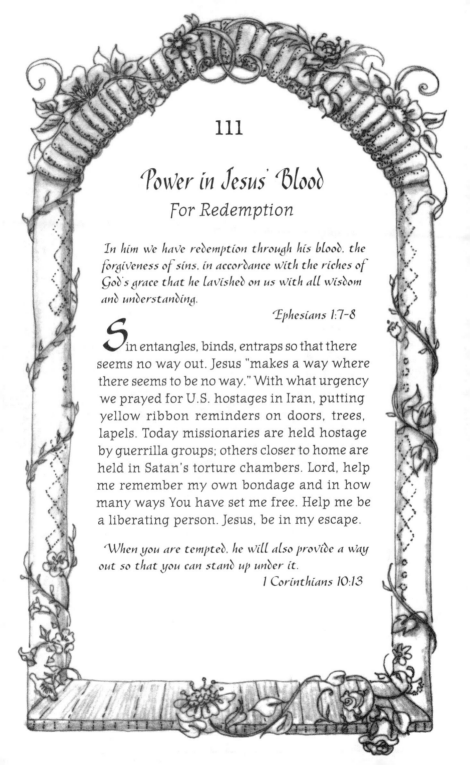

111

Power in Jesus' Blood
For Redemption

In him we have redemption through his blood, the forgiveness of sins, in accordance with the riches of God's grace that he lavished on us with all wisdom and understanding.

Ephesians 1:7-8

Sin entangles, binds, entraps so that there seems no way out. Jesus "makes a way where there seems to be no way." With what urgency we prayed for U.S. hostages in Iran, putting yellow ribbon reminders on doors, trees, lapels. Today missionaries are held hostage by guerrilla groups; others closer to home are held in Satan's torture chambers. Lord, help me remember my own bondage and in how many ways You have set me free. Help me be a liberating person. Jesus, be in my escape.

When you are tempted, he will also provide a way out so that you can stand up under it.

1 Corinthians 10:13

112

Power in Jesus' Blood
For Citizenship

Remember that at that time you were separate from Christ. . . . foreigners to the covenants of the promise, without hope and without God in the world. But now in Christ Jesus you who once were far away have been brought near through the blood of Christ.

Ephesians 2:12-13

My husband, Jim, and I live in a foreign land in which every time we walk down the street, people young and old stare—some with curiosity, others with open hostility. We are unmistakably different. But there are times of worship in which God's Spirit erases the differences or lifts us all above them. "You are Nicaraguan now," they say as the highest compliment. We smile and nod, thankful that God makes us acceptable. Jesus, be in my fellow citizens.

You are no longer foreigners and aliens, but fellow citizens with God's people and members of God's household.

Ephesians 2:19

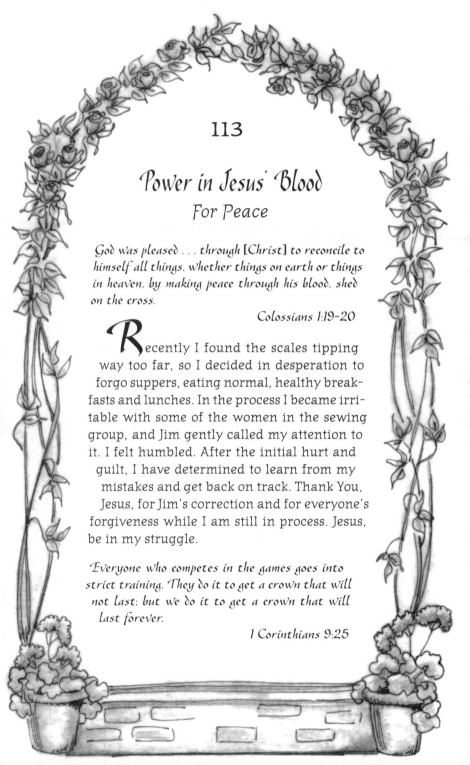

113

Power in Jesus' Blood
For Peace

God was pleased . . . through [Christ] to reconcile to himself all things, whether things on earth or things in heaven, by making peace through his blood, shed on the cross.

Colossians 1:19-20

Recently I found the scales tipping way too far, so I decided in desperation to forgo suppers, eating normal, healthy breakfasts and lunches. In the process I became irritable with some of the women in the sewing group, and Jim gently called my attention to it. I felt humbled. After the initial hurt and guilt, I have determined to learn from my mistakes and get back on track. Thank You, Jesus, for Jim's correction and for everyone's forgiveness while I am still in process. Jesus, be in my struggle.

Everyone who competes in the games goes into strict training. They do it to get a crown that will not last; but we do it to get a crown that will last forever.

1 Corinthians 9:25

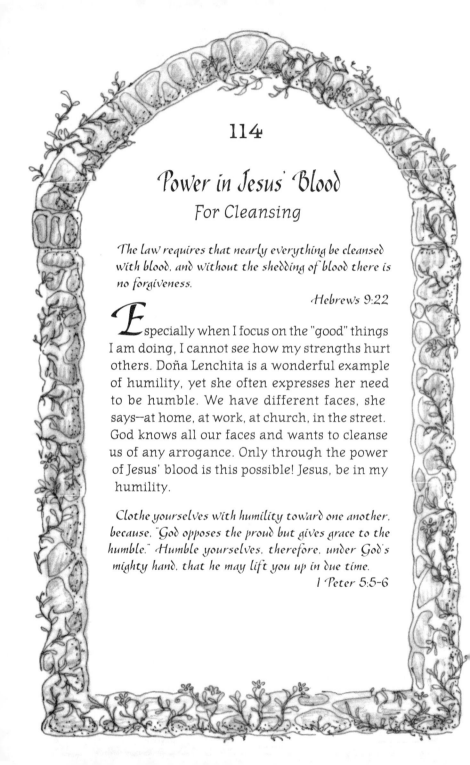

114

Power in Jesus' Blood
For Cleansing

The law requires that nearly everything be cleansed with blood, and without the shedding of blood there is no forgiveness.

Hebrews 9:22

*E*specially when I focus on the "good" things I am doing, I cannot see how my strengths hurt others. Doña Lenchita is a wonderful example of humility, yet she often expresses her need to be humble. We have different faces, she says—at home, at work, at church, in the street. God knows all our faces and wants to cleanse us of any arrogance. Only through the power of Jesus' blood is this possible! Jesus, be in my humility.

Clothe yourselves with humility toward one another, because, "God opposes the proud but gives grace to the humble." Humble yourselves, therefore, under God's mighty hand, that he may lift you up in due time.

1 Peter 5:5-6

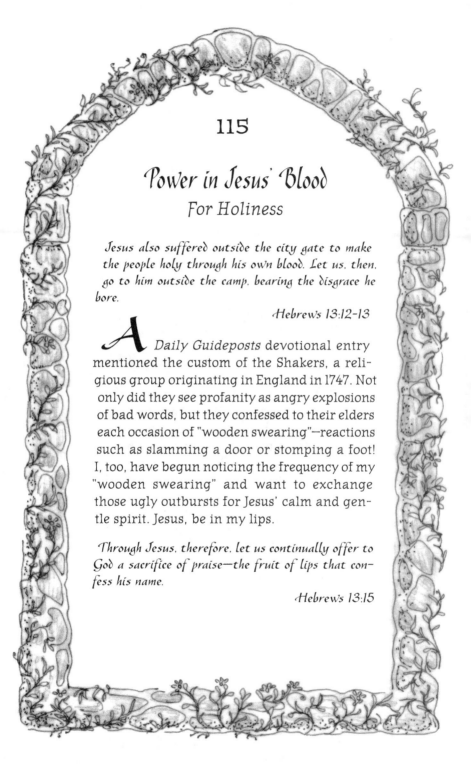

115

Power in Jesus' Blood
For Holiness

Jesus also suffered outside the city gate to make the people holy through his own blood. Let us, then, go to him outside the camp, bearing the disgrace he bore.

Hebrews 13:12-13

A *Daily Guideposts* devotional entry mentioned the custom of the Shakers, a religious group originating in England in 1747. Not only did they see profanity as angry explosions of bad words, but they confessed to their elders each occasion of "wooden swearing"—reactions such as slamming a door or stomping a foot! I, too, have begun noticing the frequency of my "wooden swearing" and want to exchange those ugly outbursts for Jesus' calm and gentle spirit. Jesus, be in my lips.

Through Jesus, therefore, let us continually offer to God a sacrifice of praise—the fruit of lips that confess his name.

Hebrews 13:15

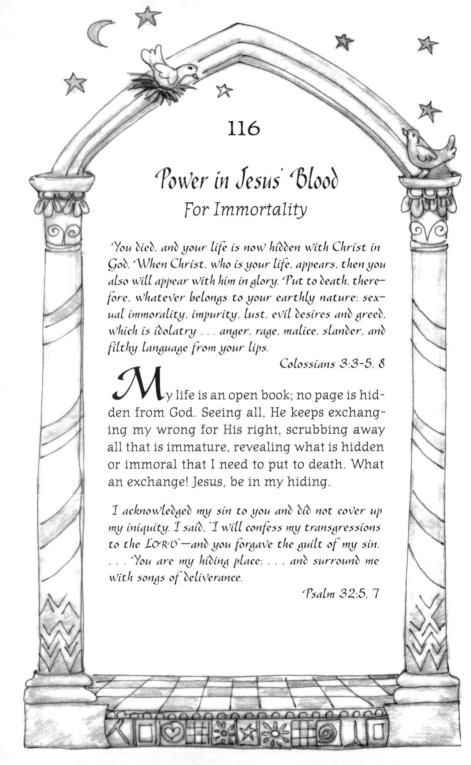

Power in Jesus' Blood
For Immortality

You died, and your life is now hidden with Christ in God. When Christ, who is your life, appears, then you also will appear with him in glory. Put to death, therefore, whatever belongs to your earthly nature: sexual immorality, impurity, lust, evil desires and greed, which is idolatry . . . anger, rage, malice, slander, and filthy language from your lips.

Colossians 3:3-5, 8

My life is an open book; no page is hidden from God. Seeing all, He keeps exchanging my wrong for His right, scrubbing away all that is immature, revealing what is hidden or immoral that I need to put to death. What an exchange! Jesus, be in my hiding.

I acknowledged my sin to you and did not cover up my iniquity. I said, "I will confess my transgressions to the LORD"—and you forgave the guilt of my sin. . . . You are my hiding place: . . . and surround me with songs of deliverance.

Psalm 32:5, 7

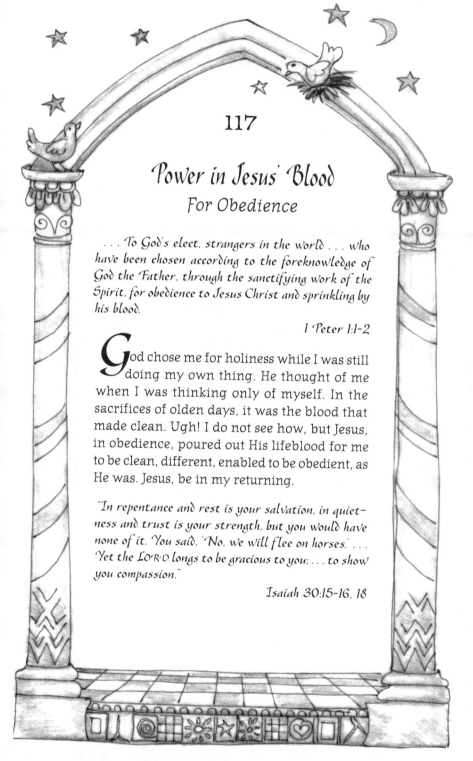

117

Power in Jesus' Blood
For Obedience

. . . To God's elect, strangers in the world . . . who have been chosen according to the foreknowledge of God the Father, through the sanctifying work of the Spirit, for obedience to Jesus Christ and sprinkling by his blood.

1 Peter 1:1-2

God chose me for holiness while I was still doing my own thing. He thought of me when I was thinking only of myself. In the sacrifices of olden days, it was the blood that made clean. Ugh! I do not see how, but Jesus, in obedience, poured out His lifeblood for me to be clean, different, enabled to be obedient, as He was. Jesus, be in my returning.

"In repentance and rest is your salvation, in quiet-ness and trust is your strength, but you would have none of it. You said, 'No, we will flee on horses.' . . . Yet the LORD longs to be gracious to you; . . . to show you compassion."

Isaiah 30:15-16, 18

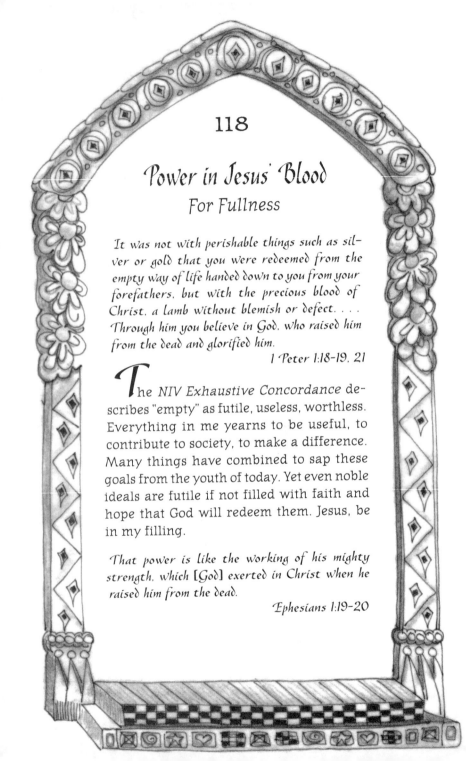

Power in Jesus' Blood
For Fullness

It was not with perishable things such as silver or gold that you were redeemed from the empty way of life handed down to you from your forefathers, but with the precious blood of Christ, a lamb without blemish or defect. . . . Through him you believe in God, who raised him from the dead and glorified him.

1 Peter 1:18-19, 21

*T*he *NIV Exhaustive Concordance* describes "empty" as futile, useless, worthless. Everything in me yearns to be useful, to contribute to society, to make a difference. Many things have combined to sap these goals from the youth of today. Yet even noble ideals are futile if not filled with faith and hope that God will redeem them. Jesus, be in my filling.

That power is like the working of his mighty strength, which [God] exerted in Christ when he raised him from the dead.

Ephesians 1:19-20

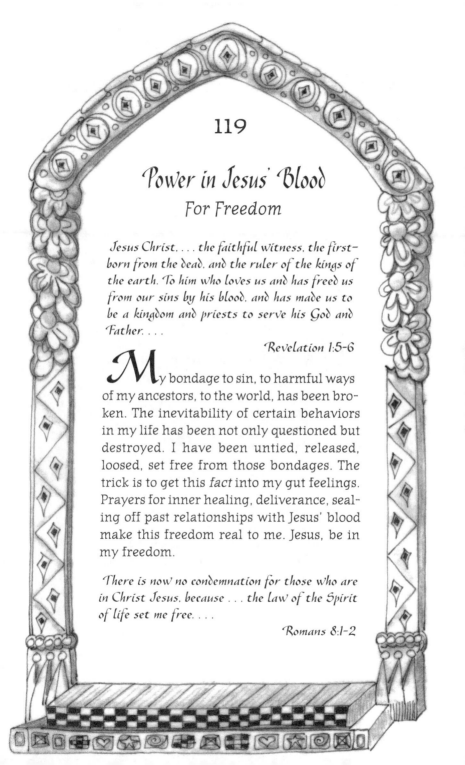

Power in Jesus' Blood
For Freedom

Jesus Christ. . . . the faithful witness, the first-born from the dead, and the ruler of the kings of the earth. To him who loves us and has freed us from our sins by his blood, and has made us to be a kingdom and priests to serve his God and Father. . . .

Revelation 1:5-6

My bondage to sin, to harmful ways of my ancestors, to the world, has been broken. The inevitability of certain behaviors in my life has been not only questioned but destroyed. I have been untied, released, loosed, set free from those bondages. The trick is to get this *fact* into my gut feelings. Prayers for inner healing, deliverance, sealing off past relationships with Jesus' blood make this freedom real to me. Jesus, be in my freedom.

There is now no condemnation for those who are in Christ Jesus, because . . . the law of the Spirit of life set me free. . . .

Romans 8:1-2

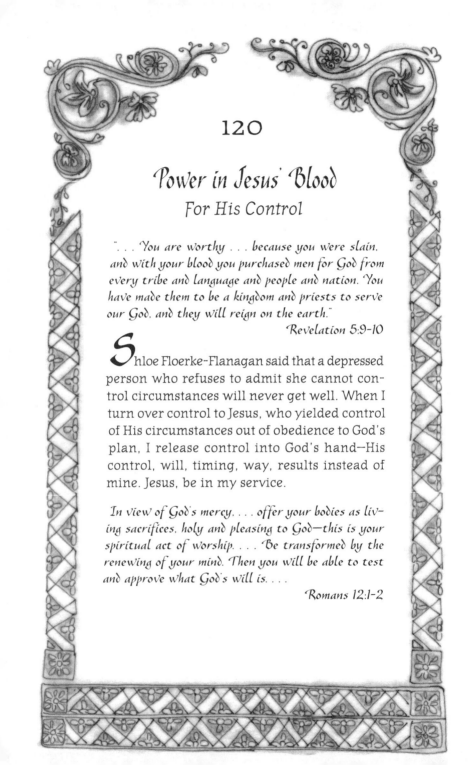

Power in Jesus' Blood
For His Control

*". . . You are worthy . . . because you were slain,
and with your blood you purchased men for God from
every tribe and language and people and nation. You
have made them to be a kingdom and priests to serve
our God, and they will reign on the earth."*
Revelation 5:9-10

Shloe Floerke-Flanagan said that a depressed
person who refuses to admit she cannot control circumstances will never get well. When I
turn over control to Jesus, who yielded control
of His circumstances out of obedience to God's
plan, I release control into God's hand—His
control, will, timing, way, results instead of
mine. Jesus, be in my service.

*In view of God's mercy. . . . offer your bodies as liv-
ing sacrifices, holy and pleasing to God—this is your
spiritual act of worship. . . . Be transformed by the
renewing of your mind. Then you will be able to test
and approve what God's will is. . . .*
Romans 12:1-2

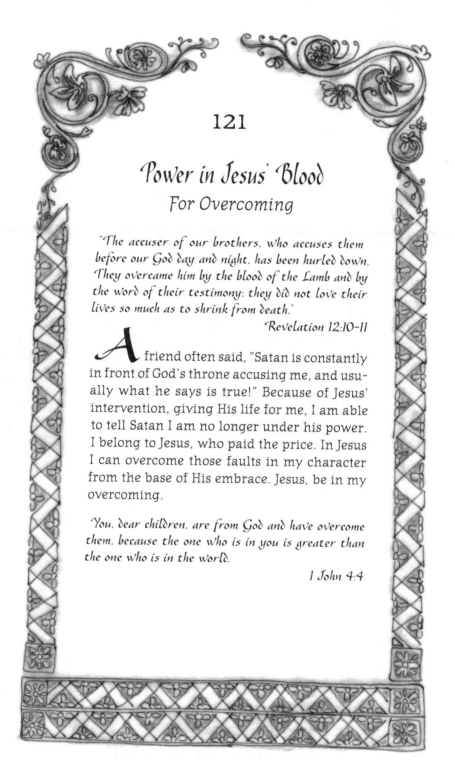

121

Power in Jesus' Blood
For Overcoming

"The accuser of our brothers, who accuses them before our God day and night, has been hurled down. They overcame him by the blood of the Lamb and by the word of their testimony; they did not love their lives so much as to shrink from death."

Revelation 12:10-11

A friend often said, "Satan is constantly in front of God's throne accusing me, and usually what he says is true!" Because of Jesus' intervention, giving His life for me, I am able to tell Satan I am no longer under his power. I belong to Jesus, who paid the price. In Jesus I can overcome those faults in my character from the base of His embrace. Jesus, be in my overcoming.

You, dear children, are from God and have overcome them, because the one who is in you is greater than the one who is in the world.

1 John 4:4

122

Power to Forgive
Others' Sins against Me

"When you stand praying, if you hold anything against anyone, forgive him, so that your Father in heaven may forgive you your sins."

Mark 11:25

Jesus knew that if I am holding anything against anyone, God cannot forgive me. "Forgive one another daily," our son James wrote in a wedding song. It is those closest to me who often offend me the most. In the Lord's Prayer, Jesus has me ask God to forgive me the same way I forgive others. Jesus, be in those who hurt me and in my forgiveness.

Jesus said, "Father, forgive them, for they do not know what they are doing."

Luke 23:34

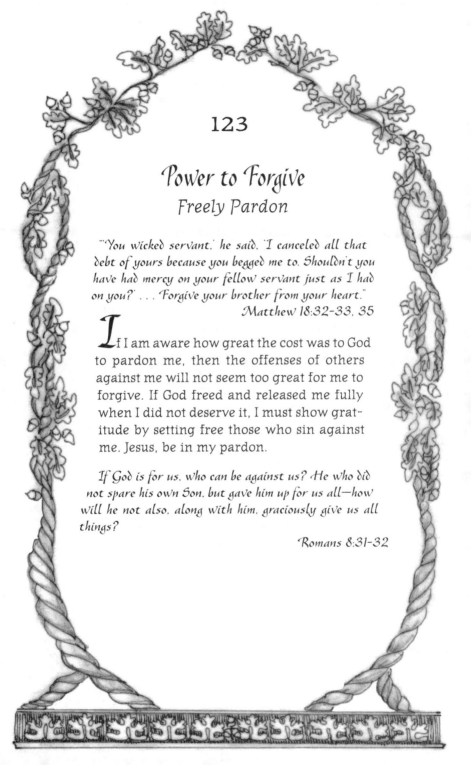

123

Power to Forgive
Freely Pardon

"'You wicked servant,' he said, 'I canceled all that debt of yours because you begged me to. Shouldn't you have had mercy on your fellow servant just as I had on you?' . . . Forgive your brother from your heart."
Matthew 18:32-33, 35

If I am aware how great the cost was to God to pardon me, then the offenses of others against me will not seem too great for me to forgive. If God freed and released me fully when I did not deserve it, I must show gratitude by setting free those who sin against me. Jesus, be in my pardon.

If God is for us, who can be against us? He who did not spare his own Son, but gave him up for us all—how will he not also, along with him, graciously give us all things?
Romans 8:31-32

Power to Forgive
Releasing Others

[He] forgives all [my] sins and heals all [my] diseases. . . . As far as the east is from the west, so far has he removed our transgressions from us.

Psalm 103:3, 12

Because God has forgiven me so completely, I learn how to forgive others. It is not easy, especially when the hurts go deep, but healing comes with forgiveness and release. I cannot hold any longer onto the past, but must allow myself and the ones who hurt me to start anew. Jesus, be in my releasing.

Peter came to Jesus and asked, "Lord, how many times shall I forgive my brother when he sins against me? Up to seven times?" Jesus answered, "I tell you, not seven times, but seventy-seven times."

Matthew 18:21

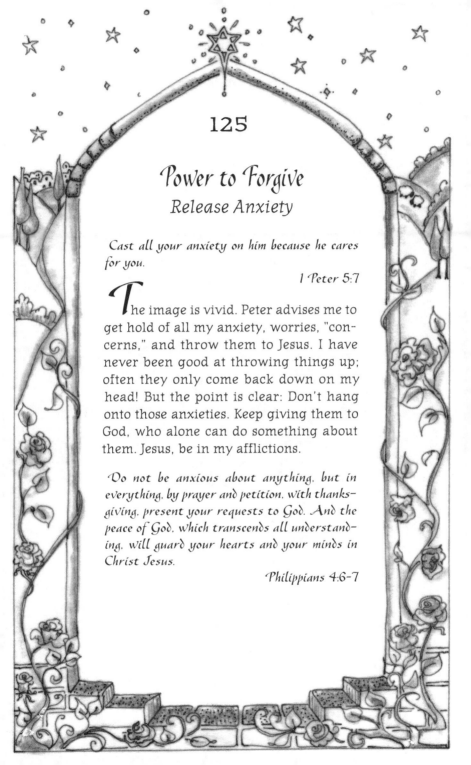

125

Power to Forgive
Release Anxiety

Cast all your anxiety on him because he cares for you.

1 Peter 5:7

The image is vivid. Peter advises me to get hold of all my anxiety, worries, "concerns," and throw them to Jesus. I have never been good at throwing things up; often they only come back down on my head! But the point is clear: Don't hang onto those anxieties. Keep giving them to God, who alone can do something about them. Jesus, be in my afflictions.

Do not be anxious about anything, but in everything, by prayer and petition, with thanksgiving, present your requests to God. And the peace of God, which transcends all understanding, will guard your hearts and your minds in Christ Jesus.

Philippians 4:6-7

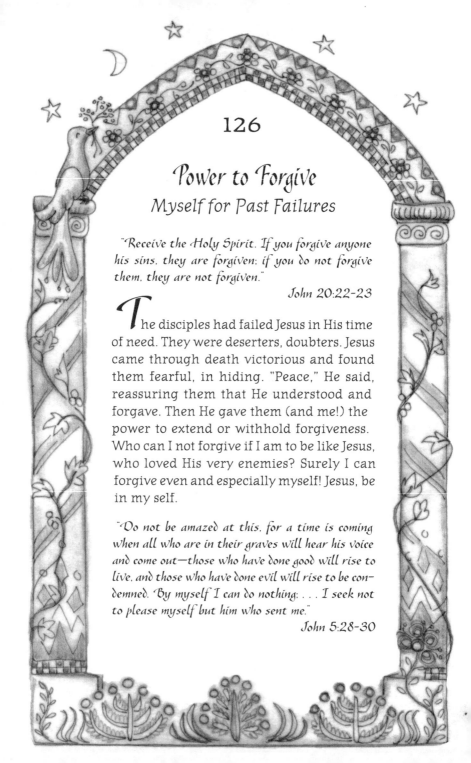

126

Power to Forgive
Myself for Past Failures

"Receive the Holy Spirit. If you forgive anyone his sins, they are forgiven; if you do not forgive them, they are not forgiven."

John 20:22-23

The disciples had failed Jesus in His time of need. They were deserters, doubters. Jesus came through death victorious and found them fearful, in hiding. "Peace," He said, reassuring them that He understood and forgave. Then He gave them (and me!) the power to extend or withhold forgiveness. Who can I not forgive if I am to be like Jesus, who loved His very enemies? Surely I can forgive even and especially myself! Jesus, be in my self.

"Do not be amazed at this, for a time is coming when all who are in their graves will hear his voice and come out—those who have done good will rise to live, and those who have done evil will rise to be condemned. By myself I can do nothing; . . . I seek not to please myself but him who sent me."

John 5:28-30

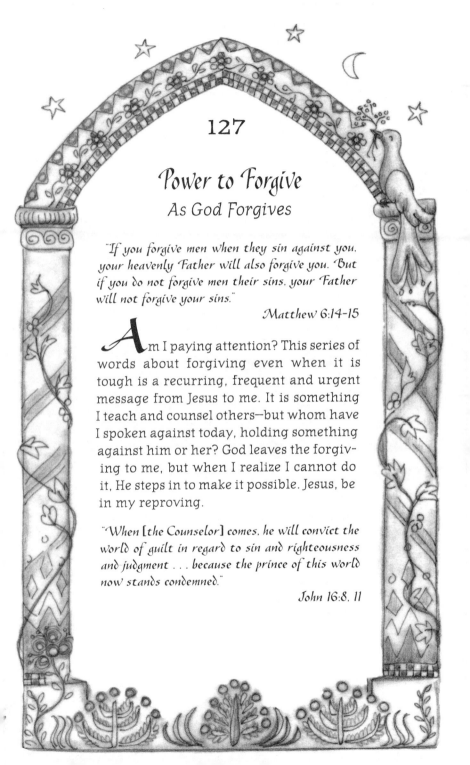

Power to Forgive
As God Forgives

"If you forgive men when they sin against you, your heavenly Father will also forgive you. But if you do not forgive men their sins, your Father will not forgive your sins."

Matthew 6:14-15

Am I paying attention? This series of words about forgiving even when it is tough is a recurring, frequent and urgent message from Jesus to me. It is something I teach and counsel others—but whom have I spoken against today, holding something against him or her? God leaves the forgiving to me, but when I realize I cannot do it, He steps in to make it possible. Jesus, be in my reproving.

"When [the Counselor] comes, he will convict the world of guilt in regard to sin and righteousness and judgment . . . because the prince of this world now stands condemned."

John 16:8, 11

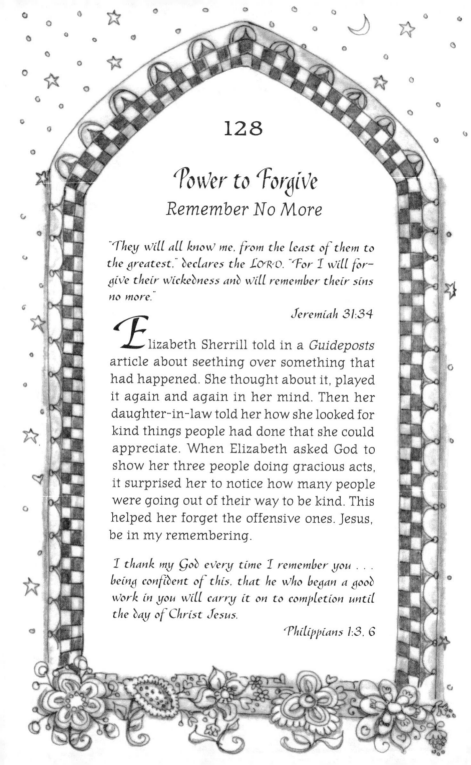

Power to Forgive
Remember No More

"They will all know me, from the least of them to the greatest," declares the LORD. "For I will forgive their wickedness and will remember their sins no more."

Jeremiah 31:34

*E*lizabeth Sherrill told in a *Guideposts* article about seething over something that had happened. She thought about it, played it again and again in her mind. Then her daughter-in-law told her how she looked for kind things people had done that she could appreciate. When Elizabeth asked God to show her three people doing gracious acts, it surprised her to notice how many people were going out of their way to be kind. This helped her forget the offensive ones. Jesus, be in my remembering.

I thank my God every time I remember you . . . being confident of this, that he who began a good work in you will carry it on to completion until the day of Christ Jesus.

Philippians 1:3, 6

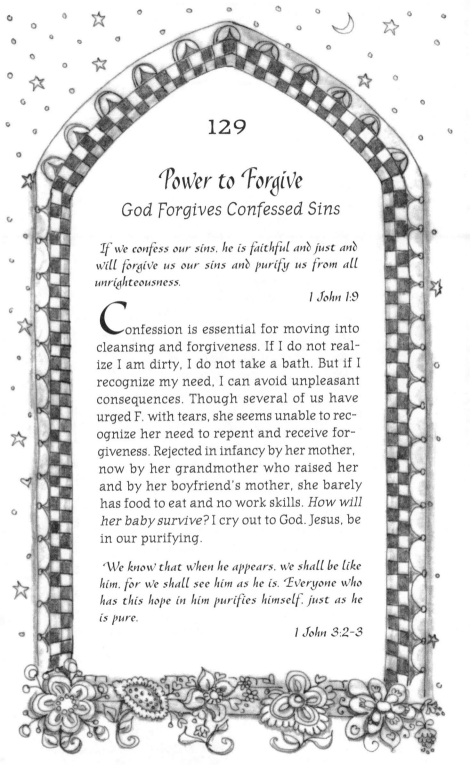

129

Power to Forgive
God Forgives Confessed Sins

If we confess our sins, he is faithful and just and will forgive us our sins and purify us from all unrighteousness.

1 John 1:9

Confession is essential for moving into cleansing and forgiveness. If I do not realize I am dirty, I do not take a bath. But if I recognize my need, I can avoid unpleasant consequences. Though several of us have urged F. with tears, she seems unable to recognize her need to repent and receive forgiveness. Rejected in infancy by her mother, now by her grandmother who raised her and by her boyfriend's mother, she barely has food to eat and no work skills. *How will her baby survive?* I cry out to God. Jesus, be in our purifying.

We know that when he appears, we shall be like him, for we shall see him as he is. Everyone who has this hope in him purifies himself, just as he is pure.

1 John 3:2-3

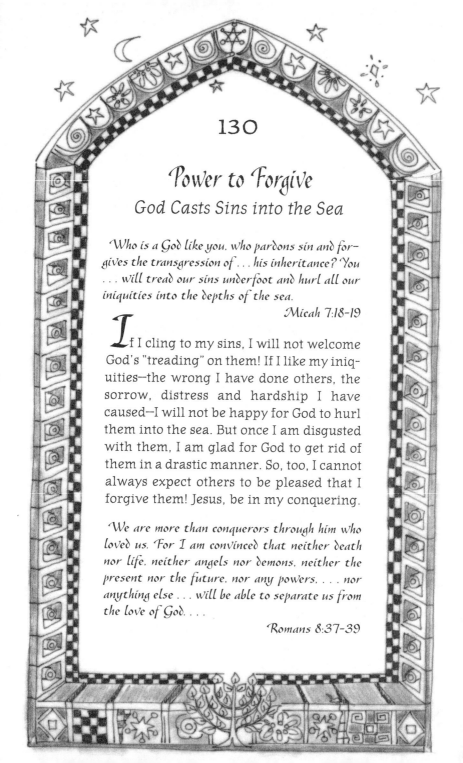

130

Power to Forgive
God Casts Sins into the Sea

Who is a God like you, who pardons sin and for-gives the transgression of . . . his inheritance? You . . . will tread our sins underfoot and hurl all our iniquities into the depths of the sea.

Micah 7:18-19

*I*f I cling to my sins, I will not welcome God's "treading" on them! If I like my iniquities—the wrong I have done others, the sorrow, distress and hardship I have caused—I will not be happy for God to hurl them into the sea. But once I am disgusted with them, I am glad for God to get rid of them in a drastic manner. So, too, I cannot always expect others to be pleased that I forgive them! Jesus, be in my conquering.

We are more than conquerors through him who loved us. For I am convinced that neither death nor life, neither angels nor demons, neither the present nor the future, nor any powers, . . . nor anything else . . . will be able to separate us from the love of God. . . .

Romans 8:37-39

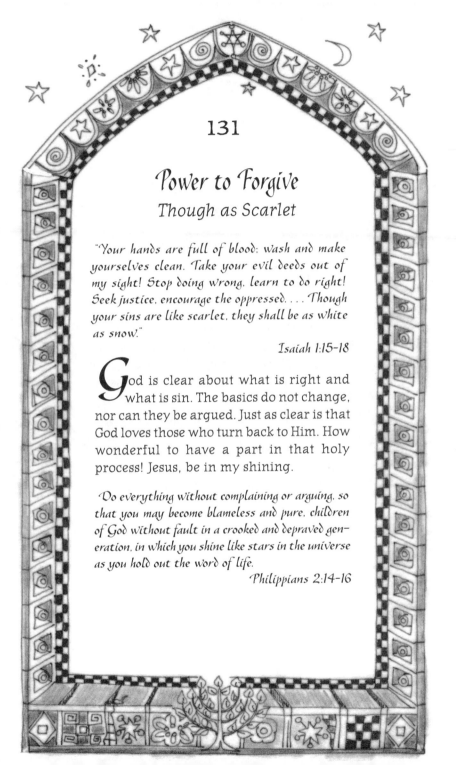

Power to Forgive
Though as Scarlet

"Your hands are full of blood: wash and make yourselves clean. Take your evil deeds out of my sight! Stop doing wrong, learn to do right! Seek justice, encourage the oppressed. . . . Though your sins are like scarlet, they shall be as white as snow."

Isaiah 1:15-18

God is clear about what is right and what is sin. The basics do not change, nor can they be argued. Just as clear is that God loves those who turn back to Him. How wonderful to have a part in that holy process! Jesus, be in my shining.

Do everything without complaining or arguing, so that you may become blameless and pure, children of God without fault in a crooked and depraved generation, in which you shine like stars in the universe as you hold out the word of life.

Philippians 2:14-16

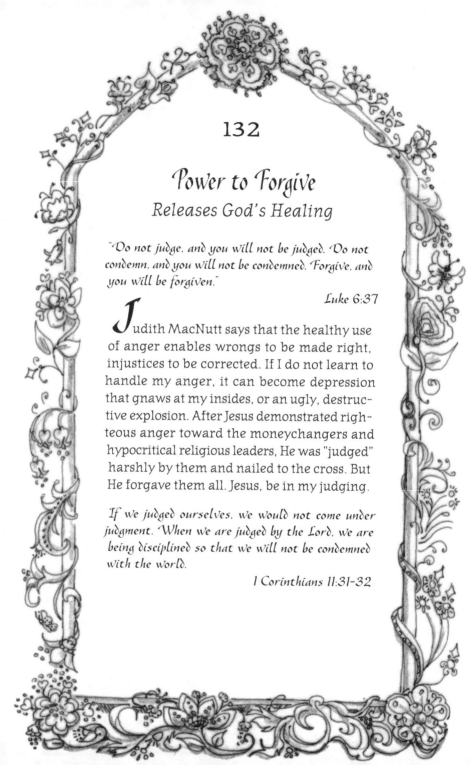

132

Power to Forgive
Releases God's Healing

"Do not judge, and you will not be judged. Do not condemn, and you will not be condemned. Forgive, and you will be forgiven."

Luke 6:37

Judith MacNutt says that the healthy use of anger enables wrongs to be made right, injustices to be corrected. If I do not learn to handle my anger, it can become depression that gnaws at my insides, or an ugly, destructive explosion. After Jesus demonstrated righteous anger toward the moneychangers and hypocritical religious leaders, He was "judged" harshly by them and nailed to the cross. But He forgave them all. Jesus, be in my judging.

If we judged ourselves, we would not come under judgment. When we are judged by the Lord, we are being disciplined so that we will not be condemned with the world.

1 Corinthians 11:31-32

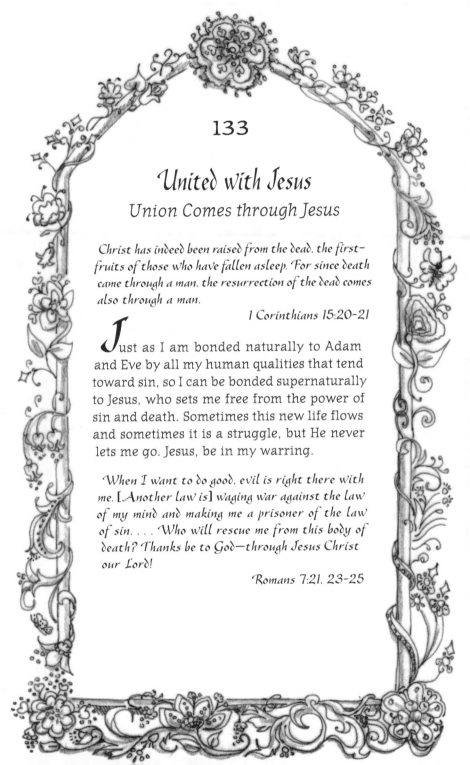

133

United with Jesus
Union Comes through Jesus

Christ has indeed been raised from the dead, the first-fruits of those who have fallen asleep. For since death came through a man, the resurrection of the dead comes also through a man.

1 Corinthians 15:20-21

Just as I am bonded naturally to Adam and Eve by all my human qualities that tend toward sin, so I can be bonded supernaturally to Jesus, who sets me free from the power of sin and death. Sometimes this new life flows and sometimes it is a struggle, but He never lets me go. Jesus, be in my warring.

When I want to do good, evil is right there with me. [Another law is] waging war against the law of my mind and making me a prisoner of the law of sin. . . . Who will rescue me from this body of death? Thanks be to God—through Jesus Christ our Lord!

Romans 7:21, 23-25

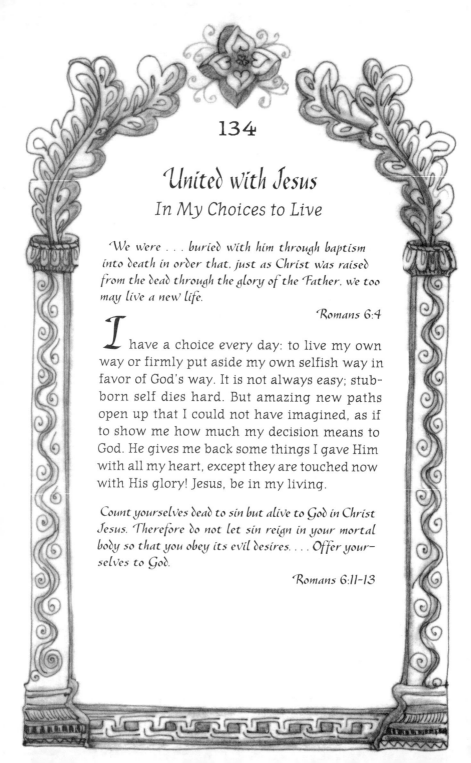

134

United with Jesus
In My Choices to Live

We were . . . buried with him through baptism into death in order that, just as Christ was raised from the dead through the glory of the Father, we too may live a new life.

Romans 6:4

I have a choice every day: to live my own way or firmly put aside my own selfish way in favor of God's way. It is not always easy; stubborn self dies hard. But amazing new paths open up that I could not have imagined, as if to show me how much my decision means to God. He gives me back some things I gave Him with all my heart, except they are touched now with His glory! Jesus, be in my living.

Count yourselves dead to sin but alive to God in Christ Jesus. Therefore do not let sin reign in your mortal body so that you obey its evil desires. . . . Offer yourselves to God.

Romans 6:11-13

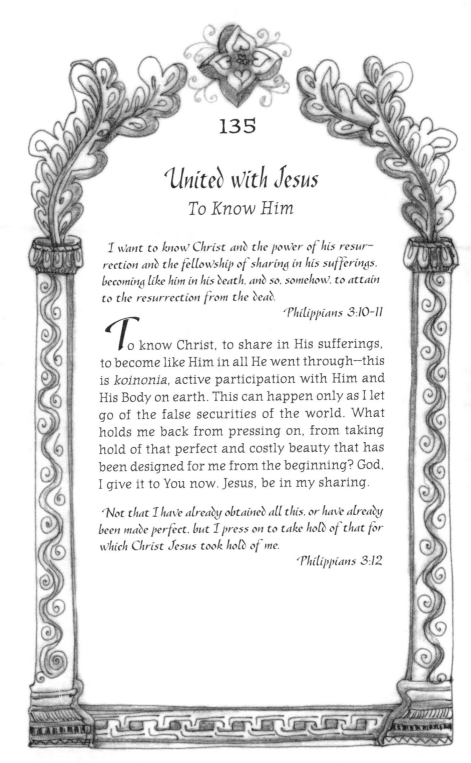

135

United with Jesus
To Know Him

I want to know Christ and the power of his resurrection and the fellowship of sharing in his sufferings, becoming like him in his death, and so, somehow, to attain to the resurrection from the dead.

Philippians 3:10-11

To know Christ, to share in His sufferings, to become like Him in all He went through—this is *koinonia*, active participation with Him and His Body on earth. This can happen only as I let go of the false securities of the world. What holds me back from pressing on, from taking hold of that perfect and costly beauty that has been designed for me from the beginning? God, I give it to You now. Jesus, be in my sharing.

Not that I have already obtained all this, or have already been made perfect, but I press on to take hold of that for which Christ Jesus took hold of me.

Philippians 3:12

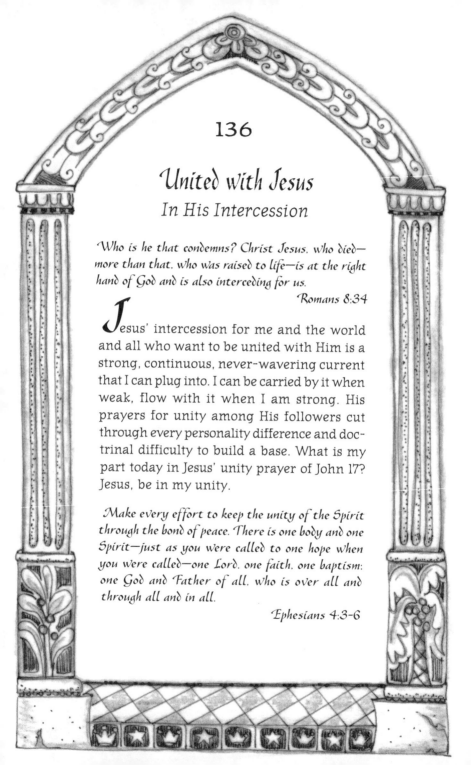

136

United with Jesus
In His Intercession

Who is he that condemns? Christ Jesus, who died—
more than that, who was raised to life—is at the right
hand of God and is also interceding for us.

Romans 8:34

Jesus' intercession for me and the world and all who want to be united with Him is a strong, continuous, never-wavering current that I can plug into. I can be carried by it when weak, flow with it when I am strong. His prayers for unity among His followers cut through every personality difference and doctrinal difficulty to build a base. What is my part today in Jesus' unity prayer of John 17? Jesus, be in my unity.

Make every effort to keep the unity of the Spirit
through the bond of peace. There is one body and one
Spirit—just as you were called to one hope when
you were called—one Lord, one faith, one baptism:
one God and Father of all, who is over all and
through all and in all.

Ephesians 4:3-6

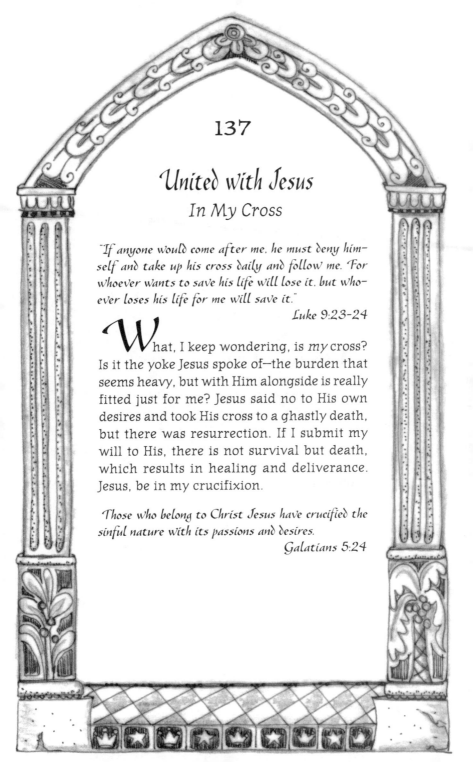

137

United with Jesus
In My Cross

"If anyone would come after me, he must deny him-self and take up his cross daily and follow me. For whoever wants to save his life will lose it, but who-ever loses his life for me will save it."
Luke 9:23-24

What, I keep wondering, is *my* cross? Is it the yoke Jesus spoke of—the burden that seems heavy, but with Him alongside is really fitted just for me? Jesus said no to His own desires and took His cross to a ghastly death, but there was resurrection. If I submit my will to His, there is not survival but death, which results in healing and deliverance. Jesus, be in my crucifixion.

Those who belong to Christ Jesus have crucified the sinful nature with its passions and desires.
Galatians 5:24

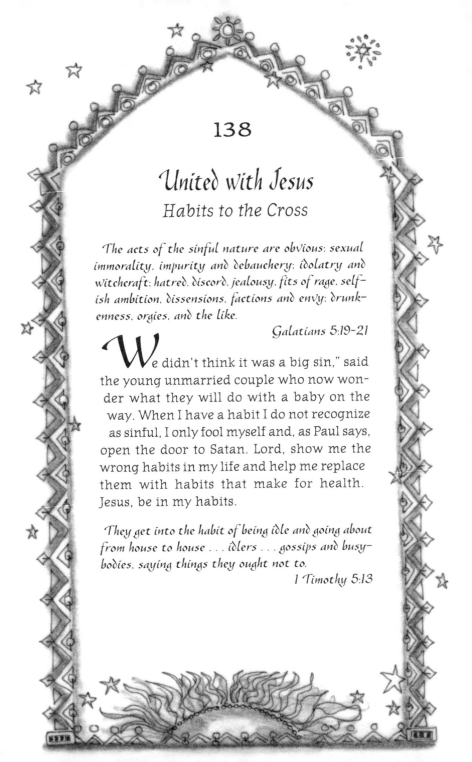

138

United with Jesus
Habits to the Cross

The acts of the sinful nature are obvious: sexual immorality, impurity and debauchery; idolatry and witchcraft; hatred, discord, jealousy, fits of rage, selfish ambition, dissensions, factions and envy; drunkenness, orgies, and the like.

Galatians 5:19-21

"We didn't think it was a big sin," said the young unmarried couple who now wonder what they will do with a baby on the way. When I have a habit I do not recognize as sinful, I only fool myself and, as Paul says, open the door to Satan. Lord, show me the wrong habits in my life and help me replace them with habits that make for health. Jesus, be in my habits.

They get into the habit of being idle and going about from house to house ... idlers ... gossips and busybodies, saying things they ought not to.

1 Timothy 5:13

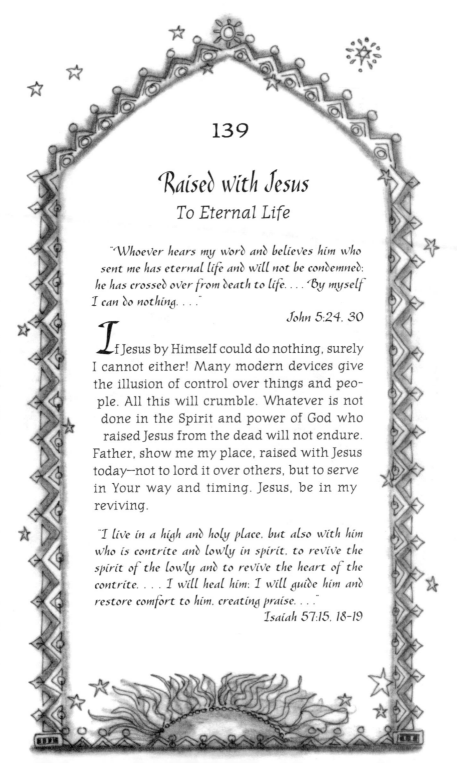

139

Raised with Jesus
To Eternal Life

"Whoever hears my word and believes him who sent me has eternal life and will not be condemned: he has crossed over from death to life. . . . By myself I can do nothing. . . ."

John 5:24, 30

*I*f Jesus by Himself could do nothing, surely I cannot either! Many modern devices give the illusion of control over things and people. All this will crumble. Whatever is not done in the Spirit and power of God who raised Jesus from the dead will not endure. Father, show me my place, raised with Jesus today—not to lord it over others, but to serve in Your way and timing. Jesus, be in my reviving.

"I live in a high and holy place, but also with him who is contrite and lowly in spirit, to revive the spirit of the lowly and to revive the heart of the contrite. . . . I will heal him; I will guide him and restore comfort to him, creating praise. . . ."

Isaiah 57:15, 18-19

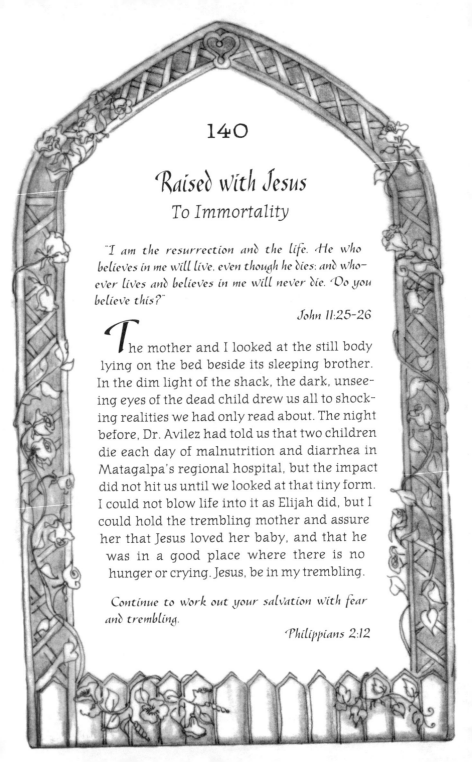

Raised with Jesus
To Immortality

"I am the resurrection and the life. He who believes in me will live, even though he dies; and who-ever lives and believes in me will never die. Do you believe this?"

John 11:25-26

The mother and I looked at the still body lying on the bed beside its sleeping brother. In the dim light of the shack, the dark, unseeing eyes of the dead child drew us all to shocking realities we had only read about. The night before, Dr. Avilez had told us that two children die each day of malnutrition and diarrhea in Matagalpa's regional hospital, but the impact did not hit us until we looked at that tiny form. I could not blow life into it as Elijah did, but I could hold the trembling mother and assure her that Jesus loved her baby, and that he was in a good place where there is no hunger or crying. Jesus, be in my trembling.

Continue to work out your salvation with fear and trembling.

Philippians 2:12

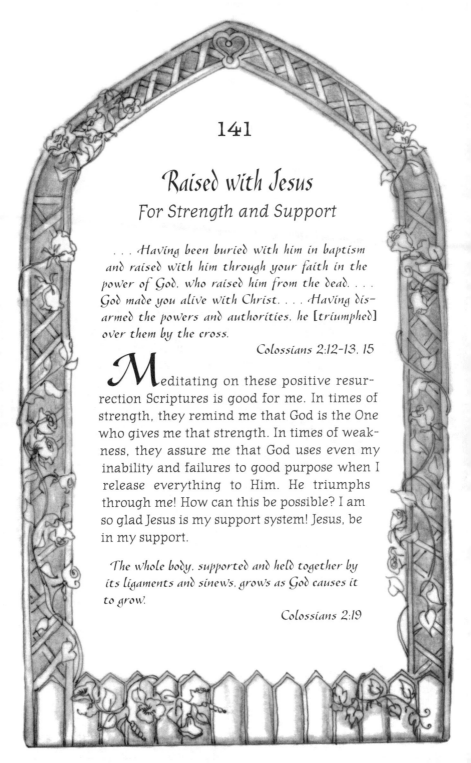

141

Raised with Jesus
For Strength and Support

... Having been buried with him in baptism and raised with him through your faith in the power of God, who raised him from the dead.... God made you alive with Christ.... Having disarmed the powers and authorities, he [triumphed] over them by the cross.

Colossians 2:12-13, 15

Meditating on these positive resurrection Scriptures is good for me. In times of strength, they remind me that God is the One who gives me that strength. In times of weakness, they assure me that God uses even my inability and failures to good purpose when I release everything to Him. He triumphs through me! How can this be possible? I am so glad Jesus is my support system! Jesus, be in my support.

The whole body, supported and held together by its ligaments and sinews, grows as God causes it to grow.

Colossians 2:19

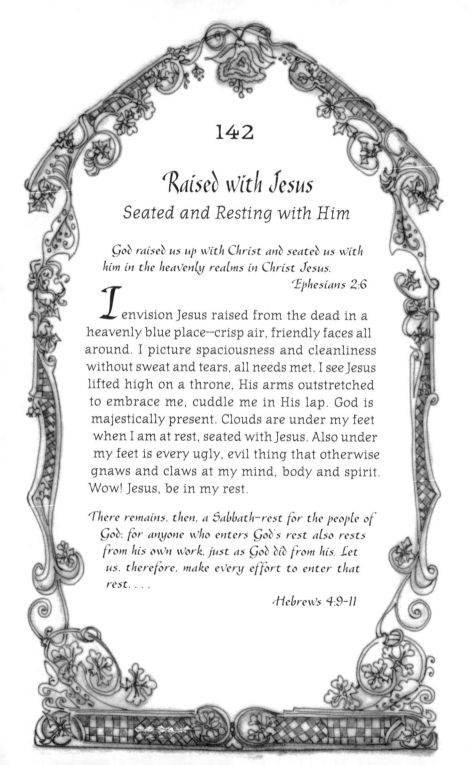

142

Raised with Jesus
Seated and Resting with Him

God raised us up with Christ and seated us with him in the heavenly realms in Christ Jesus.
Ephesians 2:6

I envision Jesus raised from the dead in a heavenly blue place—crisp air, friendly faces all around. I picture spaciousness and cleanliness without sweat and tears, all needs met. I see Jesus lifted high on a throne, His arms outstretched to embrace me, cuddle me in His lap. God is majestically present. Clouds are under my feet when I am at rest, seated with Jesus. Also under my feet is every ugly, evil thing that otherwise gnaws and claws at my mind, body and spirit. Wow! Jesus, be in my rest.

There remains, then, a Sabbath-rest for the people of God: for anyone who enters God's rest also rests from his own work, just as God did from his. Let us, therefore, make every effort to enter that rest. . . .
Hebrews 4:9-11

143

Raised with Jesus
God Raises Us

*Neither the sexually immoral nor idolaters nor
adulterers nor male prostitutes nor homosexual
offenders nor thieves nor the greedy nor drunkards
nor slanderers nor swindlers will inherit the kingdom
of God. . . . But you were washed, you were sanctified,
you were justified in the name of the Lord Jesus Christ
and by the Spirit of our God.*

1 Corinthians 6:9-11

I am known by God; but everything unlike
His perfect love was put to death with Jesus.
Now I am washed, acquitted, consecrated, made
holy! This freedom from what I was attracts others to Him. Jesus, be in my behavior.

*The overseer must be above reproach, the husband of but
one wife, temperate, self-controlled, respectable, hos-
pitable, able to teach, not given to drunkenness, not
violent but gentle, not quarrelsome, not a lover
of money. . . .*

1 Timothy 3:2-3

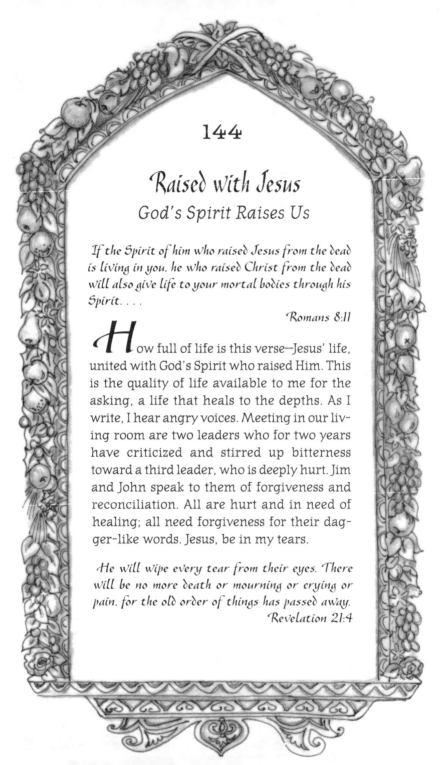

144

Raised with Jesus

God's Spirit Raises Us

If the Spirit of him who raised Jesus from the dead is living in you, he who raised Christ from the dead will also give life to your mortal bodies through his Spirit. . . .

Romans 8:11

How full of life is this verse—Jesus' life, united with God's Spirit who raised Him. This is the quality of life available to me for the asking, a life that heals to the depths. As I write, I hear angry voices. Meeting in our living room are two leaders who for two years have criticized and stirred up bitterness toward a third leader, who is deeply hurt. Jim and John speak to them of forgiveness and reconciliation. All are hurt and in need of healing; all need forgiveness for their dagger-like words. Jesus, be in my tears.

He will wipe every tear from their eyes. There will be no more death or mourning or crying or pain, for the old order of things has passed away.

Revelation 21:4

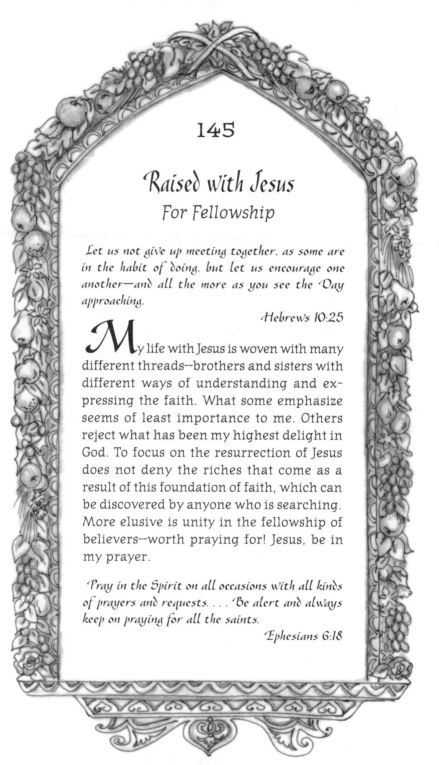

145

Raised with Jesus
For Fellowship

Let us not give up meeting together, as some are in the habit of doing, but let us encourage one another—and all the more as you see the Day approaching.

Hebrews 10:25

My life with Jesus is woven with many different threads—brothers and sisters with different ways of understanding and expressing the faith. What some emphasize seems of least importance to me. Others reject what has been my highest delight in God. To focus on the resurrection of Jesus does not deny the riches that come as a result of this foundation of faith, which can be discovered by anyone who is searching. More elusive is unity in the fellowship of believers—worth praying for! Jesus, be in my prayer.

Pray in the Spirit on all occasions with all kinds of prayers and requests. . . . Be alert and always keep on praying for all the saints.

Ephesians 6:18

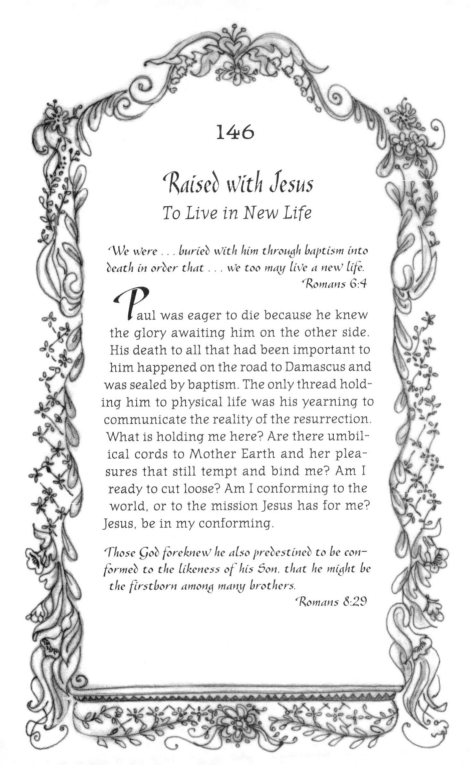

146

Raised with Jesus
To Live in New Life

*We were ... buried with him through baptism into
death in order that ... we too may live a new life.*
Romans 6:4

*P*aul was eager to die because he knew
the glory awaiting him on the other side.
His death to all that had been important to
him happened on the road to Damascus and
was sealed by baptism. The only thread holding him to physical life was his yearning to
communicate the reality of the resurrection.
What is holding me here? Are there umbil-
ical cords to Mother Earth and her plea-
sures that still tempt and bind me? Am I
ready to cut loose? Am I conforming to the
world, or to the mission Jesus has for me?
Jesus, be in my conforming.

*Those God foreknew he also predestined to be con-
formed to the likeness of his Son, that he might be
the firstborn among many brothers.*
Romans 8:29

Raised with Jesus
United with Him

If we have been united with him like this in his death, we will certainly also be united with him in his resurrection. For we know that our old self was crucified with him so that the body of sin might be done away with, that we should no longer be slaves to sin.

Romans 6:5-6

Unity with Jesus begins now when I want Him more than I want my old self and her selfish ways. Then the bonding begins, like a mother holding her newborn child on her tummy after nine months of waiting. Being united with Jesus also means bonding with many new brothers and sisters who need me in order to complete their own wholeness, just as I need them. Jesus, be in my bonding.

Forgive as the Lord forgave you. And over all these virtues put on love, which binds them all together in perfect unity.

Colossians 3:13-14

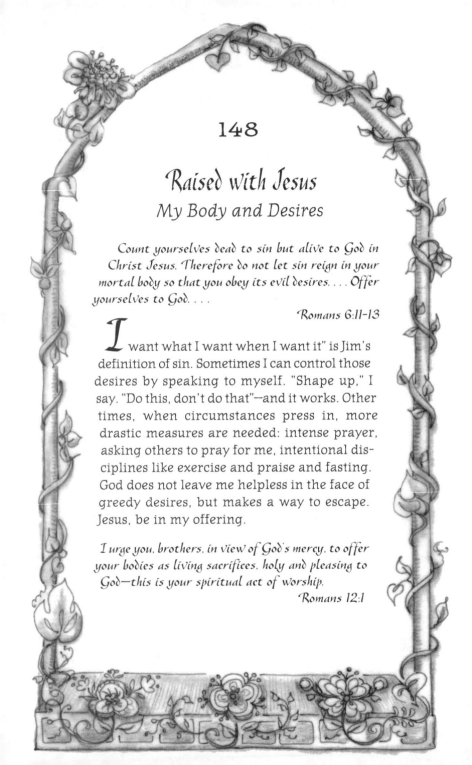

148

Raised with Jesus
My Body and Desires

Count yourselves dead to sin but alive to God in Christ Jesus. Therefore do not let sin reign in your mortal body so that you obey its evil desires. . . . Offer yourselves to God. . . .

Romans 6:11-13

I want what I want when I want it" is Jim's definition of sin. Sometimes I can control those desires by speaking to myself. "Shape up," I say. "Do this, don't do that"—and it works. Other times, when circumstances press in, more drastic measures are needed: intense prayer, asking others to pray for me, intentional disciplines like exercise and praise and fasting. God does not leave me helpless in the face of greedy desires, but makes a way to escape. Jesus, be in my offering.

I urge you, brothers, in view of God's mercy, to offer your bodies as living sacrifices, holy and pleasing to God—this is your spiritual act of worship.

Romans 12:1

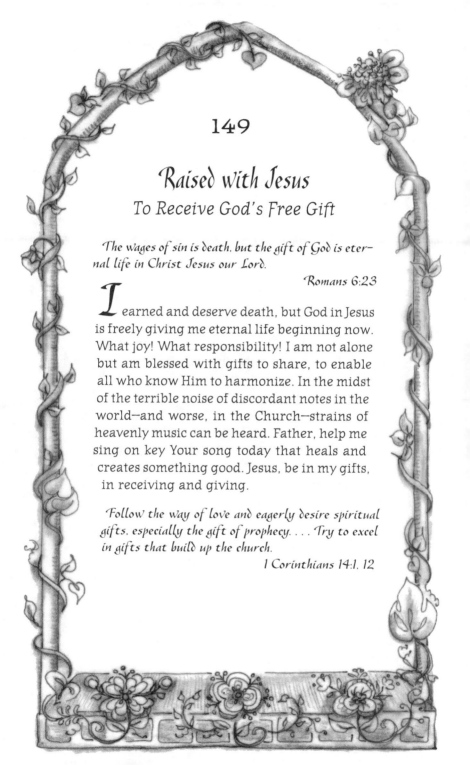

149

Raised with Jesus
To Receive God's Free Gift

The wages of sin is death, but the gift of God is eternal life in Christ Jesus our Lord.

Romans 6:23

I earned and deserve death, but God in Jesus is freely giving me eternal life beginning now. What joy! What responsibility! I am not alone but am blessed with gifts to share, to enable all who know Him to harmonize. In the midst of the terrible noise of discordant notes in the world—and worse, in the Church—strains of heavenly music can be heard. Father, help me sing on key Your song today that heals and creates something good. Jesus, be in my gifts, in receiving and giving.

Follow the way of love and eagerly desire spiritual gifts, especially the gift of prophecy. . . . Try to excel in gifts that build up the church.

1 Corinthians 14:1, 12

150

Power to Bless
Those I Have Forgiven

To him who is able to keep you from falling and to present you before his glorious presence without fault and with great joy.

Jude 24

Forgiveness is a basic ingredient of the Christian life. Blessing is what adds sweetness and savor. Even today in Jewish homes where the Sabbath is observed, the father blesses the mother with Proverbs 31, then together they lay hands on and bless each child. The quality of blessing builds up the blesser as well as the blessed and completes whatever is lacking by communicating assurance, acceptance and appreciation, which are then passed to others without being diminished. Jesus, be in my failings.

We who are strong ought to bear with the failings of the weak and not to please ourselves. Each of us should please his neighbor for his good, to build him up.

Romans 15:1-2

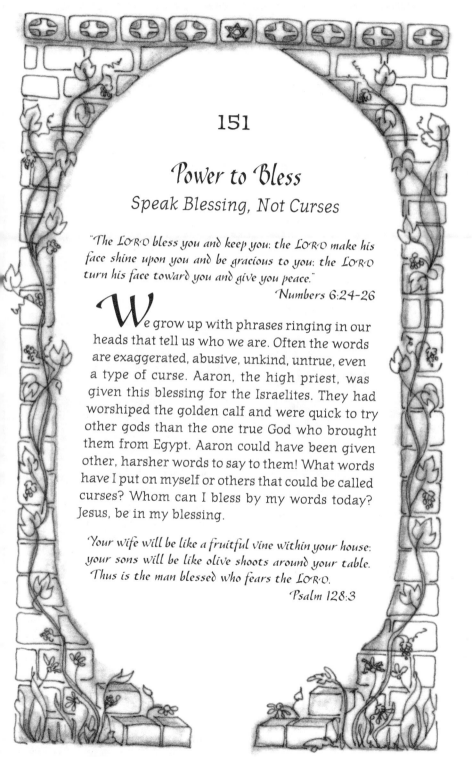

151

Power to Bless
Speak Blessing, Not Curses

"The LORD bless you and keep you; the LORD make his face shine upon you and be gracious to you; the LORD turn his face toward you and give you peace."

Numbers 6:24-26

We grow up with phrases ringing in our heads that tell us who we are. Often the words are exaggerated, abusive, unkind, untrue, even a type of curse. Aaron, the high priest, was given this blessing for the Israelites. They had worshiped the golden calf and were quick to try other gods than the one true God who brought them from Egypt. Aaron could have been given other, harsher words to say to them! What words have I put on myself or others that could be called curses? Whom can I bless by my words today? Jesus, be in my blessing.

Your wife will be like a fruitful vine within your house; your sons will be like olive shoots around your table. Thus is the man blessed who fears the LORD.

Psalm 128:3

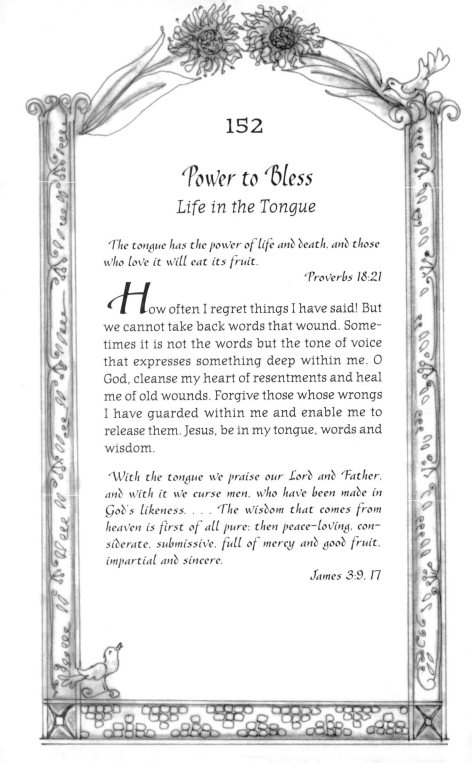

Power to Bless
Life in the Tongue

The tongue has the power of life and death, and those who love it will eat its fruit.

Proverbs 18:21

How often I regret things I have said! But we cannot take back words that wound. Sometimes it is not the words but the tone of voice that expresses something deep within me. O God, cleanse my heart of resentments and heal me of old wounds. Forgive those whose wrongs I have guarded within me and enable me to release them. Jesus, be in my tongue, words and wisdom.

With the tongue we praise our Lord and Father, and with it we curse men, who have been made in God's likeness. . . . The wisdom that comes from heaven is first of all pure; then peace-loving, considerate, submissive, full of mercy and good fruit, impartial and sincere.

James 3:9, 17

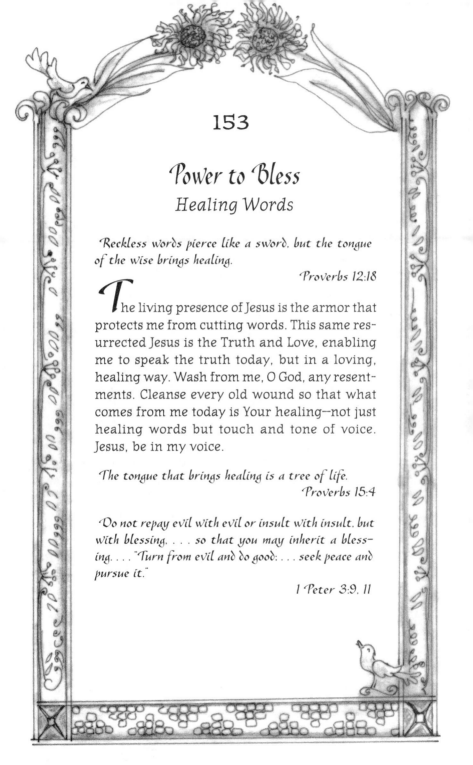

Power to Bless
Healing Words

Reckless words pierce like a sword, but the tongue of the wise brings healing.

Proverbs 12:18

*T*he living presence of Jesus is the armor that protects me from cutting words. This same resurrected Jesus is the Truth and Love, enabling me to speak the truth today, but in a loving, healing way. Wash from me, O God, any resentments. Cleanse every old wound so that what comes from me today is Your healing—not just healing words but touch and tone of voice. Jesus, be in my voice.

The tongue that brings healing is a tree of life.

Proverbs 15:4

Do not repay evil with evil or insult with insult, but with blessing. . . . so that you may inherit a blessing. . . . "Turn from evil and do good: . . . seek peace and pursue it."

1 Peter 3:9, 11

Power to Bless
Break Generational Curses

Christ redeemed us from the curse of the law by becoming a curse for us, for it is written: "Cursed is everyone who is hung on a tree."

Galatians 3:13

"The curse of the law" implies that I cannot live up to God's expectations or my own; it is impossible. Jesus made a new way by offering for me His own fulfillment of the Law. Psychologists say the personality of a child is formed *en utero*. How often I see or hear my parents in me—often those traits I did not like in them! Jesus' resurrection means that His fragrance and beauty pour out from me as from a broken vessel, and I can speak blessing to others. Jesus, be in my communication, both giving and receiving.

He redeemed us in order that the blessing given to Abraham might come to the Gentiles through Christ Jesus, so that by faith we might receive the promise of the Spirit.

Galatians 3:14

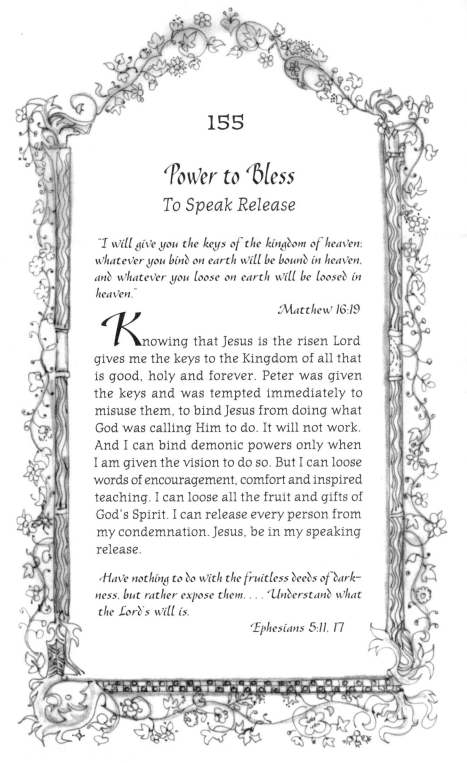

Power to Bless
To Speak Release

*"I will give you the keys of the kingdom of heaven:
whatever you bind on earth will be bound in heaven,
and whatever you loose on earth will be loosed in
heaven."*

Matthew 16:19

Knowing that Jesus is the risen Lord
gives me the keys to the Kingdom of all that
is good, holy and forever. Peter was given
the keys and was tempted immediately to
misuse them, to bind Jesus from doing what
God was calling Him to do. It will not work.
And I can bind demonic powers only when
I am given the vision to do so. But I can loose
words of encouragement, comfort and inspired
teaching. I can loose all the fruit and gifts of
God's Spirit. I can release every person from
my condemnation. Jesus, be in my speaking
release.

*Have nothing to do with the fruitless deeds of dark-
ness, but rather expose them. . . . Understand what
the Lord's will is.*

Ephesians 5:11, 17

156

Power to Bless
With Healing

I pray that out of his glorious riches he may strengthen you with power through his Spirit in your inner being.

Ephesians 3:16

After the ascension of Jesus, the Holy Spirit was released to fill believers as He filled Jesus. Those earliest disciples often gathered to pray for more of God's Spirit. He always came! Healing of body, mind and spirit as an integrated whole was always part of the Spirit's coming. Healing is not only for my well-being but for those for whom I pray. The Spirit is like a stream of living water welling up within me, healing me when I invite Him in and flowing out, touching all around with refreshing and health. Jesus, be in my spirit.

God did not give us a spirit of timidity, but a spirit of power, of love and of self-discipline.

2 Timothy 1:7

Power to Bless
With Productivity

The LORD has anointed me to preach good news to the poor . . . to bind up the brokenhearted, to proclaim freedom for the captives and release for the prisoners . . . to comfort . . . and provide for those who grieve . . . a crown of beauty . . . the oil of gladness . . . a garment of praise.

Isaiah 61:1-3

*I*f everything I am and do is dedicated to God, He will produce through me ways to bring good news to those with fewer resources and healing to hurting people. I will be a guide who opens doors to God for those who are in literal or emotional prisons. I will comfort, be a source of beauty, gladness and praise for those who grieve. Jesus, be in my productivity.

"There will be showers of blessing. The trees of the field will yield their fruit . . . the people will be secure in their land. They will know that I am the LORD. . . ."

Ezekiel 34:26-27

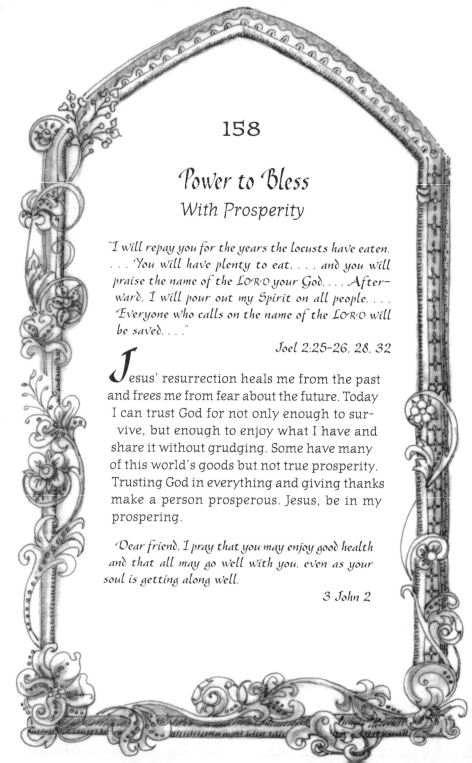

158

Power to Bless
With Prosperity

"I will repay you for the years the locusts have eaten.
. . . You will have plenty to eat. . . . and you will
praise the name of the LORD your God. . . . Afterward. I will pour out my Spirit on all people. . . .
Everyone who calls on the name of the LORD will
be saved. . . ."

Joel 2:25-26. 28. 32

Jesus' resurrection heals me from the past
and frees me from fear about the future. Today
I can trust God for not only enough to survive, but enough to enjoy what I have and
share it without grudging. Some have many
of this world's goods but not true prosperity.
Trusting God in everything and giving thanks
make a person prosperous. Jesus, be in my
prospering.

Dear friend. I pray that you may enjoy good health
and that all may go well with you. even as your
soul is getting along well.

3 John 2

Power to Bless
With Victory

Thanks be to God! He gives us the victory through our Lord Jesus Christ. Therefore, my dear brothers, stand firm. Let nothing move you. Always give yourselves fully to the work of the Lord, because you know that your labor in the Lord is not in vain.

1 Corinthians 15:57-58

Father Bob Kerner, in a talk on anger toward God, gave examples of many in the Bible who struggled with God: Jacob, Job, Jeremiah, Jonah, David, even Jesus. God can handle my anger toward circumstances and toward injustice in the world. He helps me work through anger and fear into His penetrating light, which ultimately overcomes everything, in me and in the world, not from Him. Jesus, be in my victory.

His commands are not burdensome, for everyone born of God overcomes the world. This is the victory that has overcome the world, even our faith.

1 John 5:3-4

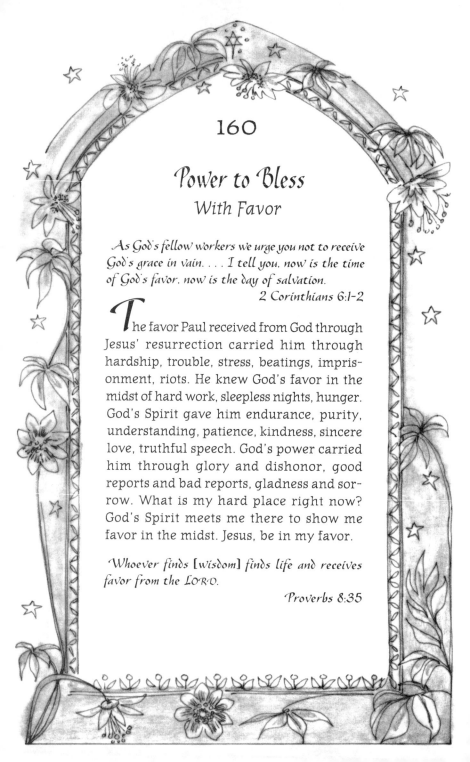

160

Power to Bless
With Favor

As God's fellow workers we urge you not to receive God's grace in vain. . . . I tell you, now is the time of God's favor, now is the day of salvation.

2 Corinthians 6:1-2

The favor Paul received from God through Jesus' resurrection carried him through hardship, trouble, stress, beatings, imprisonment, riots. He knew God's favor in the midst of hard work, sleepless nights, hunger. God's Spirit gave him endurance, purity, understanding, patience, kindness, sincere love, truthful speech. God's power carried him through glory and dishonor, good reports and bad reports, gladness and sorrow. What is my hard place right now? God's Spirit meets me there to show me favor in the midst. Jesus, be in my favor.

Whoever finds [wisdom] finds life and receives favor from the LORD.

Proverbs 8:35

Equipped for Spiritual Warfare
Truth

Put on the full armor of God so that you can take your stand against the devil's schemes. . . . Stand firm then, with the belt of truth buckled around your waist. . . .

Ephesians 6:11, 14

*B*ecause of the resurrection of Jesus, His Spirit is available and surrounds me like the armor of a soldier. Jesus, who is Truth personified, enters me and covers me with truth—with all that is honest, sincere, true. Part of my protection from evil is founding my life on and circling my being with what is true. Jesus, I would be true. Be in my surroundings.

When he, the Spirit of truth, comes, he will guide you into all truth. . . . He will . . . speak only what he hears, and he will tell you what is yet to come.

John 16:13

Equipped for Spiritual Warfare
Righteousness

"When [the Counselor] comes, he will convict the
world of guilt in regard to sin and righteousness
and judgment: . . . in regard to righteousness, because
I am going to the Father, where you can see me no
longer."

John 16:8, 10

Jesus' resurrection means I have access to
God's righteousness, God's heart. I learn from
Paul's picture of the breastplate of righteousness, that what is right and just covers my
heart and connects me to God's heart. My
heart, the seat of my emotions, feelings and
desires, comes under His control. My longings
are transformed into desires for what is truly
just and right. Jesus, be in my righteousness.

"I will put my Spirit on him and he will bring justice to
the nations. . . . A bruised reed he will not break. . . .
In faithfulness he will bring forth justice."

Isaiah 42:1, 3

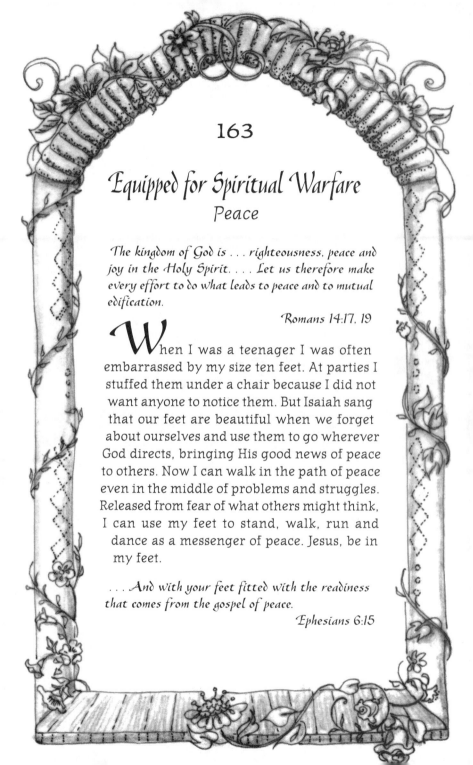

Equipped for Spiritual Warfare
Peace

The kingdom of God is . . . righteousness, peace and joy in the Holy Spirit. . . . Let us therefore make every effort to do what leads to peace and to mutual edification.

Romans 14:17, 19

When I was a teenager I was often embarrassed by my size ten feet. At parties I stuffed them under a chair because I did not want anyone to notice them. But Isaiah sang that our feet are beautiful when we forget about ourselves and use them to go wherever God directs, bringing His good news of peace to others. Now I can walk in the path of peace even in the middle of problems and struggles. Released from fear of what others might think, I can use my feet to stand, walk, run and dance as a messenger of peace. Jesus, be in my feet.

. . . And with your feet fitted with the readiness that comes from the gospel of peace.

Ephesians 6:15

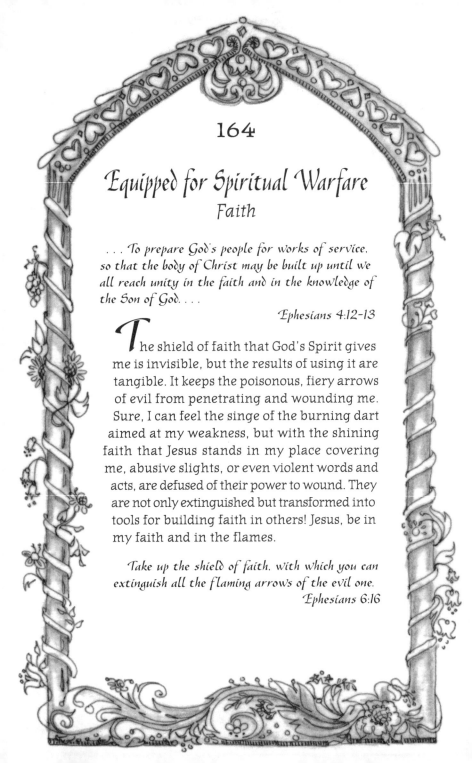

Equipped for Spiritual Warfare
Faith

*. . . To prepare God's people for works of service,
so that the body of Christ may be built up until we
all reach unity in the faith and in the knowledge of
the Son of God. . . .*

Ephesians 4:12-13

The shield of faith that God's Spirit gives
me is invisible, but the results of using it are
tangible. It keeps the poisonous, fiery arrows
of evil from penetrating and wounding me.
Sure, I can feel the singe of the burning dart
aimed at my weakness, but with the shining
faith that Jesus stands in my place covering
me, abusive slights, or even violent words and
acts, are defused of their power to wound. They
are not only extinguished but transformed into
tools for building faith in others! Jesus, be in
my faith and in the flames.

*Take up the shield of faith, with which you can
extinguish all the flaming arrows of the evil one.*
Ephesians 6:16

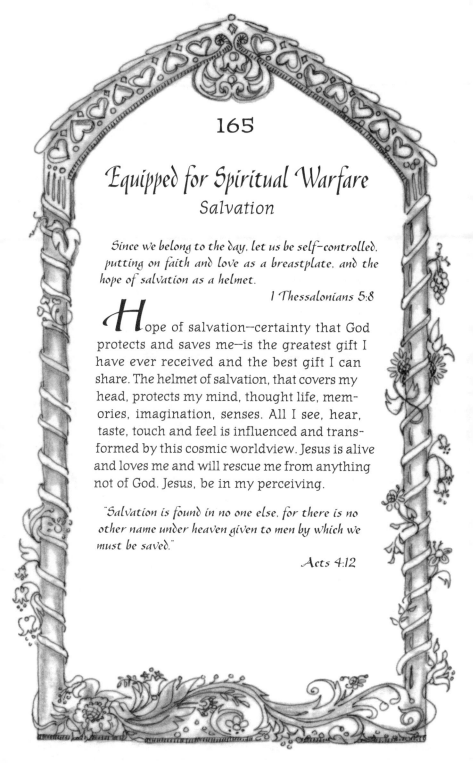

165

Equipped for Spiritual Warfare
Salvation

Since we belong to the day, let us be self-controlled, putting on faith and love as a breastplate, and the hope of salvation as a helmet.

1 Thessalonians 5:8

Hope of salvation—certainty that God protects and saves me—is the greatest gift I have ever received and the best gift I can share. The helmet of salvation, that covers my head, protects my mind, thought life, memories, imagination, senses. All I see, hear, taste, touch and feel is influenced and transformed by this cosmic worldview. Jesus is alive and loves me and will rescue me from anything not of God. Jesus, be in my perceiving.

"Salvation is found in no one else, for there is no other name under heaven given to men by which we must be saved."

Acts 4:12

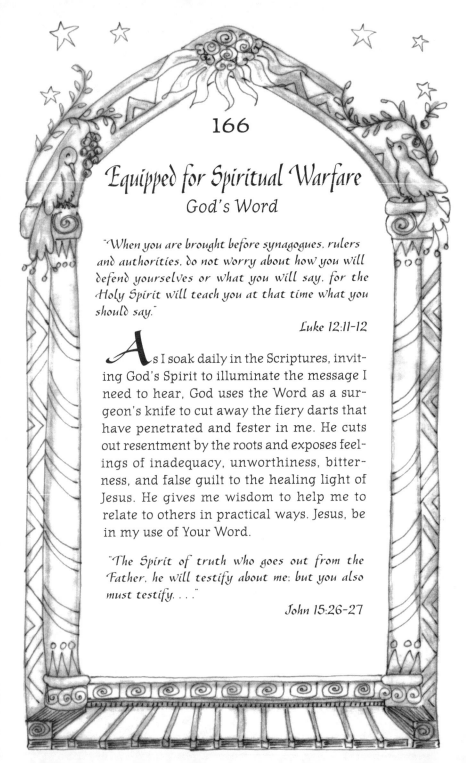

Equipped for Spiritual Warfare
God's Word

"When you are brought before synagogues, rulers and authorities, do not worry about how you will defend yourselves or what you will say, for the Holy Spirit will teach you at that time what you should say."

Luke 12:11-12

As I soak daily in the Scriptures, inviting God's Spirit to illuminate the message I need to hear, God uses the Word as a surgeon's knife to cut away the fiery darts that have penetrated and fester in me. He cuts out resentment by the roots and exposes feelings of inadequacy, unworthiness, bitterness, and false guilt to the healing light of Jesus. He gives me wisdom to help me to relate to others in practical ways. Jesus, be in my use of Your Word.

"The Spirit of truth who goes out from the Father, he will testify about me; but you also must testify. . . ."

John 15:26-27

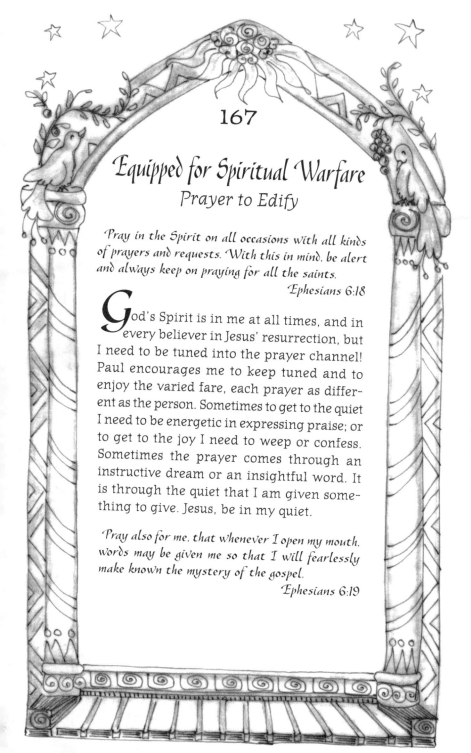

167

Equipped for Spiritual Warfare
Prayer to Edify

Pray in the Spirit on all occasions with all kinds of prayers and requests. With this in mind, be alert and always keep on praying for all the saints.

Ephesians 6:18

God's Spirit is in me at all times, and in every believer in Jesus' resurrection, but I need to be tuned into the prayer channel! Paul encourages me to keep tuned and to enjoy the varied fare, each prayer as different as the person. Sometimes to get to the quiet I need to be energetic in expressing praise; or to get to the joy I need to weep or confess. Sometimes the prayer comes through an instructive dream or an insightful word. It is through the quiet that I am given something to give. Jesus, be in my quiet.

Pray also for me, that whenever I open my mouth, words may be given me so that I will fearlessly make known the mystery of the gospel.

Ephesians 6:19

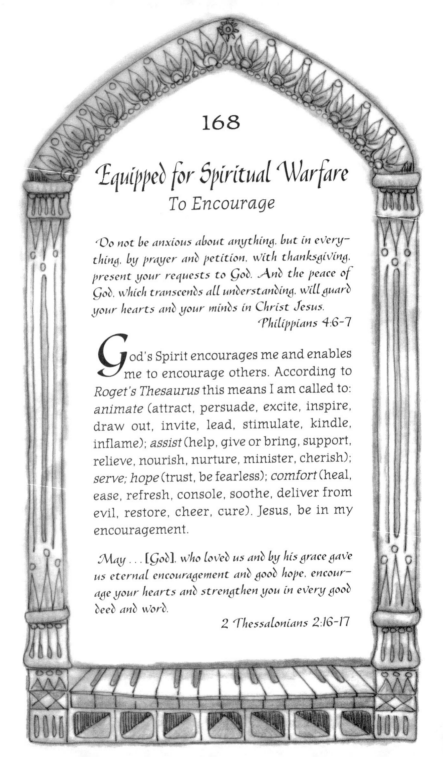

Equipped for Spiritual Warfare
To Encourage

Do not be anxious about anything, but in every-thing, by prayer and petition, with thanksgiving, present your requests to God. And the peace of God, which transcends all understanding, will guard your hearts and your minds in Christ Jesus.
Philippians 4:6-7

God's Spirit encourages me and enables me to encourage others. According to *Roget's Thesaurus* this means I am called to: *animate* (attract, persuade, excite, inspire, draw out, invite, lead, stimulate, kindle, inflame); *assist* (help, give or bring, support, relieve, nourish, nurture, minister, cherish); *serve; hope* (trust, be fearless); *comfort* (heal, ease, refresh, console, soothe, deliver from evil, restore, cheer, cure). Jesus, be in my encouragement.

May . . . [God], who loved us and by his grace gave us eternal encouragement and good hope, encour-age your hearts and strengthen you in every good deed and word.
2 Thessalonians 2:16-17

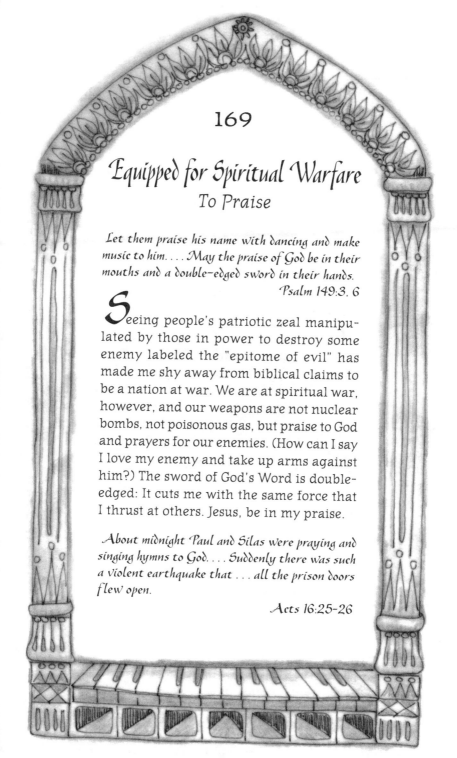

Equipped for Spiritual Warfare
To Praise

Let them praise his name with dancing and make music to him. . . . May the praise of God be in their mouths and a double-edged sword in their hands.

Psalm 149:3, 6

Seeing people's patriotic zeal manipulated by those in power to destroy some enemy labeled the "epitome of evil" has made me shy away from biblical claims to be a nation at war. We are at spiritual war, however, and our weapons are not nuclear bombs, not poisonous gas, but praise to God and prayers for our enemies. (How can I say I love my enemy and take up arms against him?) The sword of God's Word is double-edged: It cuts me with the same force that I thrust at others. Jesus, be in my praise.

About midnight Paul and Silas were praying and singing hymns to God. . . . Suddenly there was such a violent earthquake that . . . all the prison doors flew open.

Acts 16:25-26

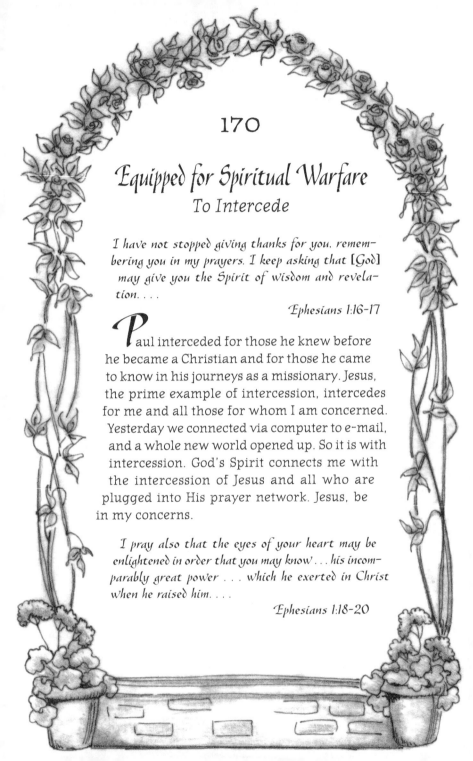

170

Equipped for Spiritual Warfare
To Intercede

I have not stopped giving thanks for you, remembering you in my prayers. I keep asking that [God] may give you the Spirit of wisdom and revelation. . . .

Ephesians 1:16-17

*P*aul interceded for those he knew before he became a Christian and for those he came to know in his journeys as a missionary. Jesus, the prime example of intercession, intercedes for me and all those for whom I am concerned. Yesterday we connected via computer to e-mail, and a whole new world opened up. So it is with intercession. God's Spirit connects me with the intercession of Jesus and all who are plugged into His prayer network. Jesus, be in my concerns.

I pray also that the eyes of your heart may be enlightened in order that you may know . . . his incomparably great power . . . which he exerted in Christ when he raised him. . . .

Ephesians 1:18-20

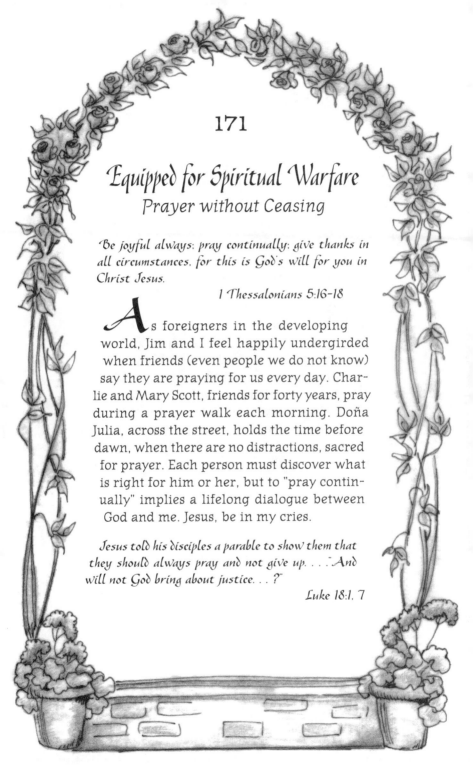

Equipped for Spiritual Warfare
Prayer without Ceasing

Be joyful always: pray continually: give thanks in all circumstances, for this is God's will for you in Christ Jesus.

1 Thessalonians 5:16-18

As foreigners in the developing world, Jim and I feel happily undergirded when friends (even people we do not know) say they are praying for us every day. Charlie and Mary Scott, friends for forty years, pray during a prayer walk each morning. Doña Julia, across the street, holds the time before dawn, when there are no distractions, sacred for prayer. Each person must discover what is right for him or her, but to "pray continually" implies a lifelong dialogue between God and me. Jesus, be in my cries.

Jesus told his disciples a parable to show them that they should always pray and not give up. . . . "And will not God bring about justice. . . ?"

Luke 18:1, 7

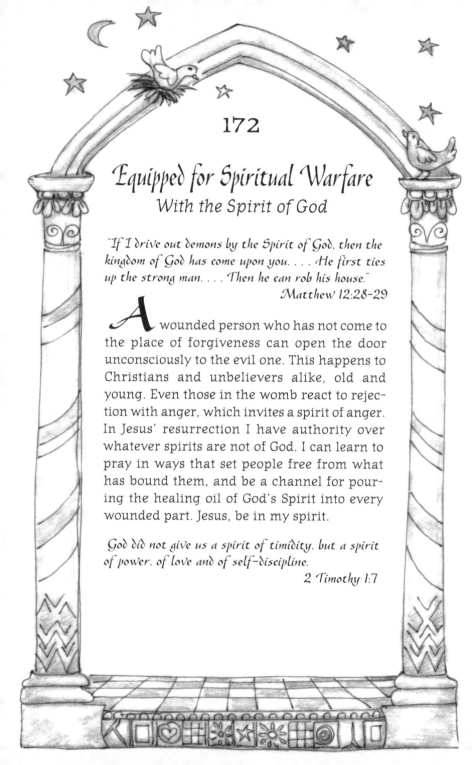

Equipped for Spiritual Warfare
With the Spirit of God

"If I drive out demons by the Spirit of God, then the kingdom of God has come upon you. . . . He first ties up the strong man. . . . Then he can rob his house."
                                    Matthew 12:28-29

A wounded person who has not come to the place of forgiveness can open the door unconsciously to the evil one. This happens to Christians and unbelievers alike, old and young. Even those in the womb react to rejection with anger, which invites a spirit of anger. In Jesus' resurrection I have authority over whatever spirits are not of God. I can learn to pray in ways that set people free from what has bound them, and be a channel for pouring the healing oil of God's Spirit into every wounded part. Jesus, be in my spirit.

God did not give us a spirit of timidity, but a spirit of power, of love and of self-discipline.
                                    2 Timothy 1:7

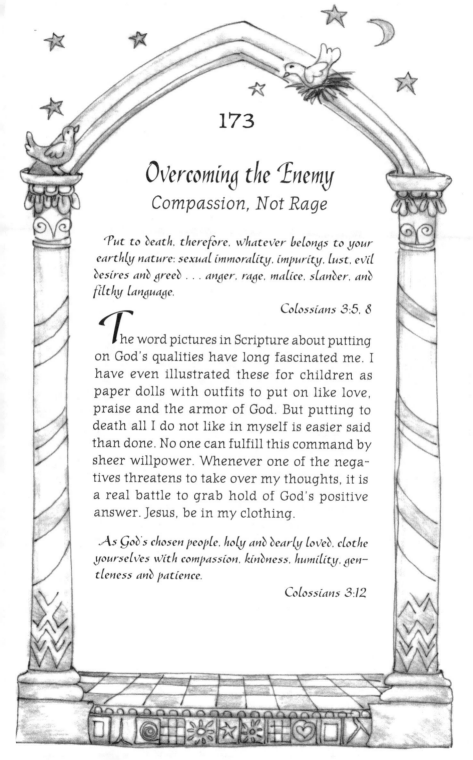

Overcoming the Enemy
Compassion, Not Rage

Put to death, therefore, whatever belongs to your earthly nature: sexual immorality, impurity, lust, evil desires and greed . . . anger, rage, malice, slander, and filthy language.

Colossians 3:5, 8

The word pictures in Scripture about putting on God's qualities have long fascinated me. I have even illustrated these for children as paper dolls with outfits to put on like love, praise and the armor of God. But putting to death all I do not like in myself is easier said than done. No one can fulfill this command by sheer willpower. Whenever one of the negatives threatens to take over my thoughts, it is a real battle to grab hold of God's positive answer. Jesus, be in my clothing.

As God's chosen people, holy and dearly loved, clothe yourselves with compassion, kindness, humility, gentleness and patience.

Colossians 3:12

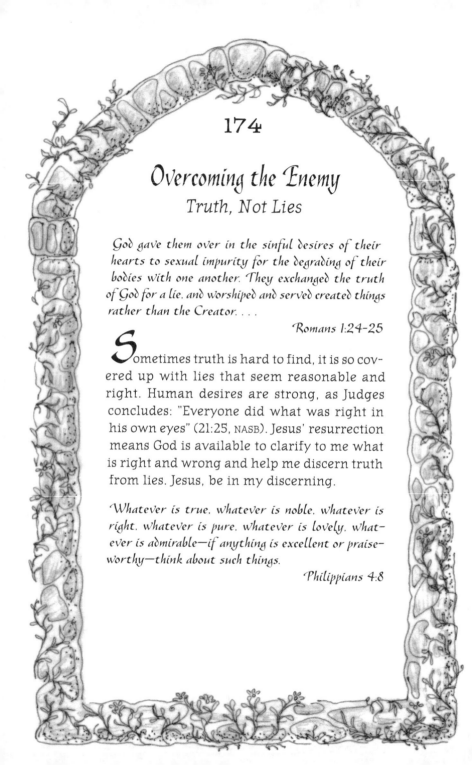

Overcoming the Enemy
Truth, Not Lies

God gave them over in the sinful desires of their hearts to sexual impurity for the degrading of their bodies with one another. They exchanged the truth of God for a lie, and worshiped and served created things rather than the Creator. . . .

Romans 1:24-25

*S*ometimes truth is hard to find, it is so covered up with lies that seem reasonable and right. Human desires are strong, as Judges concludes: "Everyone did what was right in his own eyes" (21:25, NASB). Jesus' resurrection means God is available to clarify to me what is right and wrong and help me discern truth from lies. Jesus, be in my discerning.

Whatever is true, whatever is noble, whatever is right, whatever is pure, whatever is lovely, whatever is admirable—if anything is excellent or praiseworthy—think about such things.

Philippians 4:8

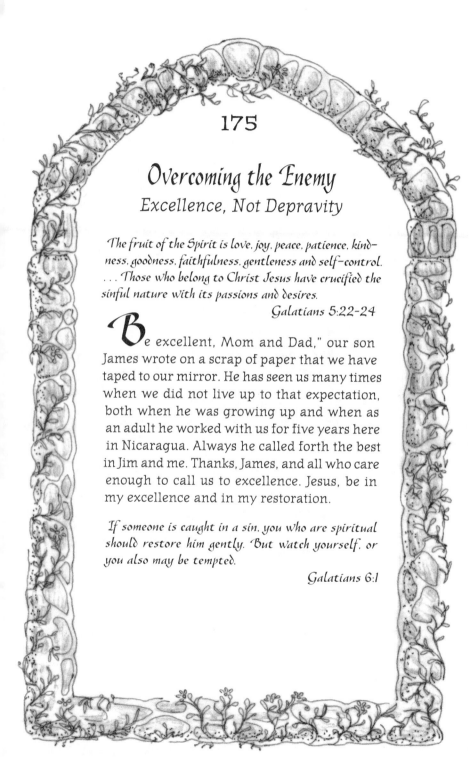

Overcoming the Enemy
Excellence, Not Depravity

The fruit of the Spirit is love, joy, peace, patience, kindness, goodness, faithfulness, gentleness and self-control. . . . Those who belong to Christ Jesus have crucified the sinful nature with its passions and desires.

Galatians 5:22-24

Be excellent, Mom and Dad," our son James wrote on a scrap of paper that we have taped to our mirror. He has seen us many times when we did not live up to that expectation, both when he was growing up and when as an adult he worked with us for five years here in Nicaragua. Always he called forth the best in Jim and me. Thanks, James, and all who care enough to call us to excellence. Jesus, be in my excellence and in my restoration.

If someone is caught in a sin, you who are spiritual should restore him gently. But watch yourself, or you also may be tempted.

Galatians 6:1

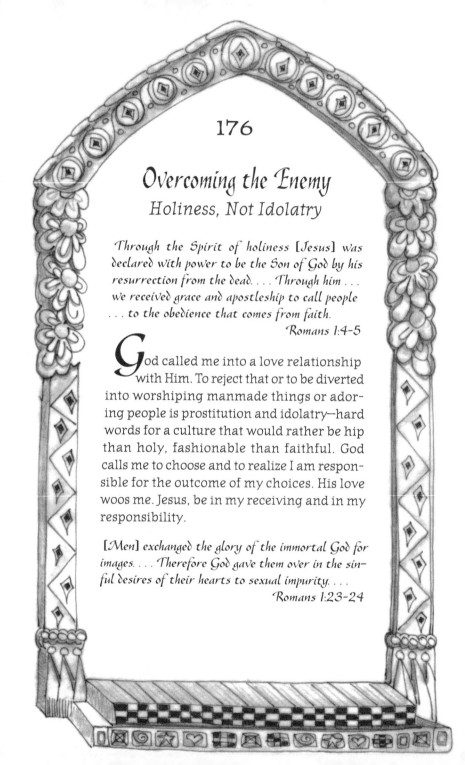

176

Overcoming the Enemy
Holiness, Not Idolatry

Through the Spirit of holiness [Jesus] was declared with power to be the Son of God by his resurrection from the dead. . . . Through him . . . we received grace and apostleship to call people . . . to the obedience that comes from faith.

Romans 1:4-5

God called me into a love relationship with Him. To reject that or to be diverted into worshiping manmade things or adoring people is prostitution and idolatry—hard words for a culture that would rather be hip than holy, fashionable than faithful. God calls me to choose and to realize I am responsible for the outcome of my choices. His love woos me. Jesus, be in my receiving and in my responsibility.

[Men] exchanged the glory of the immortal God for images. . . . Therefore God gave them over in the sinful desires of their hearts to sexual impurity. . . .

Romans 1:23-24

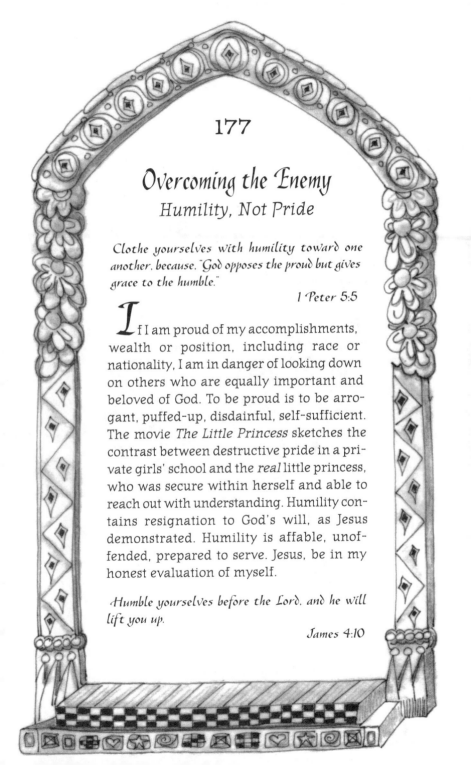

Overcoming the Enemy
Humility, Not Pride

Clothe yourselves with humility toward one another, because, "God opposes the proud but gives grace to the humble."

1 Peter 5:5

*I*f I am proud of my accomplishments, wealth or position, including race or nationality, I am in danger of looking down on others who are equally important and beloved of God. To be proud is to be arrogant, puffed-up, disdainful, self-sufficient. The movie *The Little Princess* sketches the contrast between destructive pride in a private girls' school and the *real* little princess, who was secure within herself and able to reach out with understanding. Humility contains resignation to God's will, as Jesus demonstrated. Humility is affable, unoffended, prepared to serve. Jesus, be in my honest evaluation of myself.

Humble yourselves before the Lord, and he will lift you up.

James 4:10

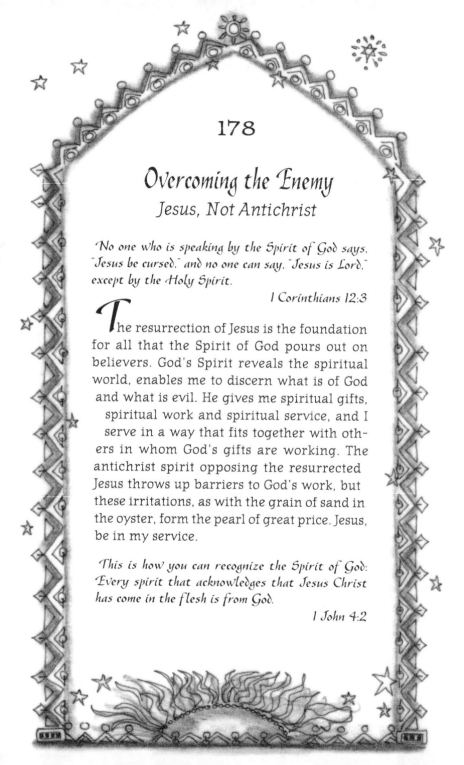

178

Overcoming the Enemy
Jesus, Not Antichrist

No one who is speaking by the Spirit of God says,
"Jesus be cursed," and no one can say, "Jesus is Lord,"
except by the Holy Spirit.

1 Corinthians 12:3

The resurrection of Jesus is the foundation for all that the Spirit of God pours out on believers. God's Spirit reveals the spiritual world, enables me to discern what is of God and what is evil. He gives me spiritual gifts, spiritual work and spiritual service, and I serve in a way that fits together with others in whom God's gifts are working. The antichrist spirit opposing the resurrected Jesus throws up barriers to God's work, but these irritations, as with the grain of sand in the oyster, form the pearl of great price. Jesus, be in my service.

This is how you can recognize the Spirit of God:
Every spirit that acknowledges that Jesus Christ
has come in the flesh is from God.

1 John 4:2

Overcoming the Enemy
Wisdom, Not Divination

"I will set my face against the person who turns to mediums and spiritists to prostitute himself by following them, and I will cut him off from his people."

Leviticus 20:6

For many years while I was a faithful church-goer but did not yet believe in the resurrection of Jesus, I also did not believe in Satan. That was fine with Satan, because I was, by default, in his camp. When the resurrection became real to me and I knew beyond question that Jesus is alive and began discovering the Holy Spirit's gifts for me, Satan shocked me by revealing himself. But everything I needed to know to take authority over every attack of evil was already explained clearly in God's Word. Jesus, be in my knowledge.

There are different kinds of gifts, but the same Spirit. . . . To one there is given through the Spirit the message of wisdom, to another the message of knowledge. . . .

1 Corinthians 12:4, 8

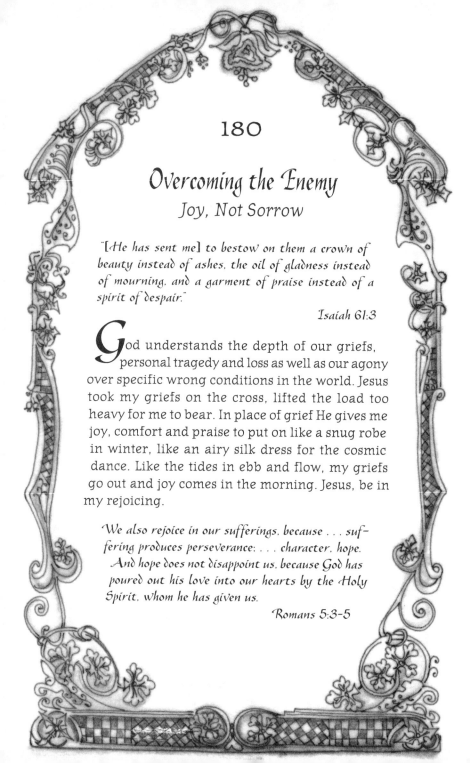

Overcoming the Enemy
Joy, Not Sorrow

"[He has sent me] to bestow on them a crown of beauty instead of ashes, the oil of gladness instead of mourning, and a garment of praise instead of a spirit of despair."

Isaiah 61:3

God understands the depth of our griefs, personal tragedy and loss as well as our agony over specific wrong conditions in the world. Jesus took my griefs on the cross, lifted the load too heavy for me to bear. In place of grief He gives me joy, comfort and praise to put on like a snug robe in winter, like an airy silk dress for the cosmic dance. Like the tides in ebb and flow, my griefs go out and joy comes in the morning. Jesus, be in my rejoicing.

We also rejoice in our sufferings, because . . . suffering produces perseverance: . . . character, hope. And hope does not disappoint us, because God has poured out his love into our hearts by the Holy Spirit, whom he has given us.

Romans 5:3-5

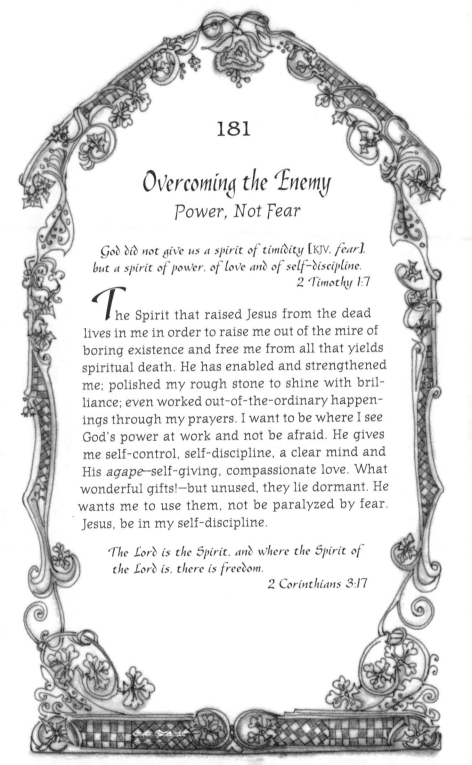

Overcoming the Enemy
Power, Not Fear

God did not give us a spirit of timidity [KJV, fear],
but a spirit of power, of love and of self-discipline.
2 Timothy 1:7

The Spirit that raised Jesus from the dead lives in me in order to raise me out of the mire of boring existence and free me from all that yields spiritual death. He has enabled and strengthened me; polished my rough stone to shine with brilliance; even worked out-of-the-ordinary happenings through my prayers. I want to be where I see God's power at work and not be afraid. He gives me self-control, self-discipline, a clear mind and His *agape*—self-giving, compassionate love. What wonderful gifts!—but unused, they lie dormant. He wants me to use them, not be paralyzed by fear. Jesus, be in my self-discipline.

The Lord is the Spirit, and where the Spirit of
the Lord is, there is freedom.
2 Corinthians 3:17

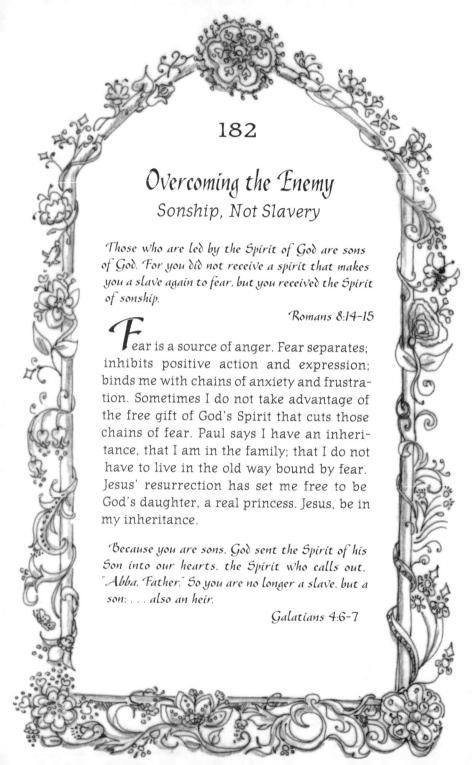

182

Overcoming the Enemy
Sonship, Not Slavery

Those who are led by the Spirit of God are sons of God. For you did not receive a spirit that makes you a slave again to fear, but you received the Spirit of sonship.

Romans 8:14-15

Fear is a source of anger. Fear separates; inhibits positive action and expression; binds me with chains of anxiety and frustration. Sometimes I do not take advantage of the free gift of God's Spirit that cuts those chains of fear. Paul says I have an inheritance, that I am in the family; that I do not have to live in the old way bound by fear. Jesus' resurrection has set me free to be God's daughter, a real princess. Jesus, be in my inheritance.

Because you are sons, God sent the Spirit of his Son into our hearts, the Spirit who calls out, "Abba, Father." So you are no longer a slave, but a son; . . . also an heir.

Galatians 4:6-7

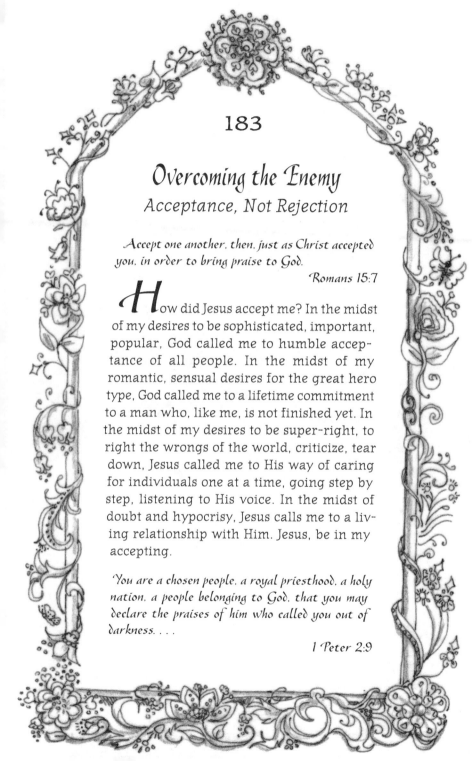

Overcoming the Enemy
Acceptance, Not Rejection

Accept one another, then, just as Christ accepted you, in order to bring praise to God.

Romans 15:7

How did Jesus accept me? In the midst of my desires to be sophisticated, important, popular, God called me to humble acceptance of all people. In the midst of my romantic, sensual desires for the great hero type, God called me to a lifetime commitment to a man who, like me, is not finished yet. In the midst of my desires to be super-right, to right the wrongs of the world, criticize, tear down, Jesus called me to His way of caring for individuals one at a time, going step by step, listening to His voice. In the midst of doubt and hypocrisy, Jesus calls me to a living relationship with Him. Jesus, be in my accepting.

You are a chosen people, a royal priesthood, a holy nation, a people belonging to God, that you may declare the praises of him who called you out of darkness. . . .

1 Peter 2:9

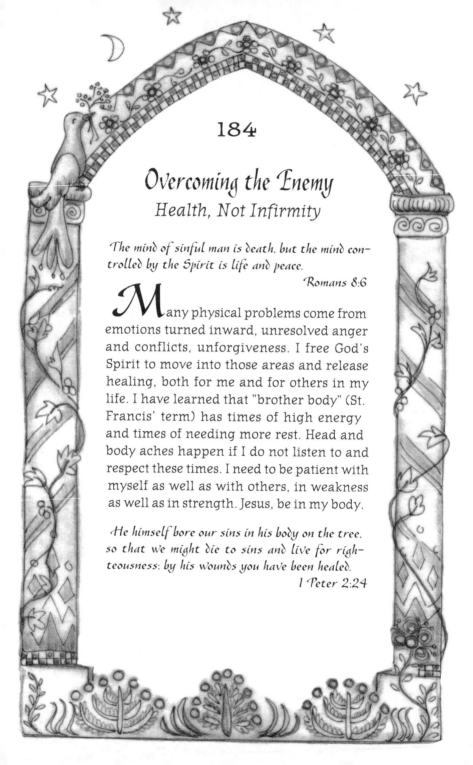

184

Overcoming the Enemy
Health, Not Infirmity

The mind of sinful man is death, but the mind controlled by the Spirit is life and peace.

Romans 8:6

Many physical problems come from emotions turned inward, unresolved anger and conflicts, unforgiveness. I free God's Spirit to move into those areas and release healing, both for me and for others in my life. I have learned that "brother body" (St. Francis' term) has times of high energy and times of needing more rest. Head and body aches happen if I do not listen to and respect these times. I need to be patient with myself as well as with others, in weakness as well as in strength. Jesus, be in my body.

He himself bore our sins in his body on the tree, so that we might die to sins and live for righteousness; by his wounds you have been healed.

1 Peter 2:24

Part Three

Jesus Reigns

in Every Corner of My Life

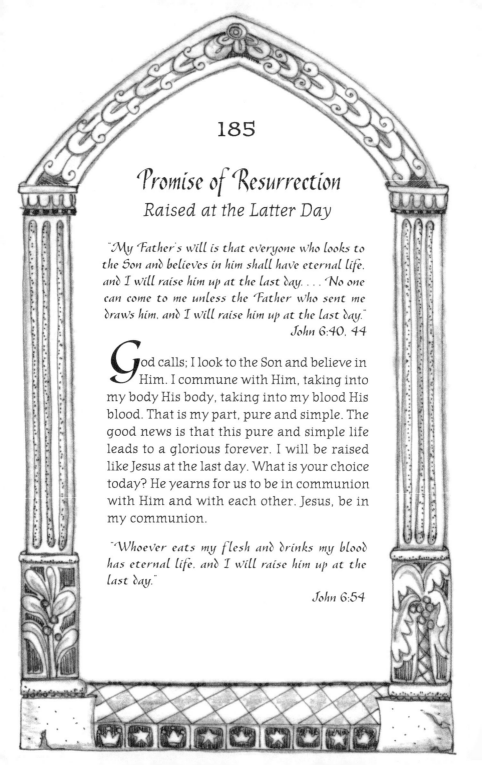

185

Promise of Resurrection
Raised at the Latter Day

"My Father's will is that everyone who looks to the Son and believes in him shall have eternal life. and I will raise him up at the last day. . . . No one can come to me unless the Father who sent me draws him, and I will raise him up at the last day."
John 6:40, 44

God calls; I look to the Son and believe in Him. I commune with Him, taking into my body His body, taking into my blood His blood. That is my part, pure and simple. The good news is that this pure and simple life leads to a glorious forever. I will be raised like Jesus at the last day. What is your choice today? He yearns for us to be in communion with Him and with each other. Jesus, be in my communion.

"Whoever eats my flesh and drinks my blood has eternal life. and I will raise him up at the last day."
John 6:54

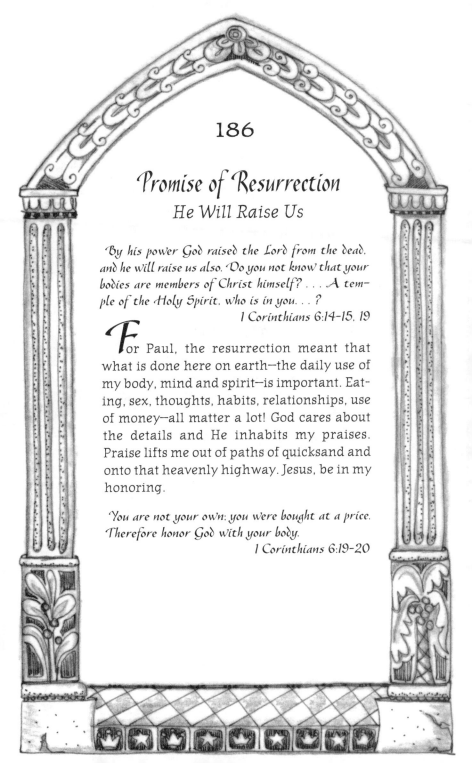

186

Promise of Resurrection
He Will Raise Us

By his power God raised the Lord from the dead, and he will raise us also. Do you not know that your bodies are members of Christ himself? . . . A temple of the Holy Spirit, who is in you. . . ?

1 Corinthians 6:14-15, 19

For Paul, the resurrection meant that what is done here on earth—the daily use of my body, mind and spirit—is important. Eating, sex, thoughts, habits, relationships, use of money—all matter a lot! God cares about the details and He inhabits my praises. Praise lifts me out of paths of quicksand and onto that heavenly highway. Jesus, be in my honoring.

You are not your own; you were bought at a price. Therefore honor God with your body.

1 Corinthians 6:19-20

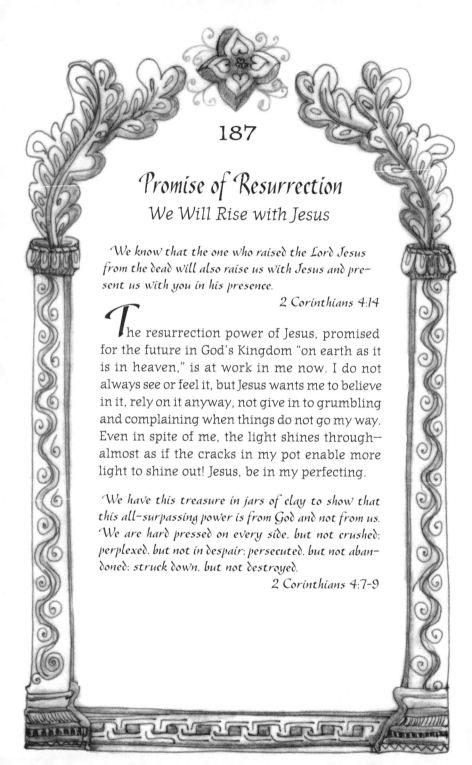

Promise of Resurrection
We Will Rise with Jesus

We know that the one who raised the Lord Jesus from the dead will also raise us with Jesus and present us with you in his presence.

2 Corinthians 4:14

The resurrection power of Jesus, promised for the future in God's Kingdom "on earth as it is in heaven," is at work in me now. I do not always see or feel it, but Jesus wants me to believe in it, rely on it anyway, not give in to grumbling and complaining when things do not go my way. Even in spite of me, the light shines through— almost as if the cracks in my pot enable more light to shine out! Jesus, be in my perfecting.

We have this treasure in jars of clay to show that this all-surpassing power is from God and not from us. We are hard pressed on every side, but not crushed; perplexed, but not in despair; persecuted, but not abandoned; struck down, but not destroyed.

2 Corinthians 4:7-9

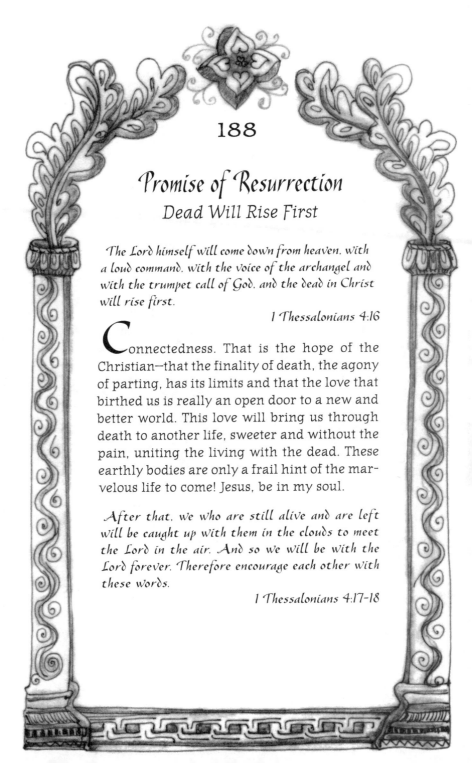

188

Promise of Resurrection
Dead Will Rise First

The Lord himself will come down from heaven, with a loud command, with the voice of the archangel and with the trumpet call of God, and the dead in Christ will rise first.

1 Thessalonians 4:16

Connectedness. That is the hope of the Christian—that the finality of death, the agony of parting, has its limits and that the love that birthed us is really an open door to a new and better world. This love will bring us through death to another life, sweeter and without the pain, uniting the living with the dead. These earthly bodies are only a frail hint of the marvelous life to come! Jesus, be in my soul.

After that, we who are still alive and are left will be caught up with them in the clouds to meet the Lord in the air. And so we will be with the Lord forever. Therefore encourage each other with these words.

1 Thessalonians 4:17-18

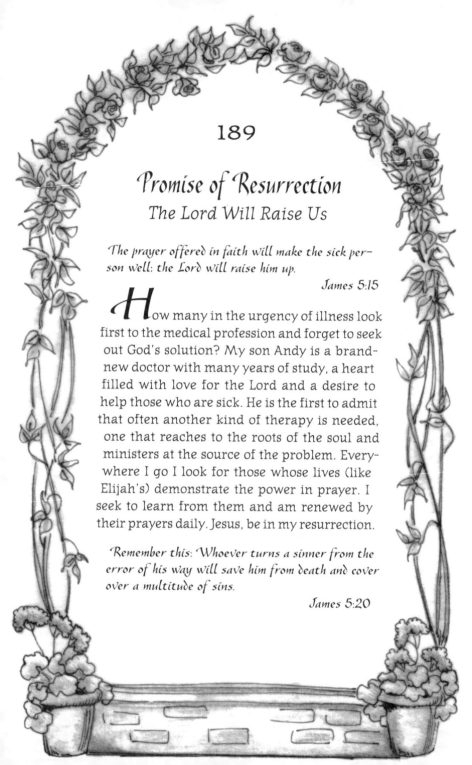

189

Promise of Resurrection
The Lord Will Raise Us

The prayer offered in faith will make the sick person well; the Lord will raise him up.

James 5:15

How many in the urgency of illness look first to the medical profession and forget to seek out God's solution? My son Andy is a brand-new doctor with many years of study, a heart filled with love for the Lord and a desire to help those who are sick. He is the first to admit that often another kind of therapy is needed, one that reaches to the roots of the soul and ministers at the source of the problem. Everywhere I go I look for those whose lives (like Elijah's) demonstrate the power in prayer. I seek to learn from them and am renewed by their prayers daily. Jesus, be in my resurrection.

Remember this: Whoever turns a sinner from the error of his way will save him from death and cover over a multitude of sins.

James 5:20

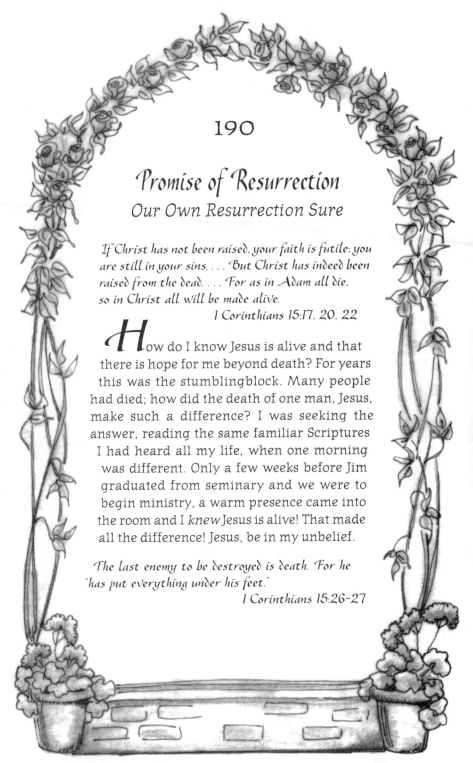

190

Promise of Resurrection
Our Own Resurrection Sure

If Christ has not been raised, your faith is futile: you are still in your sins. . . . But Christ has indeed been raised from the dead. . . . For as in Adam all die, so in Christ all will be made alive.
1 Corinthians 15:17, 20, 22

How do I know Jesus is alive and that there is hope for me beyond death? For years this was the stumblingblock. Many people had died; how did the death of one man, Jesus, make such a difference? I was seeking the answer, reading the same familiar Scriptures I had heard all my life, when one morning was different. Only a few weeks before Jim graduated from seminary and we were to begin ministry, a warm presence came into the room and I *knew* Jesus is alive! That made all the difference! Jesus, be in my unbelief.

The last enemy to be destroyed is death. For he "has put everything under his feet."
1 Corinthians 15:26-27

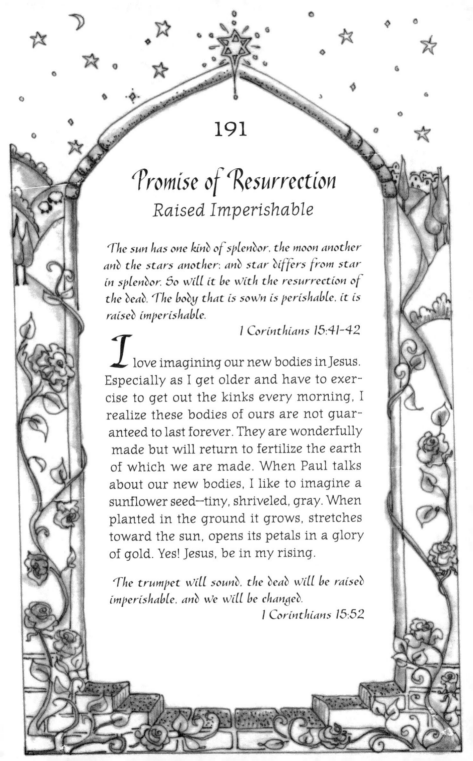

Promise of Resurrection
Raised Imperishable

The sun has one kind of splendor, the moon another and the stars another; and star differs from star in splendor. So will it be with the resurrection of the dead. The body that is sown is perishable, it is raised imperishable.

1 Corinthians 15:41-42

I love imagining our new bodies in Jesus. Especially as I get older and have to exercise to get out the kinks every morning, I realize these bodies of ours are not guaranteed to last forever. They are wonderfully made but will return to fertilize the earth of which we are made. When Paul talks about our new bodies, I like to imagine a sunflower seed—tiny, shriveled, gray. When planted in the ground it grows, stretches toward the sun, opens its petals in a glory of gold. Yes! Jesus, be in my rising.

The trumpet will sound, the dead will be raised imperishable, and we will be changed.

1 Corinthians 15:52

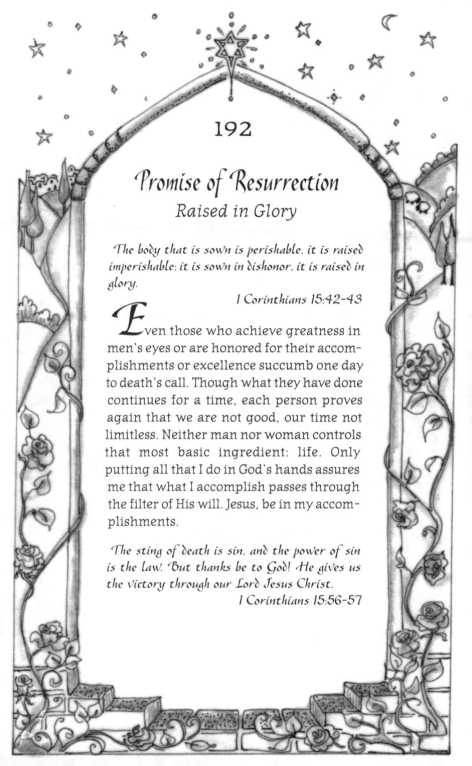

192

Promise of Resurrection
Raised in Glory

The body that is sown is perishable, it is raised imperishable; it is sown in dishonor, it is raised in glory.

1 Corinthians 15:42-43

*E*ven those who achieve greatness in men's eyes or are honored for their accomplishments or excellence succumb one day to death's call. Though what they have done continues for a time, each person proves again that we are not good, our time not limitless. Neither man nor woman controls that most basic ingredient: life. Only putting all that I do in God's hands assures me that what I accomplish passes through the filter of His will. Jesus, be in my accomplishments.

The sting of death is sin, and the power of sin is the law. But thanks be to God! He gives us the victory through our Lord Jesus Christ.

1 Corinthians 15:56-57

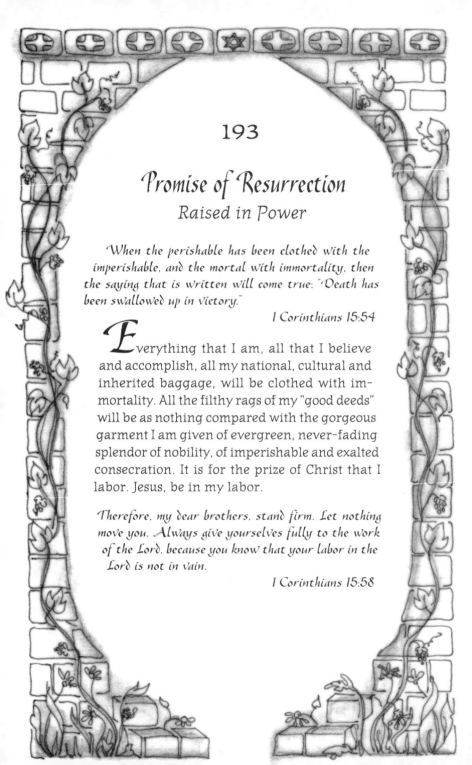

193

Promise of Resurrection
Raised in Power

*When the perishable has been clothed with the
imperishable, and the mortal with immortality, then
the saying that is written will come true: "Death has
been swallowed up in victory."*

1 Corinthians 15:54

*E*verything that I am, all that I believe
and accomplish, all my national, cultural and
inherited baggage, will be clothed with immortality. All the filthy rags of my "good deeds"
will be as nothing compared with the gorgeous
garment I am given of evergreen, never-fading
splendor of nobility, of imperishable and exalted
consecration. It is for the prize of Christ that I
labor. Jesus, be in my labor.

*Therefore, my dear brothers, stand firm. Let nothing
move you. Always give yourselves fully to the work
of the Lord, because you know that your labor in the
Lord is not in vain.*

1 Corinthians 15:58

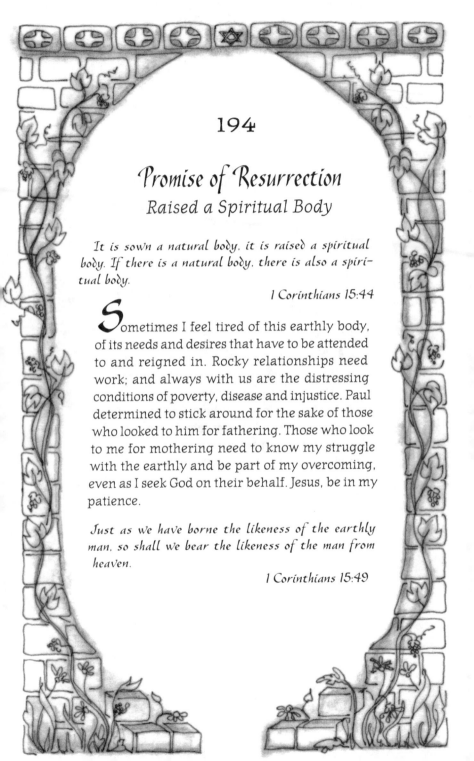

194

Promise of Resurrection
Raised a Spiritual Body

It is sown a natural body, it is raised a spiritual body. If there is a natural body, there is also a spiritual body.

1 Corinthians 15:44

Sometimes I feel tired of this earthly body, of its needs and desires that have to be attended to and reigned in. Rocky relationships need work; and always with us are the distressing conditions of poverty, disease and injustice. Paul determined to stick around for the sake of those who looked to him for fathering. Those who look to me for mothering need to know my struggle with the earthly and be part of my overcoming, even as I seek God on their behalf. Jesus, be in my patience.

Just as we have borne the likeness of the earthly man, so shall we bear the likeness of the man from heaven.

1 Corinthians 15:49

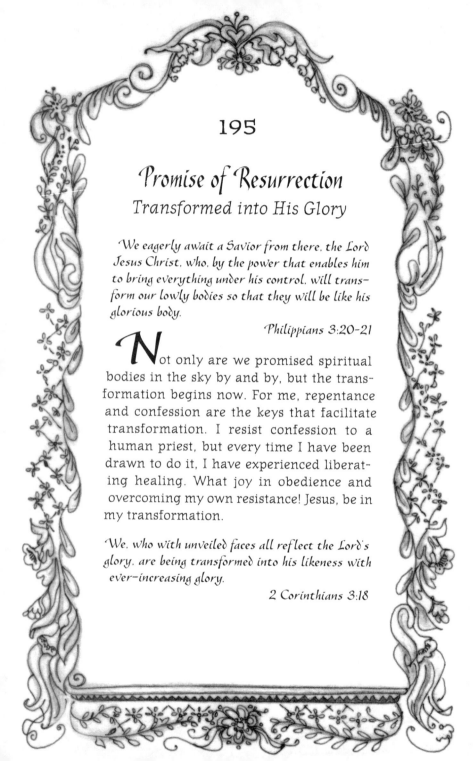

195

Promise of Resurrection
Transformed into His Glory

We eagerly await a Savior from there, the Lord Jesus Christ, who, by the power that enables him to bring everything under his control, will transform our lowly bodies so that they will be like his glorious body.

Philippians 3:20-21

Not only are we promised spiritual bodies in the sky by and by, but the transformation begins now. For me, repentance and confession are the keys that facilitate transformation. I resist confession to a human priest, but every time I have been drawn to do it, I have experienced liberating healing. What joy in obedience and overcoming my own resistance! Jesus, be in my transformation.

We, who with unveiled faces all reflect the Lord's glory, are being transformed into his likeness with ever-increasing glory.

2 Corinthians 3:18

196

Jesus, King Messiah
Savior

When you ascended on high, you led captives in your train. . . . Our God is a God who saves; from the Sovereign LORD comes escape from death.

Psalm 68:18, 20

*T*he resurrected Jesus ascended to the glorious dimensions of God's fully revealed presence. Kingly Messiah Jesus is the baby born in Bethlehem, the child who walked to Jerusalem with His parents, the itinerant preacher and healer, the crucified rebel. The difference is that anyone can meet Him now, wherever they are. His love knows no bounds of sex, age, language, race, culture. His call is urgent, demanding all of me, because without Him life is meaningless and ends in eternal death. Jesus, be in my restoration.

The LORD is my shepherd, I shall not be in want. . . . Surely goodness and love will follow me all the days of my life, and I will dwell in the house of the LORD forever.

Psalm 23:1, 6

197

Jesus, King Messiah
Covenant-Keeper

The LORD swore an oath to David. . . : "One of your own descendants I will place on your throne. . . . I will clothe [Zion's] priests with salvation. . . ."

Psalm 132:11, 16

Jesus, descendant of King David, is the only One who ever kept in every way the covenant relationship God made with Israel. Jesus fulfilled the Ten Commandments and God's intentions for all the Law, even though the Jewish leaders of His day accused Him of blasphemy and Sabbath-breaking. Mirror-image of God in human flesh, Jesus lives now in kingly glory. As His follower, His sister by adoption, I receive His pure life here on earth into my own. Father God, thank You for Jesus, for His Spirit who fills me today with strength to persevere and overcome every obstacle. Jesus, be in my endurance.

We consider blessed those who have persevered.
James 5:11

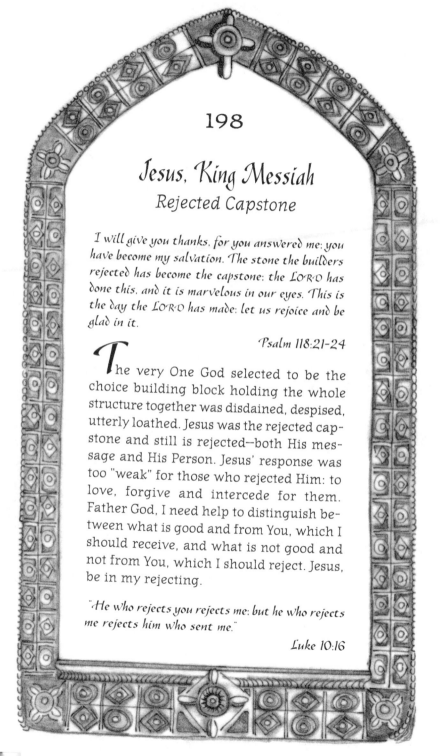

198

Jesus, King Messiah
Rejected Capstone

I will give you thanks, for you answered me: you have become my salvation. The stone the builders rejected has become the capstone: the LORD has done this, and it is marvelous in our eyes. This is the day the LORD has made: let us rejoice and be glad in it.

Psalm 118:21-24

The very One God selected to be the choice building block holding the whole structure together was disdained, despised, utterly loathed. Jesus was the rejected capstone and still is rejected—both His message and His Person. Jesus' response was too "weak" for those who rejected Him: to love, forgive and intercede for them. Father God, I need help to distinguish between what is good and from You, which I should receive, and what is not good and not from You, which I should reject. Jesus, be in my rejecting.

"He who rejects you rejects me: but he who rejects me rejects him who sent me."

Luke 10:16

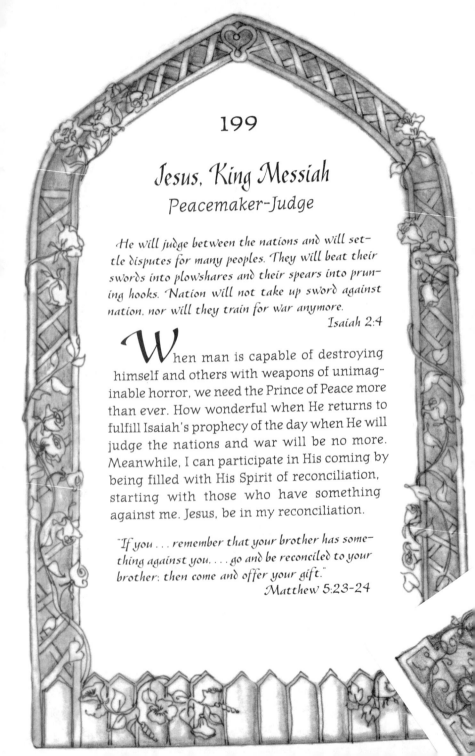

199

Jesus, King Messiah
Peacemaker-Judge

He will judge between the nations and will settle disputes for many peoples. They will beat their swords into plowshares and their spears into pruning hooks. Nation will not take up sword against nation, nor will they train for war anymore.
Isaiah 2:4

When man is capable of destroying himself and others with weapons of unimaginable horror, we need the Prince of Peace more than ever. How wonderful when He returns to fulfill Isaiah's prophecy of the day when He will judge the nations and war will be no more. Meanwhile, I can participate in His coming by being filled with His Spirit of reconciliation, starting with those who have something against me. Jesus, be in my reconciliation.

"If you . . . remember that your brother has something against you. . . . go and be reconciled to your brother; then come and offer your gift."
Matthew 5:23-24

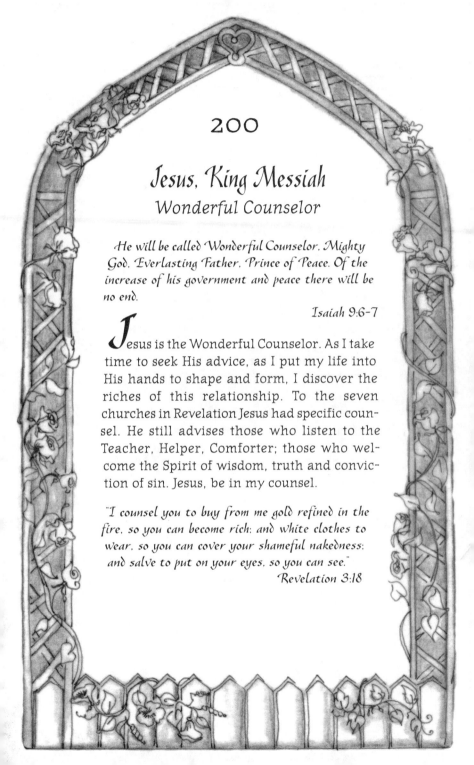

200

Jesus, King Messiah
Wonderful Counselor

He will be called Wonderful Counselor, Mighty God, Everlasting Father, Prince of Peace. Of the increase of his government and peace there will be no end.

Isaiah 9:6-7

Jesus is the Wonderful Counselor. As I take time to seek His advice, as I put my life into His hands to shape and form, I discover the riches of this relationship. To the seven churches in Revelation Jesus had specific counsel. He still advises those who listen to the Teacher, Helper, Comforter; those who welcome the Spirit of wisdom, truth and conviction of sin. Jesus, be in my counsel.

"I counsel you to buy from me gold refined in the fire, so you can become rich; and white clothes to wear, so you can cover your shameful nakedness; and salve to put on your eyes, so you can see."

Revelation 3:18

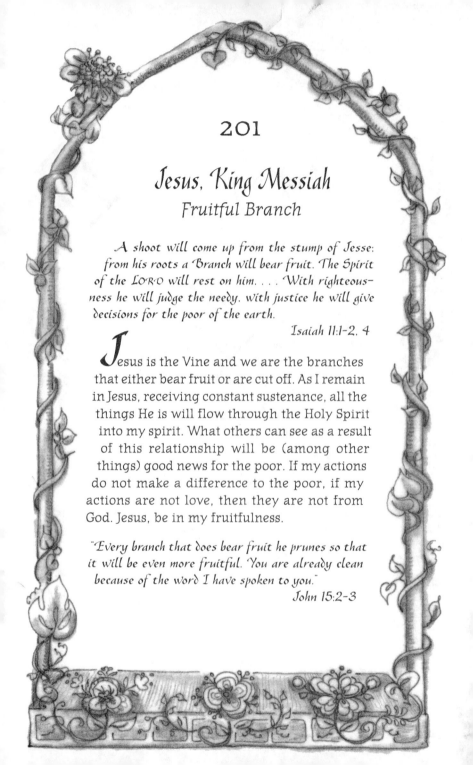

201

Jesus, King Messiah
Fruitful Branch

A shoot will come up from the stump of Jesse;
from his roots a Branch will bear fruit. The Spirit
of the LORD will rest on him. . . . With righteous-
ness he will judge the needy, with justice he will give
decisions for the poor of the earth.

Isaiah 11:1-2, 4

Jesus is the Vine and we are the branches
that either bear fruit or are cut off. As I remain
in Jesus, receiving constant sustenance, all the
things He is will flow through the Holy Spirit
into my spirit. What others can see as a result
of this relationship will be (among other
things) good news for the poor. If my actions
do not make a difference to the poor, if my
actions are not love, then they are not from
God. Jesus, be in my fruitfulness.

"Every branch that does bear fruit he prunes so that
it will be even more fruitful. You are already clean
because of the word I have spoken to you."

John 15:2-3

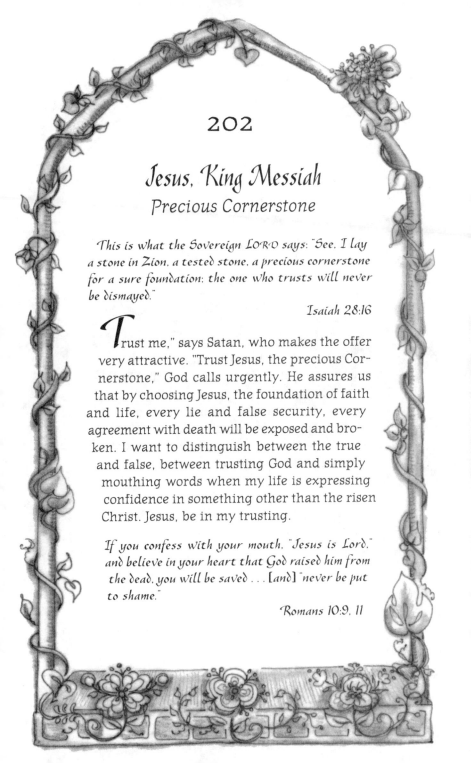

202

Jesus, King Messiah
Precious Cornerstone

This is what the Sovereign LORD says: "See, I lay a stone in Zion, a tested stone, a precious cornerstone for a sure foundation; the one who trusts will never be dismayed."

Isaiah 28:16

"Trust me," says Satan, who makes the offer very attractive. "Trust Jesus, the precious Cornerstone," God calls urgently. He assures us that by choosing Jesus, the foundation of faith and life, every lie and false security, every agreement with death will be exposed and broken. I want to distinguish between the true and false, between trusting God and simply mouthing words when my life is expressing confidence in something other than the risen Christ. Jesus, be in my trusting.

If you confess with your mouth, "Jesus is Lord," and believe in your heart that God raised him from the dead, you will be saved . . . [and] "never be put to shame."

Romans 10:9, 11

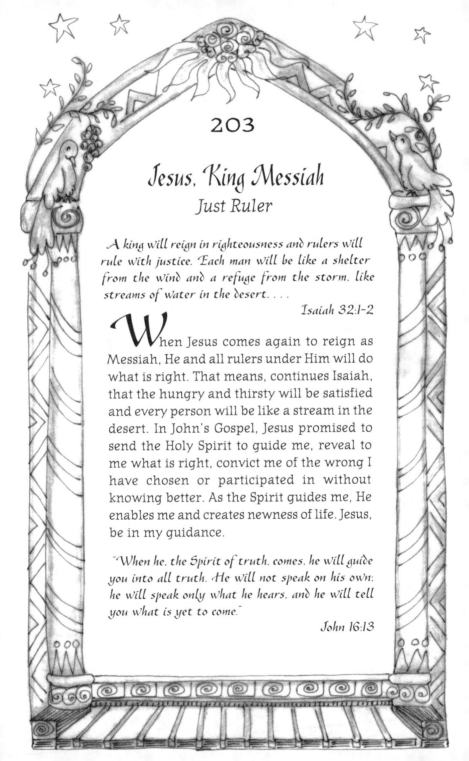

203

Jesus, King Messiah
Just Ruler

A king will reign in righteousness and rulers will rule with justice. Each man will be like a shelter from the wind and a refuge from the storm, like streams of water in the desert. . . .

Isaiah 32:1-2

When Jesus comes again to reign as Messiah, He and all rulers under Him will do what is right. That means, continues Isaiah, that the hungry and thirsty will be satisfied and every person will be like a stream in the desert. In John's Gospel, Jesus promised to send the Holy Spirit to guide me, reveal to me what is right, convict me of the wrong I have chosen or participated in without knowing better. As the Spirit guides me, He enables me and creates newness of life. Jesus, be in my guidance.

"When he, the Spirit of truth, comes, he will guide you into all truth. He will not speak on his own; he will speak only what he hears, and he will tell you what is yet to come."

John 16:13

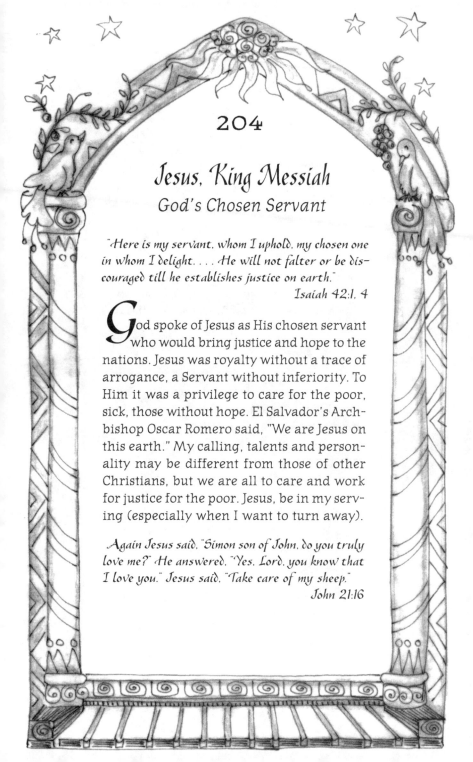

204

Jesus, King Messiah
God's Chosen Servant

"Here is my servant, whom I uphold, my chosen one in whom I delight. . . . He will not falter or be discouraged till he establishes justice on earth."

Isaiah 42:1, 4

God spoke of Jesus as His chosen servant who would bring justice and hope to the nations. Jesus was royalty without a trace of arrogance, a Servant without inferiority. To Him it was a privilege to care for the poor, sick, those without hope. El Salvador's Archbishop Oscar Romero said, "We are Jesus on this earth." My calling, talents and personality may be different from those of other Christians, but we are all to care and work for justice for the poor. Jesus, be in my serving (especially when I want to turn away).

Again Jesus said, "Simon son of John, do you truly love me?" He answered, "Yes, Lord, you know that I love you." Jesus said, "Take care of my sheep."

John 21:16

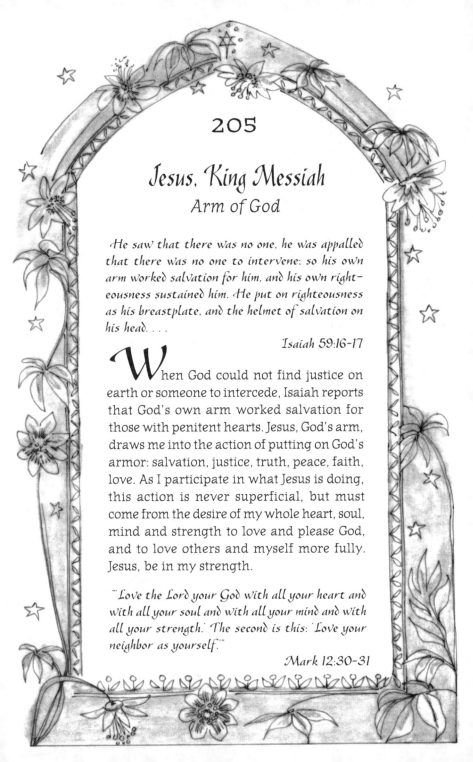

205

Jesus, King Messiah
Arm of God

*He saw that there was no one, he was appalled
that there was no one to intervene; so his own
arm worked salvation for him, and his own righteousness sustained him. He put on righteousness
as his breastplate, and the helmet of salvation on
his head. . . .*

Isaiah 59:16-17

When God could not find justice on
earth or someone to intercede, Isaiah reports
that God's own arm worked salvation for
those with penitent hearts. Jesus, God's arm,
draws me into the action of putting on God's
armor: salvation, justice, truth, peace, faith,
love. As I participate in what Jesus is doing,
this action is never superficial, but must
come from the desire of my whole heart, soul,
mind and strength to love and please God,
and to love others and myself more fully.
Jesus, be in my strength.

*"Love the Lord your God with all your heart and
with all your soul and with all your mind and with
all your strength." The second is this: "Love your
neighbor as yourself."*

Mark 12:30-31

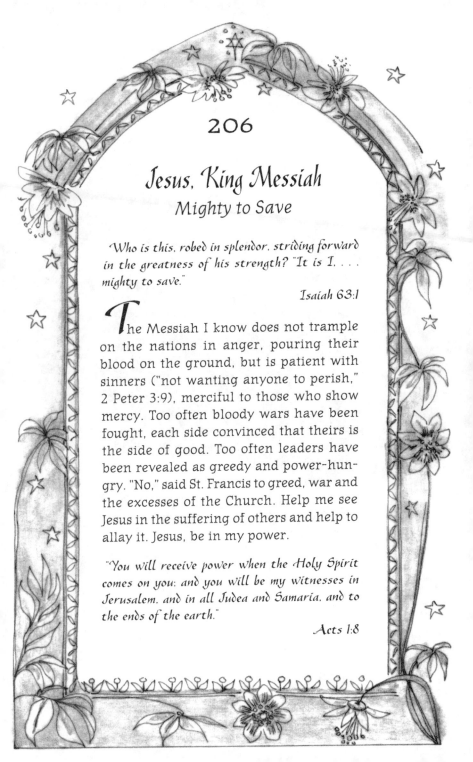

206

Jesus, King Messiah
Mighty to Save

Who is this, robed in splendor, striding forward in the greatness of his strength? "It is I, . . . mighty to save."

Isaiah 63:1

The Messiah I know does not trample on the nations in anger, pouring their blood on the ground, but is patient with sinners ("not wanting anyone to perish," 2 Peter 3:9), merciful to those who show mercy. Too often bloody wars have been fought, each side convinced that theirs is the side of good. Too often leaders have been revealed as greedy and power-hungry. "No," said St. Francis to greed, war and the excesses of the Church. Help me see Jesus in the suffering of others and help to allay it. Jesus, be in my power.

"You will receive power when the Holy Spirit comes on you; and you will be my witnesses in Jerusalem, and in all Judea and Samaria, and to the ends of the earth."

Acts 1:8

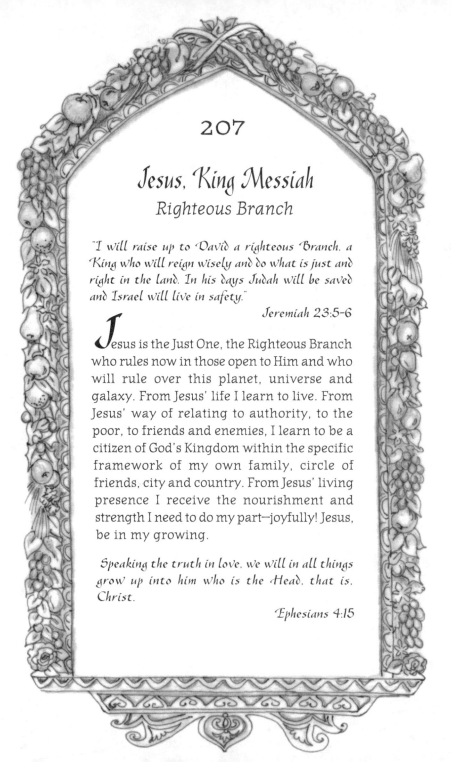

207

Jesus, King Messiah
Righteous Branch

"I will raise up to David a righteous Branch, a King who will reign wisely and do what is just and right in the land. In his days Judah will be saved and Israel will live in safety."

Jeremiah 23:5-6

Jesus is the Just One, the Righteous Branch who rules now in those open to Him and who will rule over this planet, universe and galaxy. From Jesus' life I learn to live. From Jesus' way of relating to authority, to the poor, to friends and enemies, I learn to be a citizen of God's Kingdom within the specific framework of my own family, circle of friends, city and country. From Jesus' living presence I receive the nourishment and strength I need to do my part—joyfully! Jesus, be in my growing.

Speaking the truth in love, we will in all things grow up into him who is the Head, that is, Christ.

Ephesians 4:15

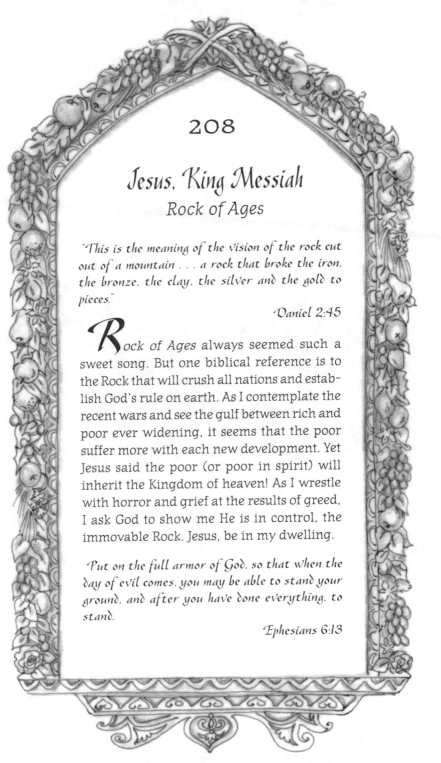

Jesus, King Messiah
Rock of Ages

"This is the meaning of the vision of the rock cut out of a mountain . . . a rock that broke the iron, the bronze, the clay, the silver and the gold to pieces."

Daniel 2:45

*R*ock of Ages always seemed such a sweet song. But one biblical reference is to the Rock that will crush all nations and establish God's rule on earth. As I contemplate the recent wars and see the gulf between rich and poor ever widening, it seems that the poor suffer more with each new development. Yet Jesus said the poor (or poor in spirit) will inherit the Kingdom of heaven! As I wrestle with horror and grief at the results of greed, I ask God to show me He is in control, the immovable Rock. Jesus, be in my dwelling.

Put on the full armor of God, so that when the day of evil comes, you may be able to stand your ground, and after you have done everything, to stand.

Ephesians 6:13

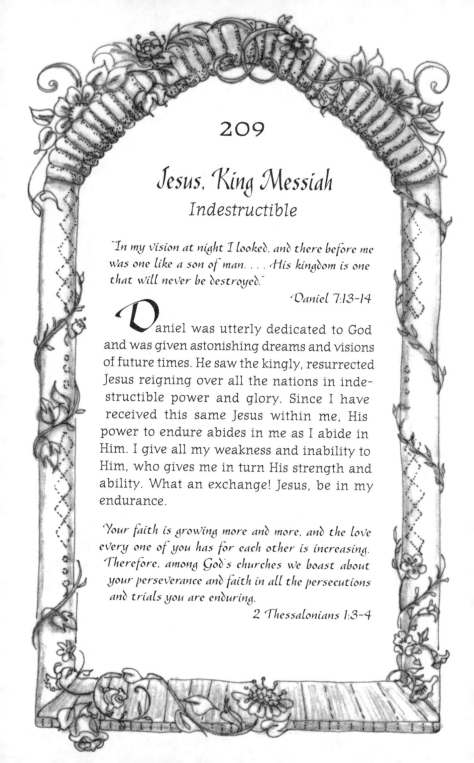

209

Jesus, King Messiah
Indestructible

"In my vision at night I looked, and there before me was one like a son of man. . . . His kingdom is one that will never be destroyed."

Daniel 7:13-14

Daniel was utterly dedicated to God and was given astonishing dreams and visions of future times. He saw the kingly, resurrected Jesus reigning over all the nations in indestructible power and glory. Since I have received this same Jesus within me, His power to endure abides in me as I abide in Him. I give all my weakness and inability to Him, who gives me in turn His strength and ability. What an exchange! Jesus, be in my endurance.

Your faith is growing more and more, and the love every one of you has for each other is increasing. Therefore, among God's churches we boast about your perseverance and faith in all the persecutions and trials you are enduring.

2 Thessalonians 1:3-4

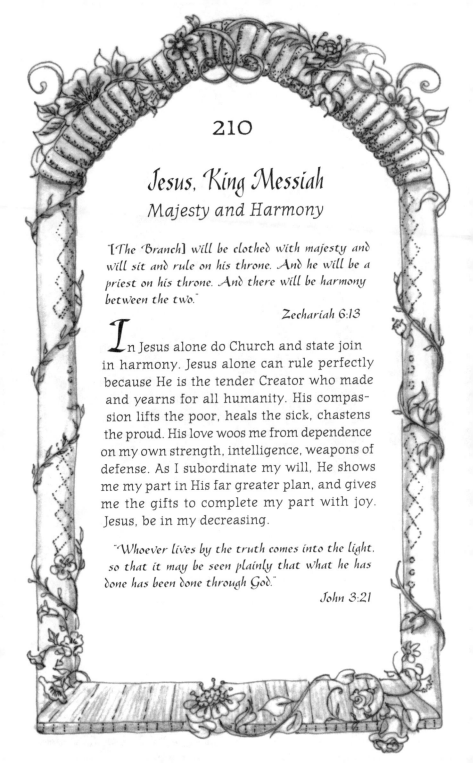

210

Jesus, King Messiah
Majesty and Harmony

"[The Branch] will be clothed with majesty and will sit and rule on his throne. And he will be a priest on his throne. And there will be harmony between the two."

Zechariah 6:13

In Jesus alone do Church and state join in harmony. Jesus alone can rule perfectly because He is the tender Creator who made and yearns for all humanity. His compassion lifts the poor, heals the sick, chastens the proud. His love woos me from dependence on my own strength, intelligence, weapons of defense. As I subordinate my will, He shows me my part in His far greater plan, and gives me the gifts to complete my part with joy. Jesus, be in my decreasing.

"Whoever lives by the truth comes into the light, so that it may be seen plainly that what he has done has been done through God."

John 3:21

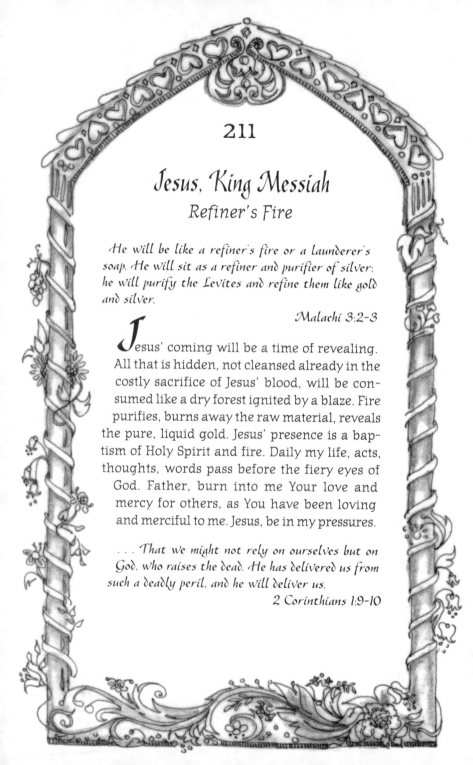

Jesus, King Messiah
Refiner's Fire

He will be like a refiner's fire or a launderer's soap. He will sit as a refiner and purifier of silver: he will purify the Levites and refine them like gold and silver.

Malachi 3:2-3

Jesus' coming will be a time of revealing. All that is hidden, not cleansed already in the costly sacrifice of Jesus' blood, will be consumed like a dry forest ignited by a blaze. Fire purifies, burns away the raw material, reveals the pure, liquid gold. Jesus' presence is a baptism of Holy Spirit and fire. Daily my life, acts, thoughts, words pass before the fiery eyes of God. Father, burn into me Your love and mercy for others, as You have been loving and merciful to me. Jesus, be in my pressures.

. . . That we might not rely on ourselves but on God. who raises the dead. He has delivered us from such a deadly peril. and he will deliver us.

2 Corinthians 1:9-10

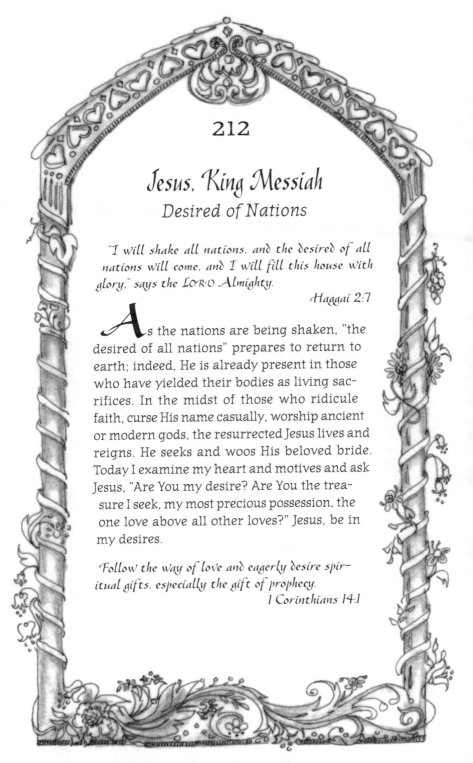

212

Jesus, King Messiah
Desired of Nations

"I will shake all nations, and the desired of all nations will come, and I will fill this house with glory," says the LORD Almighty.

Haggai 2:7

As the nations are being shaken, "the desired of all nations" prepares to return to earth; indeed, He is already present in those who have yielded their bodies as living sacrifices. In the midst of those who ridicule faith, curse His name casually, worship ancient or modern gods, the resurrected Jesus lives and reigns. He seeks and woos His beloved bride. Today I examine my heart and motives and ask Jesus, "Are You my desire? Are You the treasure I seek, my most precious possession, the one love above all other loves?" Jesus, be in my desires.

Follow the way of love and eagerly desire spiritual gifts, especially the gift of prophecy.

1 Corinthians 14:1

213

Jesus, King Messiah
Preparing a Place

"In my Father's house are many rooms. . . . I am going there to prepare a place for you. And . . . I will come back and take you to be with me that you also may be where I am."

John 14:2-3

Jesus promised that when all is ready, when the rooms in His Father's house are prepared, He will come back to take us home. I wonder if the building, preparing, renovating and restoring we do here on earth under the direction and supervision of Jesus are part of making His Father's house ready for us. Isaiah suggests that by ceasing to accuse others and by dedicating myself to a life of constructive giving, I become a restorer and a repairer. Jesus, be in my building.

"If you spend yourselves in behalf of the hungry and satisfy the needs of the oppressed . . . you will be called Repairer of Broken Walls, Restorer of Streets with Dwellings."

Isaiah 58:10, 12

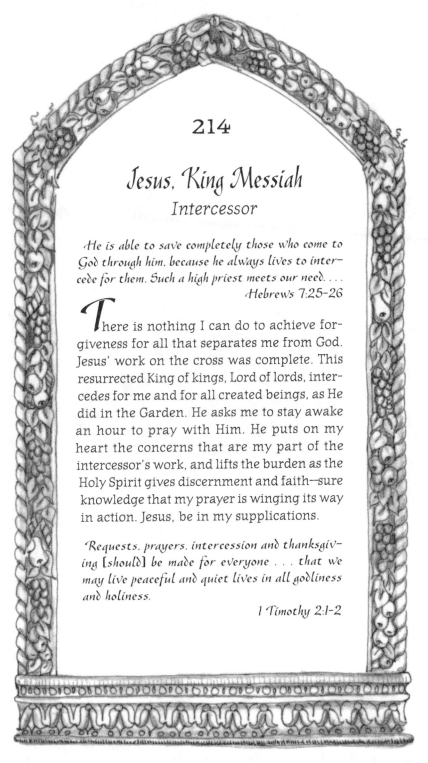

Jesus, King Messiah
Intercessor

He is able to save completely those who come to God through him, because he always lives to intercede for them. Such a high priest meets our need. . . .
Hebrews 7:25-26

There is nothing I can do to achieve forgiveness for all that separates me from God. Jesus' work on the cross was complete. This resurrected King of kings, Lord of lords, intercedes for me and for all created beings, as He did in the Garden. He asks me to stay awake an hour to pray with Him. He puts on my heart the concerns that are my part of the intercessor's work, and lifts the burden as the Holy Spirit gives discernment and faith—sure knowledge that my prayer is winging its way in action. Jesus, be in my supplications.

Requests, prayers, intercession and thanksgiving [should] be made for everyone . . . that we may live peaceful and quiet lives in all godliness and holiness.

1 Timothy 2:1-2

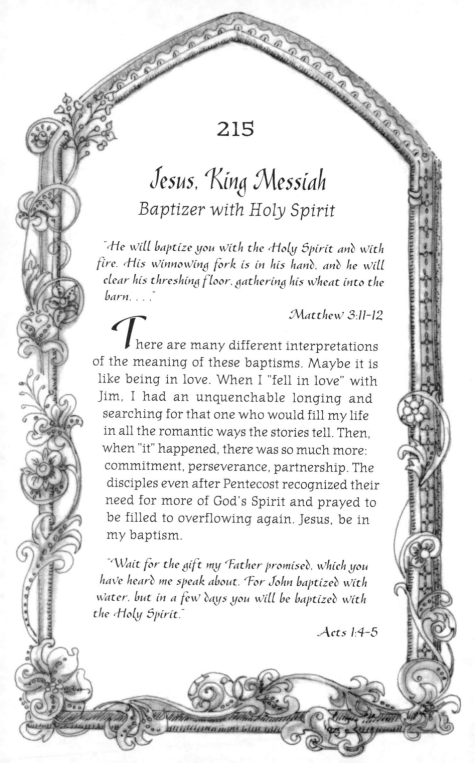

Jesus, King Messiah
Baptizer with Holy Spirit

"He will baptize you with the Holy Spirit and with fire. His winnowing fork is in his hand, and he will clear his threshing floor, gathering his wheat into the barn. . . ."

Matthew 3:11-12

There are many different interpretations of the meaning of these baptisms. Maybe it is like being in love. When I "fell in love" with Jim, I had an unquenchable longing and searching for that one who would fill my life in all the romantic ways the stories tell. Then, when "it" happened, there was so much more: commitment, perseverance, partnership. The disciples even after Pentecost recognized their need for more of God's Spirit and prayed to be filled to overflowing again. Jesus, be in my baptism.

"Wait for the gift my Father promised, which you have heard me speak about. For John baptized with water, but in a few days you will be baptized with the Holy Spirit."

Acts 1:4-5

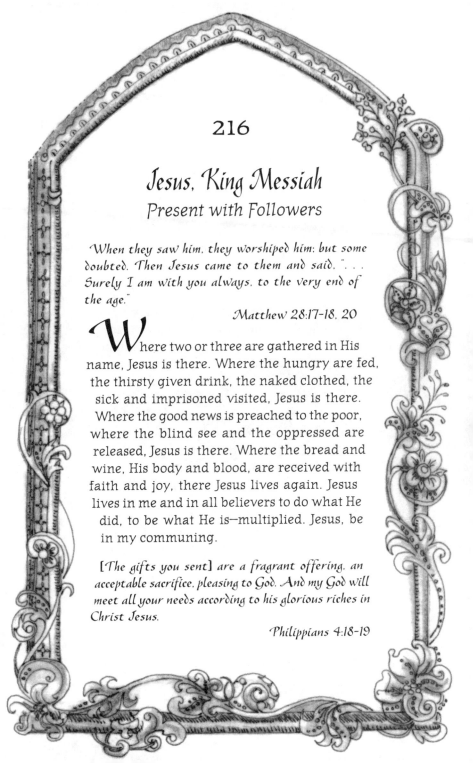

216

Jesus, King Messiah
Present with Followers

When they saw him, they worshiped him; but some doubted. Then Jesus came to them and said, "... Surely I am with you always, to the very end of the age."

Matthew 28:17-18, 20

Where two or three are gathered in His name, Jesus is there. Where the hungry are fed, the thirsty given drink, the naked clothed, the sick and imprisoned visited, Jesus is there. Where the good news is preached to the poor, where the blind see and the oppressed are released, Jesus is there. Where the bread and wine, His body and blood, are received with faith and joy, there Jesus lives again. Jesus lives in me and in all believers to do what He did, to be what He is—multiplied. Jesus, be in my communing.

[The gifts you sent] are a fragrant offering, an acceptable sacrifice, pleasing to God. And my God will meet all your needs according to his glorious riches in Christ Jesus.

Philippians 4:18-19

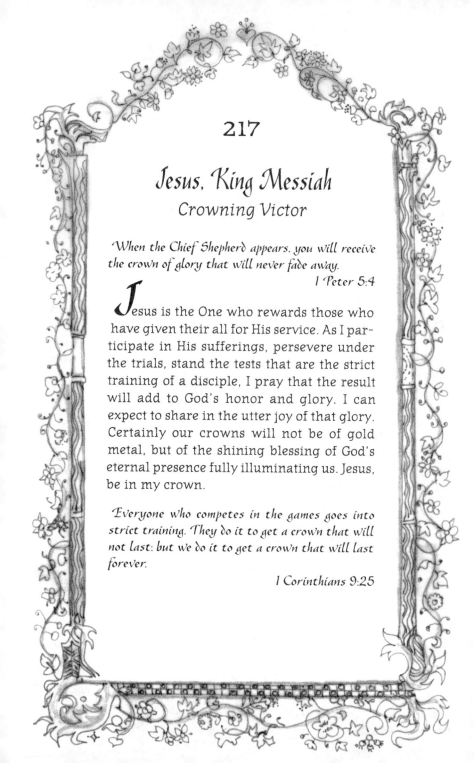

217

Jesus, King Messiah
Crowning Victor

When the Chief Shepherd appears, you will receive the crown of glory that will never fade away.
1 Peter 5:4

Jesus is the One who rewards those who have given their all for His service. As I participate in His sufferings, persevere under the trials, stand the tests that are the strict training of a disciple, I pray that the result will add to God's honor and glory. I can expect to share in the utter joy of that glory. Certainly our crowns will not be of gold metal, but of the shining blessing of God's eternal presence fully illuminating us. Jesus, be in my crown.

Everyone who competes in the games goes into strict training. They do it to get a crown that will not last: but we do it to get a crown that will last forever.

1 Corinthians 9:25

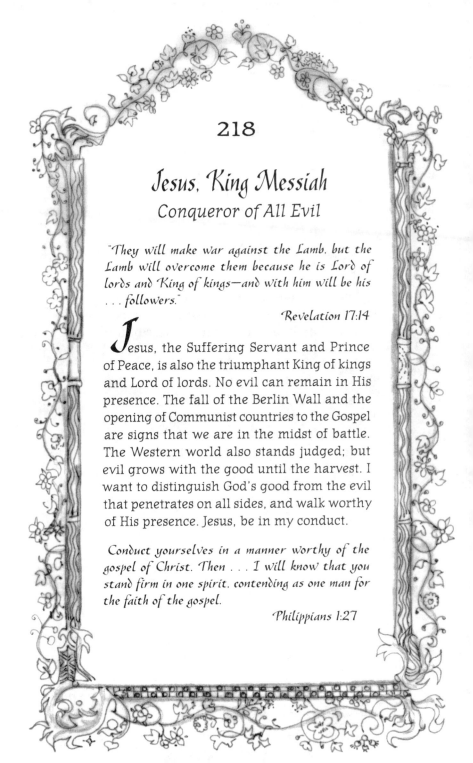

218

Jesus, King Messiah
Conqueror of All Evil

"They will make war against the Lamb, but the Lamb will overcome them because he is Lord of lords and King of kings—and with him will be his . . . followers."

Revelation 17:14

Jesus, the Suffering Servant and Prince of Peace, is also the triumphant King of kings and Lord of lords. No evil can remain in His presence. The fall of the Berlin Wall and the opening of Communist countries to the Gospel are signs that we are in the midst of battle. The Western world also stands judged; but evil grows with the good until the harvest. I want to distinguish God's good from the evil that penetrates on all sides, and walk worthy of His presence. Jesus, be in my conduct.

Conduct yourselves in a manner worthy of the gospel of Christ. Then . . . I will know that you stand firm in one spirit, contending as one man for the faith of the gospel.

Philippians 1:27

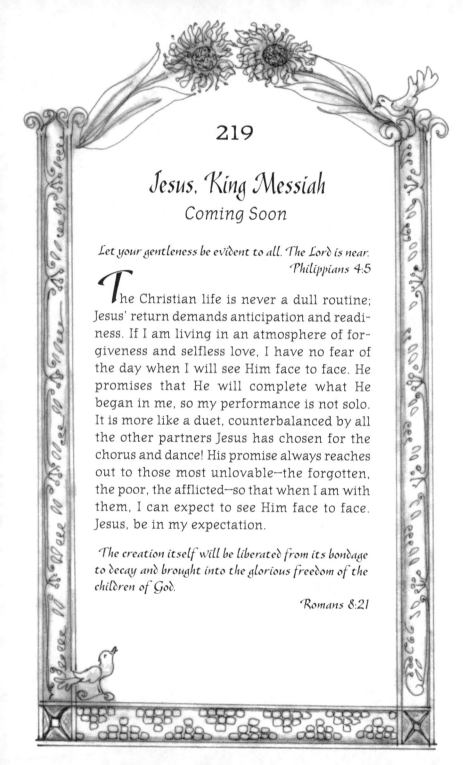

Jesus, King Messiah
Coming Soon

Let your gentleness be evident to all. The Lord is near.
Philippians 4:5

The Christian life is never a dull routine; Jesus' return demands anticipation and readiness. If I am living in an atmosphere of forgiveness and selfless love, I have no fear of the day when I will see Him face to face. He promises that He will complete what He began in me, so my performance is not solo. It is more like a duet, counterbalanced by all the other partners Jesus has chosen for the chorus and dance! His promise always reaches out to those most unlovable—the forgotten, the poor, the afflicted—so that when I am with them, I can expect to see Him face to face. Jesus, be in my expectation.

The creation itself will be liberated from its bondage to decay and brought into the glorious freedom of the children of God.

Romans 8:21

220

Jesus, King Messiah
Ascended

When Christ, who is your life, appears, then you also will appear with him in glory. Put to death, therefore, whatever belongs to your earthly nature: sexual immorality, impurity, lust, evil desires and greed, which is idolatry.

Colossians 3:4-5

Jesus, the risen Savior, now sits in the heavenly place at the right hand of God—a realm more real than our material world. If I can see through spiritual eyes that Jesus did rise from the dead, and that He does have total power over evil and all that is against God, then I must live expecting His soon coming and make the most of every moment. Everything I do is to be of praise, faith and love. Jesus, be in my fidelity.

"Behold, I come like a thief! Blessed is he who stays awake and keeps his clothes with him, so that he may not go naked and be shamefully exposed."

Revelation 16:15

221

Jesus, King Messiah
King of Kings

*There were loud voices in heaven, which said:
"The kingdom of the world has become the kingdom of our Lord and of his Christ, and he will reign
for ever and ever."*

Revelation 11:15

Where Jesus Christ is King, we have a foretaste of His reign. There His Holy Spirit is poured out, comforting those who need comfort, prodding the consciences of those who are comfortable or ignorant of their sin. A Teacher, the Holy Spirit never loses patience as I do but persists in holding me accountable, preparing me to meet Love face to face. As I learn to respect other human beings—my neighbors, my enemies, those in my own house—I learn to reverence the One who is worthy, before whom every knee shall bow and every tongue confess that Christ is Lord. Jesus, be in my revering.

*Submit to one another out of reverence for Christ.
Ephesians 5:21*

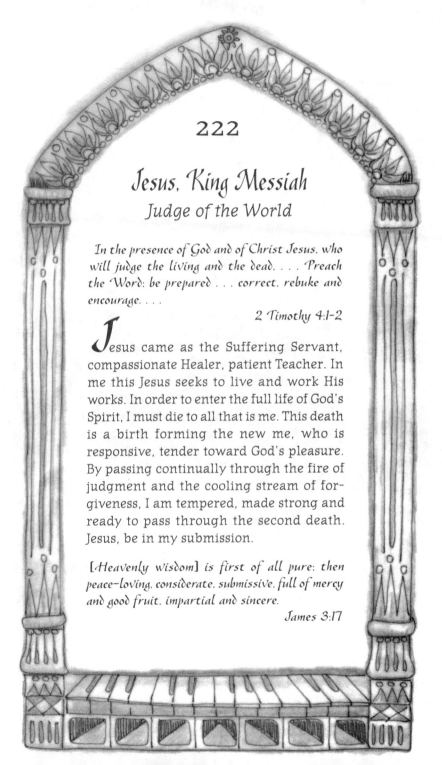

222

Jesus, King Messiah
Judge of the World

In the presence of God and of Christ Jesus, who will judge the living and the dead. . . . Preach the Word; be prepared . . . correct, rebuke and encourage. . . .

2 Timothy 4:1-2

Jesus came as the Suffering Servant, compassionate Healer, patient Teacher. In me this Jesus seeks to live and work His works. In order to enter the full life of God's Spirit, I must die to all that is me. This death is a birth forming the new me, who is responsive, tender toward God's pleasure. By passing continually through the fire of judgment and the cooling stream of forgiveness, I am tempered, made strong and ready to pass through the second death. Jesus, be in my submission.

[Heavenly wisdom] is first of all pure; then peace-loving, considerate, submissive, full of mercy and good fruit, impartial and sincere.

James 3:17

223

Jesus, King Messiah
Glorified

His head and hair were white like wool. . . . and his eyes were like blazing fire. His feet were like bronze glowing in a furnace, and his voice was like the sound of rushing waters.

Revelation 1:14-15

Jesus is the King of glory who never sought glory and gave it all to God. This glory will fill the earth. It is eternal, majestic, holy, associated with His honor and power. I am created for His glory and have glory to give to God. Telling the truth, being open and penitent before God and His people, over-looking offenses, are ways to give Him glory. I can declare His glory to the nations as well as at home. I can crown Him with glory, sing and cry glory, revere the glory, see the glory and praise His glory! Jesus, be in my glory.

"He was given authority, glory and sovereign power. . . ."

Daniel 7:14

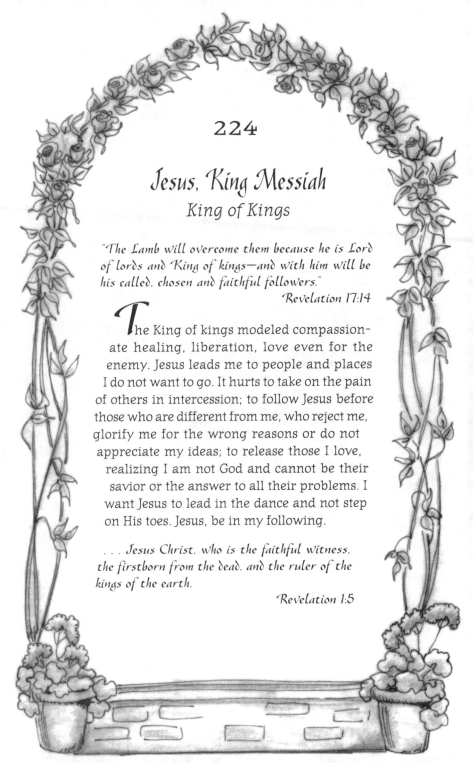

224

Jesus, King Messiah
King of Kings

"The Lamb will overcome them because he is Lord of lords and King of kings—and with him will be his called, chosen and faithful followers."
Revelation 17:14

The King of kings modeled compassionate healing, liberation, love even for the enemy. Jesus leads me to people and places I do not want to go. It hurts to take on the pain of others in intercession; to follow Jesus before those who are different from me, who reject me, glorify me for the wrong reasons or do not appreciate my ideas; to release those I love, realizing I am not God and cannot be their savior or the answer to all their problems. I want Jesus to lead in the dance and not step on His toes. Jesus, be in my following.

. . . Jesus Christ, who is the faithful witness, the firstborn from the dead, and the ruler of the kings of the earth.
Revelation 1:5

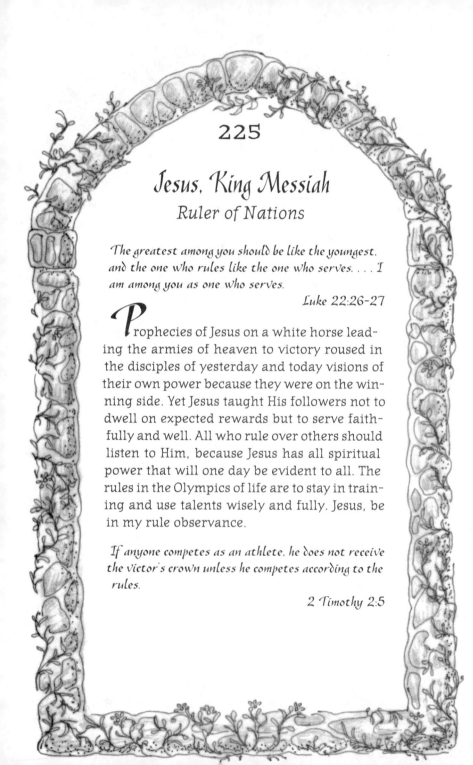

225

Jesus, King Messiah
Ruler of Nations

*The greatest among you should be like the youngest,
and the one who rules like the one who serves. . . . I
am among you as one who serves.*

Luke 22:26-27

Prophecies of Jesus on a white horse lead-
ing the armies of heaven to victory roused in
the disciples of yesterday and today visions of
their own power because they were on the win-
ning side. Yet Jesus taught His followers not to
dwell on expected rewards but to serve faith-
fully and well. All who rule over others should
listen to Him, because Jesus has all spiritual
power that will one day be evident to all. The
rules in the Olympics of life are to stay in training and use talents wisely and fully. Jesus, be
in my rule observance.

*If anyone competes as an athlete, he does not receive
the victor's crown unless he competes according to the
rules.*

2 Timothy 2:5

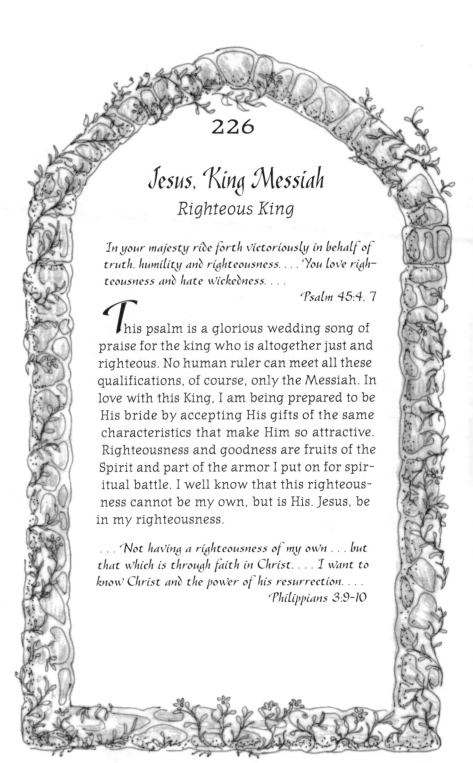

226

Jesus, King Messiah
Righteous King

In your majesty ride forth victoriously in behalf of truth, humility and righteousness. . . . You love righteousness and hate wickedness. . . .

Psalm 45:4, 7

This psalm is a glorious wedding song of praise for the king who is altogether just and righteous. No human ruler can meet all these qualifications, of course, only the Messiah. In love with this King, I am being prepared to be His bride by accepting His gifts of the same characteristics that make Him so attractive. Righteousness and goodness are fruits of the Spirit and part of the armor I put on for spiritual battle. I well know that this righteousness cannot be my own, but is His. Jesus, be in my righteousness.

. . . Not having a righteousness of my own . . . but that which is through faith in Christ. . . . I want to know Christ and the power of his resurrection. . . .

Philippians 3:9-10

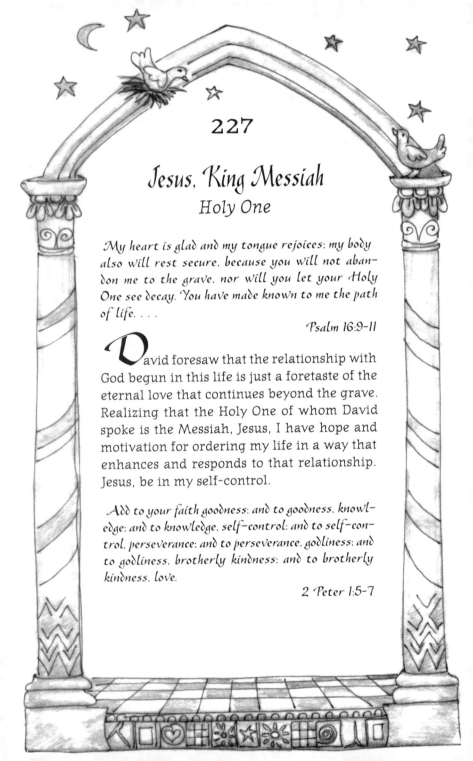

227

Jesus, King Messiah
Holy One

*My heart is glad and my tongue rejoices; my body
also will rest secure, because you will not aban-
don me to the grave, nor will you let your Holy
One see decay. You have made known to me the path
of life. . . .*

Psalm 16:9-11

David foresaw that the relationship with
God begun in this life is just a foretaste of the
eternal love that continues beyond the grave.
Realizing that the Holy One of whom David
spoke is the Messiah, Jesus, I have hope and
motivation for ordering my life in a way that
enhances and responds to that relationship.
Jesus, be in my self-control.

*Add to your faith goodness; and to goodness, knowl-
edge; and to knowledge, self-control; and to self-control, perseverance; and to perseverance, godliness; and
to godliness, brotherly kindness; and to brotherly
kindness, love.*

2 Peter 1:5-7

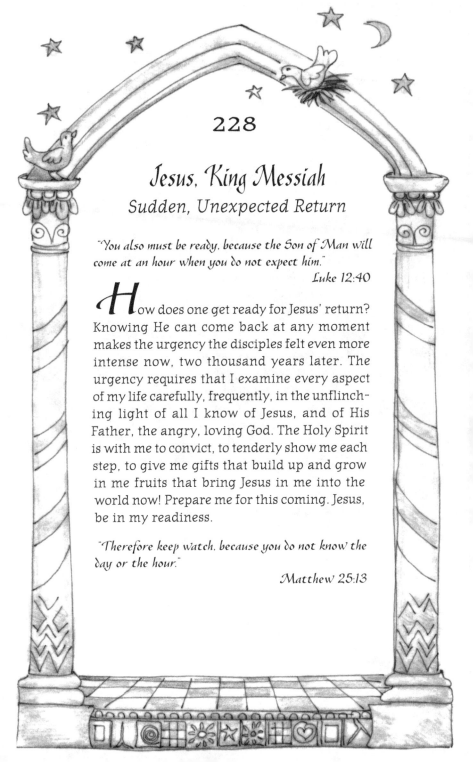

228

Jesus, King Messiah
Sudden, Unexpected Return

"You also must be ready, because the Son of Man will come at an hour when you do not expect him."
                                        Luke 12:40

*H*ow does one get ready for Jesus' return? Knowing He can come back at any moment makes the urgency the disciples felt even more intense now, two thousand years later. The urgency requires that I examine every aspect of my life carefully, frequently, in the unflinching light of all I know of Jesus, and of His Father, the angry, loving God. The Holy Spirit is with me to convict, to tenderly show me each step, to give me gifts that build up and grow in me fruits that bring Jesus in me into the world now! Prepare me for this coming. Jesus, be in my readiness.

"Therefore keep watch, because you do not know the day or the hour."
                                        Matthew 25:13

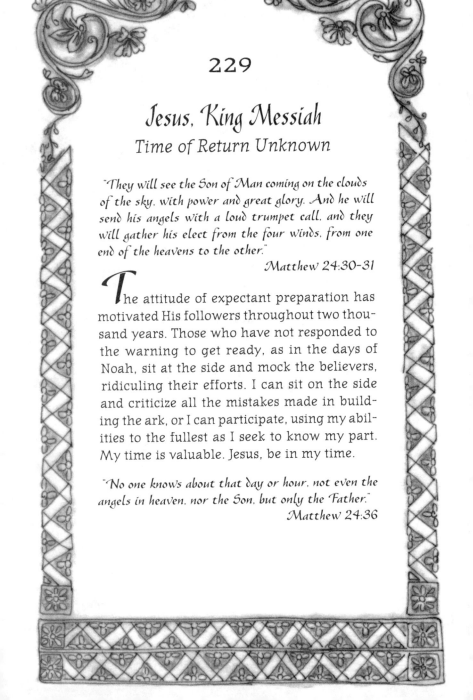

229

Jesus, King Messiah
Time of Return Unknown

"They will see the Son of Man coming on the clouds of the sky, with power and great glory. And he will send his angels with a loud trumpet call, and they will gather his elect from the four winds, from one end of the heavens to the other."

Matthew 24:30-31

The attitude of expectant preparation has motivated His followers throughout two thousand years. Those who have not responded to the warning to get ready, as in the days of Noah, sit at the side and mock the believers, ridiculing their efforts. I can sit on the side and criticize all the mistakes made in building the ark, or I can participate, using my abilities to the fullest as I seek to know my part. My time is valuable. Jesus, be in my time.

"No one knows about that day or hour, not even the angels in heaven, nor the Son, but only the Father."

Matthew 24:36

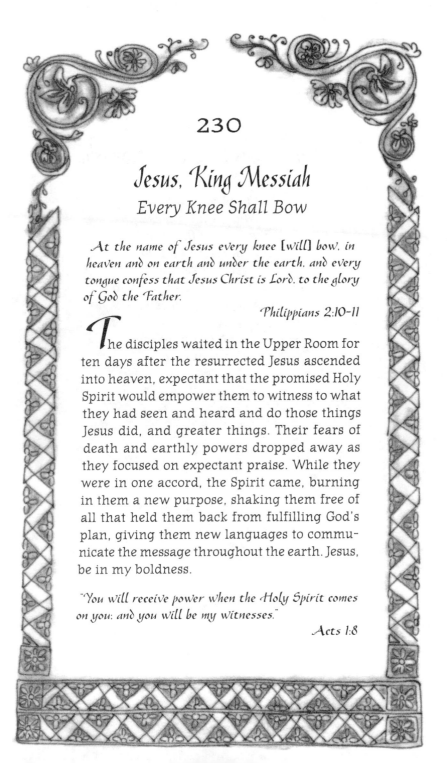

230

Jesus, King Messiah
Every Knee Shall Bow

At the name of Jesus every knee [will] bow, in heaven and on earth and under the earth, and every tongue confess that Jesus Christ is Lord, to the glory of God the Father.

Philippians 2:10-11

The disciples waited in the Upper Room for ten days after the resurrected Jesus ascended into heaven, expectant that the promised Holy Spirit would empower them to witness to what they had seen and heard and do those things Jesus did, and greater things. Their fears of death and earthly powers dropped away as they focused on expectant praise. While they were in one accord, the Spirit came, burning in them a new purpose, shaking them free of all that held them back from fulfilling God's plan, giving them new languages to communicate the message throughout the earth. Jesus, be in my boldness.

"You will receive power when the Holy Spirit comes on you; and you will be my witnesses."

Acts 1:8

Other Books by Sarah Hornsby

At the Name of Jesus
Who I Am in Jesus
The Fruit of the Spirit
Standing Firm in Jesus
Jesus, Be in Me
Getting to Know Jesus from A to Z
Jesus, Be in My Christmas
Love Is . . .
Angels All Around Me
Nicaragüense